Stock Investing

FOR

DUMMIES®

4TH EDITION

by Paul Mladjenovic

WILEY

John Wiley & Sons, Inc.

Stock Investing For Dummies® 4th Edition

Published by
John Wiley & Sons, Inc.
111 River St.
Hoboken, NJ 07030-5774
www.wiley.com

WILEY

About the Author

Paul Mladjenovic is a certified financial planner practitioner, writer, and public speaker. His businesses, PM Financial Services and ProsperityNetwork. net, have helped people with financial and business concerns since 1981. In 1985 he achieved his Certified Financial Planner (CFP) designation. Since 1983, Paul has taught thousands of investors through popular national seminars such as "The $50 Wealth-Builder" and other financial seminars. Paul has been quoted or referenced by many media outlets, including Bloomberg, MarketWatch, Comcast, CNBC, and a variety of financial and business publications and websites. As an author, he has written the books *The Unofficial Guide to Picking Stocks* (Wiley) and *Zero-Cost Marketing* (ProsperityNetwork. net). In 2002, the first edition of *Stock Investing For Dummies* was ranked in the top 10 out of 300 books reviewed by Barron's. In recent years, Paul accurately forecasted many economic events, including the rise of gold, the decline of the U.S. dollar, and the housing crisis. He edits the financial e-zine Prosperity Alert, available free at www.ProsperityNetwork.net. Paul's personal website can be found at www.RavingCapitalist.com, and you can view his video commentaries at www.youtube.com/paulmlad.

Dedication

For my fantastic wife Fran, my wonderful boys Adam and Joshua, and a loving, supportive family; I thank God for you.

I also dedicate this book to the millions of investors who deserve more knowledge and information to achieve lasting prosperity.

Author's Acknowledgments

First and foremost, I offer my appreciation and gratitude to the wonderful people at Wiley. It has been a pleasure to work with such a top-notch organization that works so hard to create products that offer readers tremendous value and information. I wish all of you continued success! Wiley has some notables whom I want to single out.

The first person is Georgette Beatty (my project editor). She has guided me from day one (for both the 3rd edition and this 4th edition). Her patience, professionalism, and guidance have kept me sane and productive. Thanks for being great!

Christy Pingleton (my copy editor) is a pro who took my bundle of words and turned them into worthy messages, and I thank her. Wiley is lucky to have her!

The technical editor, Kevin Kennedy, is a great financial pro whom I appreciate. He made sure that my logic is sound and my facts are straight. I wish him continued success.

My gratitude again goes out to my fantastic acquisitions editor, Stacy Kennedy, for making this 4th edition happen. *For Dummies* books don't magically appear at the bookstore; they happen because of the foresight and efforts of people like Stacy. Wiley is fortunate to have her (and the others also mentioned)!

Fran, Lipa Zyenska, I appreciate your great support during the writing and updating of this book. It's not always easy dealing with the world, but with you by my side, I know that God has indeed blessed me. Te amo!

Lastly, I want to acknowledge you, the reader. Over the years, you've made the *For Dummies* books what they are today. Your devotion to these wonderful books helped build a foundation that played a big part in the creation of this book and many more yet to come. Thank you!

Publisher's Acknowledgments

We're proud of this book; please send us your comments at `http://dummies.custhelp.com`. For other comments, please contact our Customer Care Department within the U.S. at 877-762-2974, outside the U.S. at 317-572-3993, or fax 317-572-4002.

Some of the people who helped bring this book to market include the following:

Acquisitions, Editorial, and Vertical Websites

Senior Project Editor: Georgette Beatty

    (Previous Edition: Georgette Beatty)

Acquisitions Editor: Stacy Kennedy

Copy Editor: Christine Pingleton

    (Previous Edition: Todd Lothery)

Assistant Editor: David Lutton

Editorial Program Coordinator: Joe Niesen

Technical Editor: Kevin L. Kennedy

Editorial Manager: Michelle Hacker

Editorial Assistant: Alexa Koschier

Cover Photo: © Harald Sund / Getty Images

Cartoons: Rich Tennant (`www.the5thwave.com`)

Composition Services

Senior Project Coordinator: Kristie Rees

Layout and Graphics: Joyce Haughey

Proofreaders: Jessica Kramer, Toni Settle

Indexer: Potomac Indexing, LLC

Publishing and Editorial for Consumer Dummies

    Kathleen Nebenhaus, Vice President and Executive Publisher

    David Palmer, Associate Publisher

    Kristin Ferguson-Wagstaffe, Product Development Director

Publishing for Technology Dummies

    Andy Cummings, Vice President and Publisher

Composition Services

    Debbie Stailey, Director of Composition Services

Contents at a Glance

Table of Contents

Introduction

．．．

*S*tock Investing For Dummies, 4th Edition, has been an honor for me to write. I'm grateful that I can share my thoughts, information, and experience with such a large and devoted group of readers.

I appreciate the timing of this edition because the world of investing and the U.S. economy seem as hazardous as ever. Volatility and risk do indeed play a greater role in today's stock market, and that means that patience and discipline are more important than ever. Fortunately, the investing tools, strategies, and vehicles at your beck and call give you the power to keep your portfolio growing even in today's financial battlefield.

Successful stock investing takes diligent work and knowledge, like any other meaningful pursuit. This book can definitely help you avoid the mistakes others have made and can point you in the right direction. It gives you a heads up about trends and conditions that are found in few other stock investing guides. Explore the pages of this book and find the topics that most interest you within the world of stock investing. Let me assure you that I've squeezed more than a quarter century of experience, education, and expertise between these covers. My track record is as good as (or better than) the track records of the experts who trumpet their successes. More important, I share information to avoid common mistakes (some of which I made myself!). Understanding what not to do can be just as important as figuring out what to do.

In all the years that I've counseled and educated investors, the single difference between success and failure, between gain and loss, has boiled down to two words: applied knowledge. Take this book as your first step in a lifelong learning adventure.

About This Book

The stock market has been a cornerstone of the investor's passive wealth-building program for over a century and continues in this role. The past ten years have been one huge roller-coaster ride for stock investors. Fortunes have been made and lost. With all the media attention and all the talking heads on radio and television, the investing public still didn't avoid losing trillions in a historic stock market debacle. Sadly, even the so-called experts who understand stocks didn't see the economic and geopolitical forces that acted like a tsunami on the market. With just a little more knowledge and a few wealth-preserving techniques, more investors could have held on to their hard-earned stock market fortunes. Cheer up, though: This book gives you an early warning on those megatrends and events that will affect your stock portfolio. While other books may tell you about stocks, this book tells you about stocks and what affects them.

This book is designed to give you a realistic approach to making money in stocks. It provides the essence of sound, practical stock investing strategies and insights that have been market-tested and proven from more than 100 years of stock market history. I don't expect you to read it cover to cover, although I'd be delighted if you read every word! Instead, this book is designed as a reference tool. Feel free to read the chapters in whatever order you choose. You can flip to the sections and chapters that interest you or those that include topics that you need to know more about.

Stock Investing For Dummies, 4th Edition, is also quite different from the "get rich with stocks" titles that have crammed the bookshelves in recent years. It doesn't take a standard approach to the topic; it doesn't assume that stocks are a sure thing and the be-all, end-all of wealth-building. In fact, at times in this book, I tell you *not* to invest in stocks (or even to bet against them!).

This book can help you succeed not only in up markets but also in down markets. Bull markets and bear markets come and go, but the informed investor can keep making money no matter what. To give you an extra edge, I've tried to include information about the investing environment for stocks. Whether it's politics or hurricanes (or both), you need to know how the big picture affects your stock investment decisions.

Conventions Used in This Book

To make navigating through this book easier, I've established the following conventions:

- **Boldface** text points out key words or the main parts of bulleted items.
- *Italics* highlight new terms that are defined.
- Monofont is used for web addresses.

   When this book was printed, some web addresses may have needed to break across two lines of text. If that happened, rest assured that I haven't put in any extra characters (such as hyphens) to indicate the break. So when using one of these web addresses, just type in exactly what you see in this book, pretending as though the line break doesn't exist.

What You're Not to Read

Sidebars (gray boxes of text) in this book give you a more in-depth look at a certain topic. Although they further illuminate a particular point, these sidebars aren't crucial to your understanding of the rest of the book. Feel free to read them or skip them. Of course, I'd love for you to read them all, but my feelings won't be hurt if you decide to skip over them.

The text that accompanies the Technical Stuff icon (see the forthcoming section "Icons Used in This Book") can be passed over as well. The text associated with this icon gives some technical details about stock investing that are certainly interesting and informative, but you can still come away with the information you need without reading this text.

Foolish Assumptions

I figure you've picked up this book for one or more of the following reasons:

- ✔ You're a beginner and want a crash course on stock investing that's an easy read.

- ✔ You're already a stock investor, and you need a book that allows you to read only those chapters that cover specific stock investing topics of interest to you.

- ✔ You need to review your own situation with the information in this book to see if you missed anything when you invested in that hot stock that your brother-in-law recommended.

- ✔ You need a great gift! When Uncle Mo is upset over his poor stock picks, you can give him this book so he can get back on his financial feet. Be sure to get a copy for his broker, too. (Odds are that the broker was the one who made those picks to begin with.)

How This Book Is Organized

The information is laid out in a straightforward format. The parts progress in a logical approach that any investor interested in stocks can follow very easily.

Part 1: The Essentials of Stock Investing

This part is for everyone. Understanding the essentials of stock investing and investing in general will only help you, especially in uncertain economic times. Stocks may even touch your finances in ways not readily apparent. For example, stocks aren't only in individual accounts; they're also in mutual funds and pension plans.

An important point is that stocks are really financial tools that are a means to an end. Investors should be able to answer the question, "Why am I considering stocks at all?" Stocks are a great vehicle for wealth-building, but only if investors realize what they can accomplish and how to use them. Chapter 2 explains how to take stock of your current financial situation and goals, and Chapter 3 defines common approaches to stock investing.

One of the essentials of stock investing is understanding risk. Most people are clueless about risk. You can't avoid every type of risk out there (life itself embodies risk). However, Chapter 4 can help you recognize it and find ways to minimize it in your stock investing program. It's one of the most important chapters that serious stock investors should read. While I'm at it, I also discuss volatility because that concept is frequently tied at the hip with risk.

There's more than one way to invest in stocks. The bulk of this book is about direct stock investing. But for some, indirect stock investing is the way to go. Exchange-traded funds (ETFs) provide some opportunities for conservative investors that I can't ignore! Therefore, check out Chapter 5 on this great approach to stock investing.

Part 11: Before You Start Buying

When you're ready to embark on your career as a stock investor, you need to use some resources to gather information about the stocks you're interested in. Fortunately, you live in the information age. I pity the investors from the 1920s who didn't have access to so many resources, but today's investors are in an enviable position. This part tells you where to find information and how to use it to be a more knowledgeable investor (a rarity in recent years!). For example, I explain that stocks can be used for both growth and income purposes, and I discuss the characteristics of each; see Chapters 8 and 9 for more information.

Chapter 6 is a great starting place for your information gathering; I show you how to stay on top of financial news and read stock tables, among other topics.

When you're ready to invest, you'll invariably have to turn to a broker. Several types of brokers are out there, so you should know which is which. The wrong broker can make you . . . uh . . . broker. Chapter 7 helps you choose.

New to this edition is Chapter 10, which gives you the lowdown on the basics of technical analysis, which is critical to know, especially if you have a short-term investing focus.

Part III: Picking Winners

I compare buying stock to picking goldfish. If you look at a bunch of goldfish to choose which ones to buy, you want to make sure that you pick the healthiest ones. With stocks, you also need to pick companies that are healthy. Part III can help you do that. It's about picking good stocks by using microeconomics, meaning that you look at the stocks of individual companies. I explain how to evaluate a company's products, services, and other factors so that you can determine whether a company is strong and healthy.

If I can steer you toward those segments of the stock market that show solid promise for the coming years, that alone would make your stock portfolio thrive. Putting your money into solid companies in thriving industries has been the hallmark of superior stock investing throughout history. It's no different now. Check out Chapter 13 if you want to know more about emerging sector opportunities.

Where do you turn to find out about a company's financial health? In Chapters 11 and 12, I show you the documents you should review to make a more informed decision. When you find the information, you'll discover how to make sense of that data as well. While you're at it, check out Chapter 14 (on investing with megatrends) and Chapter 15 (on understanding the big picture with the economy and politics, which affects the art of stock-picking).

Part IV: Investment Strategies and Tactics

Investing in stocks isn't just about what you invest in; it's also about how you go about doing it. Part IV reveals tips, strategies, and resources that you shouldn't ignore to enhance your approach to prudent stock investing.

Investing is a long-term activity, but stocks can also be short-term buying and selling opportunities, so I discuss stock trading in Chapter 16. This chapter covers the fine art of speculating, too.

In Chapter 17, I provide guidance on understanding brokerage orders. Even using the basic types will definitely enhance your chance of success. After you master the basics, you can move on to Chapter 18, which gets a little more advanced. Triggers and advanced conditional orders are the newest tools for investors, so be sure to take a look.

You may be an investor, but that doesn't mean that you have deep pockets. Chapter 19 tells you how to buy stocks with low (or no) transaction costs. If you're going to buy the stock anyway, why not save on commissions and other costs?

As an investor, you must keep an eye on what company insiders are doing. In Chapter 20, I explain what it may mean if a company's management is buying or selling the same stock that you're considering. I even touch on insider buying by politicians (nothing is sacred!).

After you spend all your time, money, and effort to grow your money in the world of stocks, you have yet another concern: holding on to your hard-earned gains. This challenge is summarized in one word: taxes. Sound tax planning is crucial for everyone who works hard. After all, taxes are the biggest expense in your lifetime (right after children!). See Chapter 21 for more information.

Part V: The Part of Tens

I wrap up the book with a hallmark of *For Dummies* books — the Part of Tens. These chapters give you a mini crash course in stock investing.

In this part, I discuss what to do when your portfolio is down (Chapter 22) and what to consider when your portfolio is up (Chapter 23). Chapter 24 covers ten opportunities and challenges that face stock investors. I also offer some tips on nonstock strategies that go well with stocks (Chapter 25).

Part VI: Appendixes

Don't overlook the appendixes. I pride myself on the resources I can provide my students and readers so that they can make informed investment decisions. Whether the topic is stock investing terminology, economics, or avoiding capital gains taxes, I include a treasure trove of resources to help you. Whether you go to a bookstore, the library, or the Internet, Appendix A gives you some great places to turn to for help. In Appendix B, I explain financial ratios. These important numbers help you better determine whether to invest in a particular company's stock.

Icons Used in This Book

Useful icons appear in the margins of this book; here's what they mean.

When you see this icon, I'm reminding you about some information that you should always keep stashed in your memory, whether you're new to investing or an old pro.

The text attached to this icon may not be crucial to your success as an investor, but it may enable you to talk shop with investing gurus and better understand the financial pages of your favorite business publication or website.

This icon flags a particular bit of advice that just may give you an edge over other investors.

Pay special attention to this icon because the advice can prevent headaches, heartaches, and financial aches.

Where to Go from Here

You may not need to read every chapter to make you more confident as a stock investor, so feel free to jump around to suit your personal needs. Because every chapter is designed to be as self-contained as possible, it won't do you any harm to cherry-pick what you really want to read. But if you're like me, you may still want to check out every chapter because you never know when you may come across a new tip or resource that will make a profitable difference in your stock portfolio. I want you to be successful so that I can brag about you in the next edition!

Part I
The Essentials of Stock Investing

The 5th Wave   By Rich Tennant

"I told my broker I wanted him to be more aggressive, so he called me an idiot and hung up the phone."

In this part . . .

The latest market turmoil and uncertainty tell investors to get back to square one. Your success is dependent on doing your homework before you invest your first dollar in stocks. Most investors don't realize that they should be scrutinizing their own situations and financial goals at least as much as they scrutinize stocks. How else can you know which stocks are right for you? Too many people risk too much simply because they don't take stock of their current needs, goals, and risk tolerance before they invest. The chapters in this part tell you what you need to know to choose the stocks that best suit you. I even include a chapter on exchange-traded funds (ETFs) because they give you an easier venue into the world of stocks.

Chapter 1

Surveying the World of Stock Investing

In This Chapter

▶ Knowing the essentials

▶ Getting ready to purchase stocks

▶ Recognizing winners

For newbies to stock investing, the stock market hasn't been offering the warmest welcome in recent years. I wrote much of this 4th Edition as the United States and the rest of the world were wondering who the next U.S. president would be and what country (Greece?) or state (California?) would head for the abyss. (Events such as these impact stock investing because our world and our financial markets are more interrelated than ever.) Too many folks are pining for the good 'ol days of 1982–1999, when choosing winning stocks was easier than finding aliens in *Star Wars*. Alas, today's stock market is a little more puzzling . . . but it can still be rewarding. I can only promise you that if you read this book seriously, you'll do *much* better than the average investor. Just keep in mind that patience and discipline count now more than ever.

The purpose of this book is not only to tell you about the basics of stock investing but also to let you in on solid strategies that can help you profit from the stock market. Before you invest, you need to understand the fundamentals of stock investing, which I introduce in this chapter. Then I give you an overview of how to put your money where it will count the most.

Understanding the Basics

The basics of stock investing are so elementary that few people recognize them. When you lose track of the basics, you lose track of why you invested to begin with. Part I of this book helps you grasp these basics:

- **Knowing the risk and volatility involved:** Perhaps the most fundamental (and therefore most important) concept to grasp is the risk you face whenever you put your hard-earned money in an investment such as a stock.

  Related to risk is the concept of volatility: Volatility refers to a condition in which there is rapid movement in the price of a particular stock (or other investment); investors use this term especially when there's a sudden drop in price in a relatively short period of time. Find out more about risk and volatility in Chapter 4.

- **Assessing your financial situation:** You need a firm awareness of your starting point and where you want to go. Chapter 2 helps you take stock of your current financial status and your goals.

- **Understanding approaches to investing:** You want to approach investing in a way that works best for you. Chapter 3 defines the most common approaches to investing.

- **Seeing what exchange-traded funds have to offer:** Exchange-traded funds are like mutual funds, but they can be traded like stocks. See Chapter 5 for the lowdown on exchange-traded funds.

The bottom line in stock investing is that you shouldn't immediately send your money to a brokerage account or go to a website and click "buy stock." The first thing you should do is find out as much as you can about what stocks are and how to use them to achieve your wealth-building goals.

Before you continue, I want to get straight exactly what a stock is. *Stock* is a type of security that indicates ownership in a corporation and represents a claim on a part of that corporation's assets and earnings. The two primary types of stocks are common and preferred:

- **Common stock:** *Common stock* (the type I cover throughout this book) entitles the owner to vote at shareholders' meetings and receive any dividends that the company issues.

- **Preferred stock:** *Preferred stock* doesn't usually confer voting rights, but it does include some rights that exceed those of common stock. Preferred stockholders, for example, have priority in certain conditions, such as receiving dividends before common stockholders in the event that the corporation goes bankrupt. Additionally, preferred stock seeks to operate similarly to a bond for investors seeking stable income. (In this book I mostly cover common stock.)

In addition to common stock, in this edition, I also cover exchange-traded funds because they can be a valuable part of the stock investor's portfolio (see Chapter 5 for more details on exchange-traded funds).

Preparing to Buy Stocks

Gathering information is critical in your stock-investing pursuits. You should gather information on your stock picks two times: before you invest and after. Obviously, you should become more informed before you invest your first dollar, but you also need to stay informed about what's happening to the company whose stock you buy as well as about the industry and the general economy. To find the best information sources, check out Chapter 6.

When you're ready to invest, you need a brokerage account. How do you know which broker to use? Chapter 7 provides some answers and resources to help you choose a broker.

Knowing How to Pick Winners

When you get past the basics, you can get to the meat of stock-picking. Successful stock-picking isn't mysterious, but it does take some time, effort, and analysis. And the effort is worthwhile because stocks are a convenient and important part of most investors' portfolios. Read the following sections and be sure to leapfrog to the relevant chapters to get the inside scoop on hot stocks.

Recognizing stock value

Imagine that you like eggs and you're buying them at the grocery store. In this example, the eggs are like companies, and the prices represent the prices that you would pay for the companies' stock. The grocery store is the stock market. What if two brands of eggs are similar, but one costs $2.99 a carton, and the other costs $3.99? Which would you choose? Odds are that you'd look at both brands, judge their quality, and, if they're indeed similar, take the cheaper eggs. The eggs at $3.99 are overpriced. The same is true of stocks. What if you compare two companies that are similar in every respect but have different share prices? All things being equal, the cheaper price has greater value for the investor.

But the egg example has another side. What if the quality of the two brands of eggs is significantly different, but their prices are the same? If one brand of eggs is stale, of poor quality, and priced at $2.99 and the other brand is fresh, of superior quality, and also priced at $2.99, which would you get? I'd take the good brand because they're better eggs. Perhaps the lesser eggs are an acceptable purchase at $1.99, but they're definitely overpriced at $2.99. The same example works with stocks. A poorly run company isn't a good choice if you can buy a better company in the marketplace at the same — or a better — price.

Comparing the value of eggs may seem overly simplistic, but doing so does cut to the heart of stock investing. Eggs and egg prices can be as varied as companies and stock prices. As an investor, you must make it your job to find the best value for your investment dollars. (Otherwise, you get egg on your face. You saw that one coming, right?)

Understanding how market capitalization affects stock value

You can determine a company's value (and thus the value of its stock) in many ways. The most basic way is to look at the company's market value, also known as market capitalization (or market cap). *Market capitalization* is simply the value you get when you multiply all the outstanding shares of a stock by the price of a single share. Calculating the market cap is easy; for example, if a company has 1 million shares outstanding and its share price is $10, the market cap is $10 million.

Small cap, mid cap, and large cap aren't references to headgear; they're references to how large a company is as measured by its market value. Here are the five basic stock categories of market capitalization:

- ✔ **Micro cap (less than $250 million):** These stocks are the smallest, and hence the riskiest, available. (There's even a subsection of micro cap called *nano cap,* which refers to stocks under $50 million, but they're not appropriate for this book.)

- ✔ **Small cap ($250 million to $1 billion):** These stocks fare better than the micro caps and still have plenty of growth potential. The key word here is "potential."

- ✔ **Mid cap ($1 billion to $10 billion):** For many investors, this category offers a good compromise between small caps and large caps. These stocks have some of the safety of large caps while retaining some of the growth potential of small caps.

- ✔ **Large cap ($10 billion to $50 billion):** This category is usually best reserved for conservative stock investors who want steady appreciation with greater safety. Stocks in this category are frequently referred to as *blue chips.*

- ✔ **Ultra cap (more than $50 billion):** These stocks are also called *mega caps* and obviously refer to companies that are the biggest of the big. Stocks such as Google and Apple are examples.

From a safety point of view, a company's size and market value do matter. All things being equal, large cap stocks are considered safer than small cap stocks. However, small cap stocks have greater potential for growth. Compare these stocks to trees: Which tree is sturdier, a giant California redwood or a small oak tree that's just a year old? In a great storm, the redwood holds up well, whereas the smaller tree has a rough time. But you also have to ask yourself which tree has more opportunity for growth. The redwood may not have much growth left, but the small oak tree has plenty of growth to look forward to.

For beginning investors, comparing market cap to trees isn't so far-fetched. You want your money to branch out without becoming a sap.

Although market capitalization is important to consider, don't invest (or not invest) based solely on it. It's just one measure of value. As a serious investor, you need to look at numerous factors that can help you determine whether any given stock is a good investment. Keep reading — this book is full of information to help you decide.

Sharpening your investment skills

Investors who analyze a company can better judge the value of its stock and profit from buying and selling it. Your greatest asset in stock investing is knowledge (and a little common sense). To succeed in the world of stock investing, keep in mind these key success factors:

- ✔ **Understand why you want to invest in stocks.** Are you seeking appreciation (capital gains) or income (dividends)? Look at Chapters 8 and 9 for information on these topics.

- ✔ **Timing your buys and sells does matter.** Terms like "overbought" and "oversold" can give you an edge when you're deciding whether to purchase or sell a stock. *Technical analysis* is a way to analyze securities through their market activity (past prices and volume) to find patterns that suggest where those investments may be headed in the short term. For more information, see Chapter 10.

- ✔ **Do some research.** Look at the company whose stock you're considering to see whether it's a profitable business worthy of your investment dollars. Chapters 11 and 12 help you scrutinize companies.

- ✔ **Understand and identify what's up with "The Big Picture."** It is a small world after all, and you should be aware of how the world can affect your stock portfolio. Everyone from the bureaucrats in Europe to the politicians in the U.S. Capitol can affect a stock or industry like a match in a dry haystack. Chapters 13, 14, and 15 give you lots of guidance on sector opportunities, megatrends, and, yes, the Big Picture (both economic and political).

✔ **Use investing strategies like the pros do.** In other words, how you go about investing can be just as important as what you invest in. I'm very big on strategies such as trailing stops and limit orders, and fortunately, today's technology gives you even more tools to help you grow or protect your money. Chapters 16, 17, and 18 highlight techniques for investing to help you make more money from your stocks.

✔ **Consider buying in smaller quantities.** Buying stocks doesn't always mean that you must buy through a broker and that it must be 100 shares. You can buy stock for as little as $25 using programs such as dividend reinvestment plans. Chapter 19 tells you more.

✔ **Do as others do, not as they say.** Sometimes, what people tell you to do with stocks is not as revealing as what people are actually doing. This is why I like to look at company insiders before I buy or sell a particular stock. I even touch on insider trading done by Congress. To find out more about insider buying and selling, read Chapter 20.

✔ **Keep more of the money you earn.** After all your great work in getting the right stocks and making the big bucks, you should know about keeping more of the fruits of your investing. I cover taxes in stock investing in Chapter 21.

Every chapter in this book offers you valuable guidance on some essential aspect of the fantastic world of stocks. The knowledge you pick up and apply from these pages has been tested over nearly a century of stock-picking. The investment experience of the past — the good, the bad, and some of the ugly — is here for your benefit. Use this information to make a lot of money (and make me proud!). And don't forget to check out the appendixes, where I provide a wide variety of investing resources and financial ratios!

Stock market insanity

Have you ever noticed a stock going up even though the company is reporting terrible results? How about seeing a stock nose-dive despite the fact that the company is doing well? What gives? Well, judging the direction of a stock in a short-term period — over the next few days or weeks — is almost impossible.

Yes, in the short term, stock investing is irrational. The price of a stock and the value of its company seem disconnected and crazy. The key phrase to remember is "short term." A stock's price and the company's value become more logical over an extended period of time. The longer a stock is in the public's view, the more rational the performance of the stock's price. In other words, a good company continues to draw attention to itself; hence, more people want its stock, and the share price rises to better match the company's value. Conversely, a bad company doesn't hold up to continued scrutiny over time. As more and more people see that the company isn't doing well, the share price declines. Over the long run, a stock's share price and the company's value eventually become equal for the most part.

Chapter 2

Taking Stock of Your Current Financial Situation and Goals

*Y*es, you want to make the big bucks. Or maybe you just want to get back the big bucks you lost in stocks during the *bear market* (a long period of falling prices) of 2000–2002 or perhaps in the infamous global financial crisis of 2008–09. (Investors who followed the guidelines from previous editions of this book did much better than the crowd!) Either way, you want your money to grow so that you can have a better life. But before you make reservations for that Caribbean cruise you're dreaming about, you have to map out your action plan for getting there. Stocks can be a great component of most wealth-building programs, but you must first do some homework on a topic that you should be very familiar with — yourself. That's right. Understanding your current financial situation and clearly defining your financial goals are the first steps in successful investing.

Let me give you an example. I met an investor at one of my seminars who had a million dollars' worth of Procter & Gamble (PG) stock, and he was nearing retirement. He asked me whether he should sell his stock and become more growth-oriented by investing in a batch of *small cap* stocks (stocks of a company worth $250 million to $1 billion; see Chapter 1 for more information). Because he already had enough assets to retire on at that time, I said that he didn't need to get more aggressive. In fact, I told him that he had too much tied to a single stock, even though it was a solid, large company. What would happen to his assets if problems arose at PG? Telling him to shrink his stock portfolio and put that money elsewhere — by paying off debt or adding investment-grade bonds for diversification, for example — seemed obvious.

This chapter is undoubtedly one of the most important chapters in this book. At first, you may think it's a chapter more suitable for some general book on personal finance. Wrong! Unsuccessful investors' greatest weakness is not understanding their financial situations and how stocks fit in. Often, I counsel people to stay out of the stock market if they aren't prepared for the responsibilities of stock investing, such as regularly reviewing the financial statements and progress of the companies they invest in.

Investing in stocks requires balance. Investors sometimes tie up too much money in stocks, putting themselves at risk of losing a significant portion of their wealth if the market plunges. Then again, other investors place little or no money in stocks and therefore miss out on excellent opportunities to grow their wealth. Investors should make stocks a part of their portfolios, but the operative word is *part*. You should let stocks take up only a *portion* of your money. A disciplined investor also has money in bank accounts, investment-grade bonds, precious metals, and other assets that offer growth or income opportunities. Diversification is the key to minimizing risk. (For more on risk, see Chapter 4. I even touch on volatility there.)

Establishing a Starting Point by Preparing a Balance Sheet

Whether you already own stocks or are looking to get into the stock market, you need to find out about how much money you can afford to invest. No matter what you hope to accomplish with your stock investing plan, the first step you should take is to figure out how much you own and how much you owe. To do this, prepare and review your personal balance sheet. A *balance sheet* is simply a list of your assets, your liabilities, and what each item is currently worth so you can arrive at your net worth. Your *net worth* is total assets minus total liabilities. (I know these terms sound like accounting mumbo jumbo, but knowing your net worth is important to your future financial success, so just do it.)

Composing your balance sheet is simple. Pull out a pencil and a piece of paper. For the computer savvy, a spreadsheet software program accomplishes the same task. Gather all your financial documents, such as bank and brokerage statements and other such paperwork — you need figures from these documents. Then follow the steps that I outline in the following sections. Update your balance sheet at least once a year to monitor your financial progress (is your net worth going up or down?).

Note: Your personal balance sheet is really no different from balance sheets that giant companies prepare. (The main difference is a few zeros, but you can use my advice in this book to work on changing that.) In fact, the more you find out about your own balance sheet, the easier it is to understand the balance sheet of companies in which you're seeking to invest. See Chapter 11 for details on reviewing company balance sheets.

Step 1: Make sure you have an emergency fund

First, list cash on your balance sheet. Your goal is to have a reserve of at least three to six months' worth of your gross living expenses in cash and cash equivalents. The cash is important because it gives you a cushion. Three to six months' worth is usually enough to get you through the most common forms of financial disruption, such as losing your job.

If your monthly expenses (or *outgo*) are $2,000, you should have at least $6,000, and probably closer to $12,000, in a secure, FDIC-insured, interest-bearing bank account (or another relatively safe, interest-bearing vehicle such as a money market fund). Consider this account an emergency fund, not an investment. Don't use this money to buy stocks.

Too many Americans don't have an emergency fund, meaning that they put themselves at risk. Walking across a busy street while wearing a blindfold is a great example of putting yourself at risk, and in recent years, investors have done the financial equivalent. Investors piled on tremendous debt, put too much into investments (such as stocks) that they didn't understand, and had little or no savings. One of the biggest problems during this past decade was that savings were sinking to record lows while debt levels were reaching new heights. People then sold many stocks because they needed funds for — you guessed it — paying bills and debt.

Resist the urge to start thinking of your investment in stocks as a savings account generating more than 20 percent per year. This is dangerous thinking! If your investments tank, or if you lose your job, you'll have financial difficulty and that will affect your stock portfolio (you may have to sell some stocks in your account just to get money to pay the bills). An emergency fund helps you through a temporary cash crunch.

Step 2: List your assets in decreasing order of liquidity

Liquid assets aren't references to beer or cola (unless you're Anheuser-Busch). Instead, *liquidity* refers to how quickly you can convert a particular *asset* (something you own that has value) into cash. If you know the liquidity of your assets, including investments, you have some options when you need cash to buy some stock (or pay some bills). All too often, people are short on cash and have too much wealth tied up in *illiquid* investments such as real estate. *Illiquid* is just a fancy way of saying that you don't have the immediate cash to meet a pressing need. (Hey, we've all had those moments!) Review your assets and take measures to ensure that enough of them are liquid (along with your illiquid assets).

Listing your assets in order of liquidity on your balance sheet gives you an immediate picture of which assets you can quickly convert to cash and which ones you can't. If you need money *now,* you can see that cash in hand, your checking account, and your savings account are at the top of the list. The items last in order of liquidity become obvious; they're things like real estate and other assets that can take a long time to convert to cash.

Selling real estate, even in a seller's market, can take months. Investors who don't have adequate liquid assets run the danger of selling assets quickly and possibly at a loss as they scramble to accumulate the cash for their short-term financial obligations. For stock investors, this scramble may include prematurely selling stocks that they originally intended to use as long-term investments.

Table 2-1 shows a typical list of assets in order of liquidity. Use it as a guide for making your own asset list.

Table 2-1 Listing Personal Assets in Decreasing Order of Liquidity

Asset Item	Market Value	Annual Growth Rate %
Current assets		
Cash on hand and in checking	$150	
Bank savings accounts and certificates of deposit	$5,000	2%
Stocks	$2,000	11%
Mutual funds	$2,400	9%
Other assets (collectibles and so on)	$240	
Total current assets	**$9,790**	
Long-term assets		
Auto	$1,800	–10%
Residence	$150,000	5%
Real estate investment	$125,000	6%
Personal stuff (such as jewelry)	$4,000	
Total long-term assets	**$280,800**	
Total assets	**$290,590**	

Here's how to break down the information in Table 2-1:

- ✔ **The first column** describes the asset. You can quickly convert *current assets* to cash — they're more liquid; *long-term assets* have value, but you can't necessarily convert them to cash quickly — they aren't very liquid.

  Note: I have stocks listed as short-term in the table. The reason is that this balance sheet is meant to list items in order of liquidity. Liquidity is best embodied in the question, "How quickly can I turn this asset into cash?" Because a stock can be sold and converted to cash very quickly, it's a good example of a liquid asset. (However, that's not the main purpose for buying stocks.)

- ✔ **The second column** gives the current market value for that item. Keep in mind that this value isn't the purchase price or original value; it's the amount you'd realistically get if you sold the asset in the current market at that moment.

- ✔ **The third column** tells you how well that investment is doing compared to one year ago. If the percentage rate is 5 percent, that item is worth 5 percent more today than it was a year ago. You need to know how well all your assets are doing. Why? So you can adjust your assets for maximum growth or get rid of assets that are losing money. Assets that are doing well should be kept (consider increasing your holdings in these assets), and assets that are down in value should be scrutinized to see whether they're candidates for removal. Perhaps you can sell them and reinvest the money elsewhere. In addition, the realized loss has tax benefits (see Chapter 21).

Figuring the annual growth rate (in the third column) as a percentage isn't difficult. Say that you buy 100 shares of the stock Gro-A-Lot Corp. (GAL), and its market value on December 31, 2011, is $50 per share for a total market value of $5,000 (100 shares × $50 per share). When you check its value on December 31, 2012, you find out that the stock is at $60 per share for a total market value of $6,000 (100 shares × $60). The annual growth rate is 20 percent. You calculate this percentage by taking the amount of the gain ($60 per share less $50 per share = $10 gain per share), which is $1,000 (100 shares times the $10 gain), and dividing it by the value at the beginning of the time period ($5,000). In this case, you get 20 percent ($1,000 ÷ $5,000).

What if GAL also generates a dividend of $2 per share during that period — now what? In that case, GAL generates a total return of 24 percent. To calculate the total return, add the appreciation ($10 per share × 100 shares = $1,000) and the dividend income ($2 per share × 100 shares = $200) and divide that sum ($1,000 + $200, or $1,200) by the value at the beginning of the year ($50 per share × 100 shares, or $5,000). The total is $1,200 ÷ $5,000, or 24 percent.

- ✔ **The last line** lists the total for all the assets and their current market value.

Step 3: List your liabilities

Liabilities are simply the bills that you're obligated to pay. Whether it's a credit card bill or a mortgage payment, a liability is an amount of money you have to pay back eventually (usually with interest). If you don't keep track of your liabilities, you may end up thinking that you have more money than you really do.

Table 2-2 lists some common liabilities. Use it as a model when you list your own. You should list the liabilities according to how soon you need to pay them. Credit card balances tend to be short-term obligations, whereas mortgages are long-term.

Table 2-2	Listing Personal Liabilities	
Liabilities	**Amount**	**Paying Rate %**
Credit cards	$4,000	15%
Personal loans	$13,000	10%
Mortgage	$100,000	8%
Total liabilities	**$117,000**	

Here's a summary of the information in Table 2-2:

✔ **The first column** names the type of debt. Don't forget to include student loans and auto loans if you have them.

Never avoid listing a liability because you're embarrassed to see how much you really owe. Be honest with yourself — doing so helps you improve your financial health.

✔ **The second column** shows the current value (or current balance) of your liabilities. List the most current balance to see where you stand with your creditors.

✔ **The third column** reflects how much interest you're paying for carrying that debt. This information is an important reminder about how debt can be a wealth zapper. Credit card debt can have an interest rate of 18 percent or more, and to add insult to injury, it isn't even tax-deductible. Using a credit card to make even a small purchase costs you if you don't pay off the balance each month. Within a year, a $50 sweater at 18 percent costs $59 when you add in the potential interest you pay.

If you compare your liabilities in Table 2-2 and your personal assets in Table 2-1, you may find opportunities to reduce the amount you pay for interest. Say, for example, that you pay 15 percent on a credit card balance of $4,000 but also have a personal asset of $5,000 in a bank savings account that's earning 2 percent in interest. In that case, you may want to consider taking $4,000 out of the savings account to pay off the credit card balance. Doing so saves you $520; the $4,000 in the bank was earning only $80 (2 percent of $4,000), while you were paying $600 on the credit card balance (15 percent of $4,000).

If you can't pay off high-interest debt, at least look for ways to minimize the cost of carrying the debt. The most obvious ways include the following:

- **Replace high-interest cards with low-interest cards.** Many companies offer incentives to consumers, including signing up for cards with favorable rates (recently under 10 percent) that can be used to pay off high-interest cards (typically 12 to 18 percent or higher).

- **Replace unsecured debt with secured debt.** Credit cards and personal loans are _unsecured_ (you haven't put up any collateral or other asset to secure the debt); therefore, they have higher interest rates because this type of debt is considered riskier for the creditor. Sources of _secured debt_ (such as home equity line accounts and brokerage accounts) provide you with a means to replace your high-interest debt with lower-interest debt. You get lower interest rates with secured debt because it's less risky for the creditor — the debt is backed up by collateral (your home or your stocks).

- **Replace variable-interest debt with fixed-interest debt.** Think about how homeowners got blindsided when their monthly payments on adjustable-rate mortgages went up drastically in the wake of the housing bubble that popped during 2005–2008. If you can't lower your debt, at least make it fixed and predictable.

The year 2011 was the 15th consecutive year that personal bankruptcies surpassed the million mark in the United States. Corporate bankruptcies were also at record levels. In 2012, total college debt surpassed $1 trillion. Make a diligent effort to control and reduce your debt; otherwise, the debt can become too burdensome. If you don't control it, you may have to sell your stocks just to stay liquid. Remember, Murphy's Law states that you _will_ sell your stock at the worst possible moment! Don't go there.

I owe, I owe, so off to work I go

One reason you continue to work is probably so that you can pay off your bills. But many people today are losing their jobs because their company owes, too!

Debt is one of the biggest financial problems in the United States today. Companies and individuals holding excessive debt contributed to the stock market's painful plunge in 2008 and 2009. The general economy and financial markets are still a major danger zone for 2012–14. If individuals and companies managed their liabilities more responsibly, the general economy would be much better off.

The greatest debt problems (in terms of size) come from the public sector. Federal, state, and municipal debt are at all-time highs. This is debt that everyone has to deal with indirectly because it's incurred by politicians and government bureaucrats but must be addressed by us. The pressure is on for higher income taxes, real estate taxes, and other taxes. Yikes! (Now I know why some people become cave-dwelling hermits.) And yes . . . the stock market (and the stocks in your portfolio) will be affected!

Step 4: Calculate your net worth

Your *net worth* is an indication of your total wealth. You can calculate your net worth with this basic equation: total assets (Table 2-1) less total liabilities (Table 2-2) equal net worth (net assets or net equity).

Table 2-3 shows this equation in action with a net worth of $173,590 — a very respectable number. For many investors, just being in a position where assets exceed liabilities (a positive net worth) is great news. Use Table 2-3 as a model to analyze your own financial situation. Your mission (if you choose to accept it — and you should) is to ensure that your net worth increases from year to year as you progress toward your financial goals (I discuss financial goals later in this chapter).

Table 2-3	Figuring Your Personal Net Worth	
Totals	*Amounts ($)*	*Increase from Year Before*
Total assets (from Table 2-1)	$290,590	+5%
Total liabilities (from Table 2-2)	($117,000)	–2%
Net worth (total assets less total liabilities)	**$173,590**	**+3%**

Step 5: Analyze your balance sheet

After you create a balance sheet (based on the steps in the preceding sections) to illustrate your current finances, take a close look at it and try to identify any changes you can make to increase your wealth. Sometimes, reaching your financial goals can be as simple as refocusing the items on your balance sheet (use Table 2-3 as a general guideline). Here are some brief points to consider:

- **Is the money in your emergency (or rainy day) fund sitting in an ultra-safe account and earning the highest interest available?** Bank money market accounts or money market funds are recommended. The safest type of account is a U.S. Treasury money market fund. Banks are backed by the Federal Deposit Insurance Corporation (FDIC), while U.S. treasury securities are backed by the "full faith and credit" of the federal government. Shop around for the best rates.

- **Can you replace depreciating assets with appreciating assets?** Say that you have two stereo systems. Why not sell one and invest the proceeds? You may say, "But I bought that unit two years ago for $500, and if I sell it now, I'll get only $300." That's your choice. You need to decide what helps your financial situation more — a $500 item that keeps shrinking in value (a *depreciating asset*) or $300 that can grow in value when invested (an *appreciating asset*).

- **Can you replace low-yield investments with high-yield investments?** Maybe you have $5,000 in a bank certificate of deposit (CD) earning 3 percent. You can certainly shop around for a better rate at another bank, but you can also seek alternatives that can offer a higher yield, such as U.S. savings bonds or short-term bond funds. Just keep in mind that if you already have a CD and you withdraw the funds before it matures, you may face a penalty (such as losing some interest).

- **Can you pay off any high-interest debt with funds from low-interest assets?** If, for example, you have $5,000 earning 2 percent in a taxable bank account, and you have $2,500 on a credit card charging 18 percent (which is not tax-deductible), you may as well pay off the credit card balance and save on the interest.

- **If you're carrying debt, are you using that money for an investment return that's greater than the interest you're paying?** Carrying a loan with an interest rate of 8 percent is acceptable if that borrowed money is yielding more than 8 percent elsewhere. Suppose that you have $6,000 in cash in a brokerage account. If you qualify, you can actually make a stock purchase greater than $6,000 by using margin (essentially a loan from the broker). You can buy $12,000 of stock using your $6,000 in cash, with the remainder financed by the broker. Of course, you pay interest on that margin loan. But what if the interest rate is 6 percent and the stock you're about to invest in has a dividend that yields 9 percent? In that case, the dividend can help you pay off the margin loan, and you keep the additional income. (For more on buying on margin, see Chapter 17.)

✓ **Can you sell any personal stuff for cash?** You can replace unproductive assets with cash from garage sales and auction websites.

✓ **Can you use your home equity to pay off consumer debt?** Borrowing against your home has more favorable interest rates, and this interest is still tax-deductible.

Paying off consumer debt by using funds borrowed against your home is a great way to wipe the slate clean. What a relief to get rid of your credit card balances! Just don't turn around and run up the consumer debt again. You can get overburdened and experience financial ruin (not to mention homelessness). Not a pretty picture.

The important point to remember is that you can take control of your finances with discipline (and with the advice I offer in this book).

Funding Your Stock Program

If you're going to invest money in stocks, the first thing you need is . . . money! Where can you get that money? If you're waiting for an inheritance to come through, you may have to wait a long time, considering all the advances being made in healthcare lately. (What's that? You were going to invest in healthcare stocks? How ironic.) Yet, the challenge still comes down to how to fund your stock program.

Many investors can reallocate their investments and assets to do the trick. *Reallocating* simply means selling some investments or other assets and reinvesting that money into something else (such as stocks). It boils down to deciding what investment or asset you can sell or liquidate. Generally, you want to consider those investments and assets that give you a low return on your money (or no return at all). If you have a complicated mix of investments and assets, you may want to consider reviewing your options with a financial planner. Reallocation is just part of the answer; your cash flow is the other part.

Ever wonder why there's so much month left at the end of the money? Consider your cash flow. Your *cash flow* refers to what money is coming in (income) and what money is being spent (outgo). The net result is either a positive cash flow or a negative cash flow, depending on your cash management skills. Maintaining a positive cash flow (more money coming in than going out) helps you increase your net worth. A negative cash flow ultimately depletes your wealth and wipes out your net worth if you don't turn it around immediately.

The following sections show you how to calculate and analyze your cash flow. The first step is to do a cash flow statement. With a cash flow statement, you ask yourself three questions:

- **What money is coming in?** In your cash flow statement, jot down all sources of income. Calculate income for the month and then for the year. Include everything: salary, wages, interest, dividends, and so on. Add them all up and get your grand total for income.

- **What is your outgo?** Write down all the things that you spend money on. List all your expenses. If possible, categorize them as essential and nonessential. You can get an idea of all the expenses that you can reduce without affecting your lifestyle. But before you do that, make as complete a list as possible of what you spend your money on.

- **What's left?** If your income is greater than your outgo, you have money ready and available for stock investing. No matter how small the amount seems, it definitely helps. I've seen fortunes built when people started to diligently invest as little as $25 to $50 per week or per month. If your outgo is greater than your income, you better sharpen your pencil. Cut down on nonessential spending and/or increase your income. If your budget is a little tight, hold off on your stock investing until your cash flow improves.

Dot-com-and-go

If you were publishing a book about negative cash flow, you could look for the employees of any one of 100 dot-com companies to write it. Their qualifications include working for a company that flew sky-high in 1999 and crashed in 2000 and 2001. Companies such as eToys.com, Pets.com, and DrKoop.com were given millions, yet they couldn't turn a profit and eventually closed for business. You may as well call them "dot-com-and-go." You can learn from their mistakes. (Actually, they could have learned from you.) In the same way that profit is the most essential single element in a business, a positive cash flow is important for your finances in general and for funding your stock investment program in particular.

Don't confuse a cash flow statement with an income statement (also called a *profit and loss statement* or an *income and expense statement*). A cash flow statement is simple to calculate because you can easily track what goes in and what goes out. Income statements are a little different (especially for businesses) because they take into account things that aren't technically cash flow (such as depreciation or amortization). Find out more about income statements in Chapter 11.

Step 1: Tally up your income

Using Table 2-4 as a worksheet, list and calculate the money you have coming in. The first column describes the source of the money, the second column indicates the monthly amount from each respective source, and the last column indicates the amount projected for a full year. Include all income, such as wages, business income, dividends, interest income, and so on. Then project these amounts for a year (multiply by 12) and enter those amounts in the third column.

Table 2-4	Listing Your Income	
Item	*Monthly $ Amount*	*Yearly $ Amount*
Salary and wages		
Interest income and dividends		
Business net (after taxes) income		
Other income		
Total income		

Your total income is the amount of money you have to work with. To ensure your financial health, don't spend more than this amount. Always be aware of and carefully manage your income.

Step 2: Add up your outgo

Using Table 2-5 as a worksheet, list and calculate the money that's going out. How much are you spending and on what? The first column describes the source of the expense, the second column indicates the monthly amount, and the third column shows the amount projected for a full year. Include all the money you spend: credit card and other debt payments; household expenses, such as food, utility bills, and medical expenses; and nonessential expenses such as video games and elephant-foot umbrella stands.

Table 2-5	Listing Your Expenses (Outgo)	
Item	*Monthly $ Amount*	*Yearly $ Amount*
Payroll taxes		
Rent or mortgage		
Utilities		
Food		
Clothing		
Insurance (medical, auto, homeowners, and so on)		
Telephone		
Real estate taxes		
Auto expenses		
Charity		
Recreation		
Credit card payments		
Loan payments		
Other		
Total outgo		

Payroll taxes is just a category in which to lump all the various taxes that the government takes out of your paycheck. Feel free to put each individual tax on its own line if you prefer. The important thing is creating a comprehensive list that's meaningful to you.

You may notice that the outgo doesn't include items such as payments to a 401(k) plan and other savings vehicles. Yes, these items do impact your cash flow, but they're not expenses; the amounts that you invest (or your employer invests for you) are essentially assets that benefit your financial situation versus expenses that don't help you build wealth. To account for the 401(k), simply deduct it from the gross pay before you calculate the preceding worksheet (Table 2-5). If, for example, your gross pay is $2,000 and your 401(k) contribution is $300, then use $1,700 as your income figure.

Step 3: Create a cash flow statement

Okay, you're almost to the end. The next step is creating a cash flow statement so that you can see (all in one place) how your money moves — how much comes in and how much goes out and where it goes.

Plug the amount of your total income (from Table 2-4) and the amount of your total expenses (from Table 2-5) into the Table 2-6 worksheet to see your *cash flow*. Do you have positive cash flow — more coming in than going out — so that you can start investing in stocks (or other investments), or are expenses overpowering your income? Doing a cash flow statement isn't just about finding money in your financial situation to fund your stock program. First and foremost, it's about your financial well-being. Are you managing your finances well or not?

Table 2-6	Looking at Your Cash Flow	
Item	*Monthly $ Amount*	*Yearly $ Amount*
Total income (from Table 2-4)		
Total outgo (from Table 2-5)		
Net inflow/outflow		

At the time of this writing, 2012 was shaping up to be yet another record year for personal and business bankruptcies. Personal debt and expenses far exceeded whatever income they generated. That announcement is another reminder to watch your cash flow; keep your income growing and your expenses and debt as low as possible.

Step 4: Analyze your cash flow

Use your cash flow statement in Table 2-6 to identify sources of funds for your investment program. The more you can increase your income and decrease your outgo, the better. Scrutinize your data. Where can you improve the results? Here are some questions to ask yourself:

✔ How can you increase your income? Do you have hobbies, interests, or skills that can generate extra cash for you?

✔ Can you get more paid overtime at work? How about a promotion or a job change?

✔ Where can you cut expenses?

✔ Have you categorized your expenses as either "necessary" or "nonessential"?

✔ Can you lower your debt payments by refinancing or consolidating loans and credit card balances?

✔ Have you shopped around for lower insurance or telephone rates?

✔ Have you analyzed your tax withholdings in your paycheck to make sure that you're not overpaying your taxes (just to get your overpayment back next year as a refund)?

Another option: Finding investment money in tax savings

According to the Tax Foundation (taxfoundation.org), the average U.S. citizen pays more in taxes than in food, clothing, and shelter combined. Sit down with your tax advisor and try to find ways to reduce your taxes. A home-based business, for example, is a great way to gain new income and increase your tax deductions, resulting in a lower tax burden. Your tax advisor can make recommendations that work for you.

One tax strategy to consider is doing your stock investing in a tax-sheltered account such as a traditional Individual Retirement Account (IRA) or a Roth Individual Retirement Account (Roth IRA). Again, check with your tax advisor for deductions and strategies available to you. For more on the tax implications of stock investing, see Chapter 21.

Setting Your Sights on Your Financial Goals

Consider stocks as tools for living, just like any other investment — no more, no less. Stocks are among the many tools you use to accomplish something — to achieve a goal. Yes, successfully investing in stocks is the goal that you're probably shooting for if you're reading this book. However, you must complete the following sentence: "I want to be successful in my stock investing program to accomplish _____ short." You must consider stock investing as a means to an end. When people buy a computer, they don't (or shouldn't) think of buying a computer just to have a computer. People buy a computer because doing so helps them achieve a particular result, such as being more efficient in business, playing fun games, or having a nifty paperweight (tsk, tsk).

Know the difference between long-term, intermediate-term, and short-term goals, and then set some of each (see Chapter 3 for more information).

- ✔ Long-term goals refer to projects or financial goals that need funding five or more years from now.
- ✔ Intermediate-term goals refer to financial goals that need funding two to five years from now.
- ✔ Short-term goals need funding less than two years from now.

Stocks, in general, are best suited for long-term goals such as these:

- ✔ Achieving financial independence (think retirement funding)
- ✔ Paying for future college costs
- ✔ Paying for any long-term expenditure or project

Some categories of stock (such as conservative or large cap) may be suitable for intermediate-term financial goals. If, for example, you'll retire four years from now, conservative stocks can be appropriate. If you're optimistic (or *bullish*) about the stock market and confident that stock prices will rise, go ahead and invest. However, if you're negative about the market (you're *bearish*, or you believe that stock prices will decline), you may want to wait until the economy starts to forge a clear path. To help you figure out some mega-trends for the U.S. economy, flip to Chapter 14.

Stocks generally aren't suitable for short-term investing goals because stock prices can behave irrationally in a short period of time. Stocks fluctuate from day to day, so you don't know what the stock will be worth in the near future. You may end up with less money than you expected. For investors seeking to reliably accrue money for short-term needs, short-term bank certificates of deposit or money market funds are more appropriate.

In recent years, investors have sought quick, short-term profits by trading and speculating in stocks. Lured by the fantastic returns generated by the stock market in the late 1990s, investors saw stocks as a get-rich-quick scheme. It's very important for you to understand the difference between *investing, saving,* and *speculating*. Which one do you want to do? Knowing the answer to this question is crucial to your goals and aspirations. Investors who don't know the difference tend to get burned. Here's some information to help you distinguish among these three actions:

✔ *Investing* **is the act of putting your current funds into securities or tangible assets for the purpose of gaining future appreciation, income, or both.** You need time, knowledge, and discipline to invest. The investment can fluctuate in price, but it has been chosen for long-term potential.

✔ *Saving* **is the safe accumulation of funds for a future use.** Savings don't fluctuate and are generally free of financial risk. The emphasis is on safety and liquidity.

✔ *Speculating* **is the financial world's equivalent of gambling.** An investor who speculates is seeking quick profits gained from short-term price movements in a particular asset or investment. (In recent years, many folks have been trading stocks [buying and selling in the short term with frequency], which is in the realm of short-term speculating.)

These distinctly different concepts are often confused, even among so-called financial experts. I know of one financial advisor who actually put a child's college fund money into an Internet stock fund, only to lose more than $17,000 in less than ten months! For more on the distinctions between investing and speculating (and trading too!) go to Chapter 16.

Chapter 3

Defining Common Approaches to Stock Investing

"Investing for the long term" isn't just some perfunctory investment slogan. It's a culmination of proven stock market experience that goes back many decades. Unfortunately, investor buying and selling habits have deteriorated in recent years due to impatience. Today's investors think that short term is measured in days, intermediate term is measured in weeks, and long term is measured in months. Yeesh! No wonder so many folks are complaining about lousy investment returns. Investors have lost the profitable art of patience!

What should you do? Become an investor with a time horizon greater than one year (the emphasis is on "greater"). Give your investments time to grow. Everybody dreams about emulating the success of someone like Warren Buffett, but few emulate his patience (a huge part of his investment success).

Stocks are tools you can use to build your wealth. When used wisely, for the right purpose and in the right environment, they do a great job. But when improperly applied, they can lead to disaster. In this chapter, I show you how to choose the right types of investments based on your short-term, intermediate-term, and long-term financial goals. I also show you how to decide on your purpose for investing (growth or income investing) and your style of investing (conservative or aggressive).

Matching Stocks and Strategies with Your Goals

Various stocks are out there, as well as various investment approaches. The key to success in the stock market is matching the right kind of stock with the right kind of investment situation. You have to choose the stock and the approach that match your goals. (Check out Chapter 2 for more on defining your financial goals.)

Before investing in a stock, ask yourself, "When do I want to reach my financial goal?" Stocks are a means to an end. Your job is to figure out what that end is — or, more important, when it is. Do you want to retire in ten years or next year? Must you pay for your kid's college education next year or 18 years from now? The length of time you have before you need the money you hope to earn from stock investing determines what stocks you should buy. Table 3-1 gives you some guidelines for choosing the kind of stock best suited for the type of investor you are and the goals you have.

Table 3-1	Investor Types, Financial Goals, and Stock Types	
Type of Investor	*Time Frame for Financial Goals*	*Type of Stock Most Suitable*
Conservative (worries about risk)	Long term (more than 5 years)	Large cap stocks and mid cap stocks
Aggressive (high tolerance to risk)	Long term (more than 5 years)	Small cap stocks and mid cap stocks
Conservative (worries about risk)	Intermediate term (2 to 5 years)	Large cap stocks, preferably with dividends
Aggressive (high tolerance to risk)	Intermediate term (2 to 5 years)	Small cap stocks and mid cap stocks
Short term	1 to 2 years	Stocks are not suitable for the short term. Instead, look at vehicles such as savings accounts and money market funds.
Very short term	Less than 1 year	Stocks? Don't even think about it! Well . . . you *can* invest in stocks for less than a year, but seriously, you're not really investing — you're either trading or speculating (see Chapter 16). Instead, use savings accounts and money market funds.

Dividends are payments made to a stock-owner (unlike *interest,* which is payment to a creditor). Dividends are a great form of income, and companies that issue dividends tend to have more stable stock prices as well. For more information on dividend-paying stocks, see the section "Steadily making money: Income investing," later in this chapter, and also see Chapter 9.

Table 3-1 gives you general guidelines, but not everyone fits into a particular profile. Every investor has a unique situation, set of goals, and level of risk tolerance. The terms *large cap, mid cap,* and *small cap* refer to the size (or *market capitalization,* also known as *market cap*) of the company. All factors being equal, large companies are safer (less risky) than small companies. For more on market caps, see the section "Investing for Your Personal Style," later in this chapter, as well as Chapter 1.

Investing for the Future

Are your goals long-term or short-term? Answering this question is important because individual stocks can be either great or horrible choices, depending on the time period you want to focus on. Generally, the length of time you plan to invest in stocks can be short-term, intermediate-term, or long-term. The following sections outline what kinds of stocks are most appropriate for each term length.

Investing in quality stocks becomes less risky as the time frame lengthens. Stock prices tend to fluctuate daily, but they have a tendency to trend up or down over an extended period of time. Even if you invest in a stock that goes down in the short term, you're likely to see it rise and possibly exceed your investment if you have the patience to wait it out and let the stock price appreciate.

Focusing on the short term

Short term generally means one year or less, although some people extend the period to two years or less. Short-term investing isn't about making a quick buck on your stock choices — it refers to when you may need the money.

Every person has short-term goals. Some are modest, such as setting aside money for a vacation next month or paying for medical bills. Other short-term goals are more ambitious, such as accruing funds for a down payment to purchase a new home within six months. Whatever the expense or purchase, you need a predictable accumulation of cash soon. If this sounds like your situation, stay away from the stock market!

Because stocks can be so unpredictable in the short term, they're a bad choice for short-term considerations. I get a kick out of market analysts on TV saying things such as, "At $25 a share, XYZ is a solid investment, and we feel that its stock should hit our target price of $40 within six to nine months." You know that an eager investor hears that and says, "Gee, why bother with 3 percent at the bank when this stock will rise by more than 50 percent? I better call my broker." It may hit that target amount (or surpass it), or it may not. Most of the time, the stock doesn't reach the target price, and the investor is disappointed. The stock can even go down!

The reason that target prices are frequently missed is that it's difficult to figure out what millions of investors will do in the short term. The short term can be irrational because so many investors have so many reasons for buying and selling that it can be difficult to analyze. If you invest for an important short-term need, you can lose very important cash quicker than you think.

During the raging bull market of the late 1990s, investors watched as some high-profile stocks went up 20 to 50 percent in a matter of months. Hey, who needs a savings account earning a measly interest rate when stocks grow like that! Of course, when the bear market hit from 2000 to 2003 and those same stocks fell 50 to 85 percent, a savings account earning a measly interest rate suddenly didn't seem so bad.

Short-term stock investing is very unpredictable. Stocks — even the best ones — fluctuate in the short term. In a negative environment, they can be very volatile. No one can accurately predict the price movement (unless he has some inside information), so stocks are definitely inappropriate for any financial goal you need to reach within one year. You can better serve your short-term goals with stable, interest-bearing investments like certificates of deposit at your local bank. Refer to Table 3-1 for suggestions about your short-term strategies.

Short-term investing = speculating

My case files are littered with examples of long-term stock investors who morphed into short-term speculators. I know of one fellow who had $80,000 and was set to get married within 12 months and then put a down payment on a new home for him and his bride. He wanted to surprise her by growing his nest egg quickly so they could have a glitzier wedding and a larger down payment. What happened? The money instead shrunk to $11,000 as his stock choices pulled back sharply. Ouch! How does that go again? For better or for worse . . . uh . . . for richer or for poorer? I'm sure they had to adjust their plans accordingly. I recall some of the stocks he chose, and now, years later, those stocks have recovered and gone on to new highs.

The bottom line is that investing in stocks for the short term is nothing more than speculating. Your only possible strategy is luck.

Considering intermediate-term goals

Intermediate term refers to the financial goals you plan to reach in two to five years. For example, if you want to accumulate funds to put money down for investment in real estate four years from now, some growth-oriented investments may be suitable. (I discuss growth investing in more detail later in this chapter.)

Although some stocks *may* be appropriate for a two- or three-year period, not all stocks are good intermediate-term investments. Some stocks are fairly stable and hold their value well, such as the stock of large or established dividend-paying companies. Other stocks have prices that jump all over the place, such as those of untested companies that haven't been in existence long enough to develop a consistent track record.

If you plan to invest in the stock market to meet intermediate-term goals, consider large, established companies or dividend-paying companies in industries that provide the necessities of life (like the food and beverage industry, or electric utilities). In today's economic environment, I strongly believe that stocks attached to companies that serve basic human needs should have a major presence in most stock portfolios. They're especially well-suited for intermediate investment goals.

Just because a particular stock is labeled as being appropriate for the intermediate term doesn't mean you should get rid of it by the stroke of midnight five years from now. After all, if the company is doing well and going strong, you can continue holding the stock indefinitely. The more time you give a well-positioned, profitable company's stock to grow, the better you'll do.

Preparing for the long term

Stock investing is best suited for making money over a long period of time. Usually, when you measure stocks against other investments in terms of five to (preferably) ten or more years, they excel. Even investors who bought stocks during the depths of the Great Depression saw profitable growth in their stock portfolios over a ten-year period. In fact, if you examine any ten-year period over the past fifty years, you see that stocks beat out other financial investments (such as bonds or bank investments) in almost every period when measured by total return (taking into account reinvesting and compounding of capital gains and dividends)!

Of course, your work doesn't stop at deciding on a long-term investment. You still have to do your homework and choose stocks wisely, because even in good times, you can lose money if you invest in companies that go out of business. Part III of this book shows you how to evaluate specific companies and industries and alerts you to factors in the general economy that can affect stock behavior. Appendix A provides plenty of resources you can turn to.

Because so many different types and categories of stocks are available, virtually any investor with a long-term perspective should add stocks to his investment portfolio. Whether you want to save for a young child's college fund or for future retirement goals, carefully selected stocks have proven to be a superior long-term investment.

Investing for a Purpose

When someone asked the lady why she bungee jumped off the bridge that spanned a massive ravine, she answered, "Because it's fun!" When someone asked the fellow why he dove in to a pool chock-full of alligators and snakes, he responded, "Because someone pushed me." You shouldn't invest in stocks unless you have a purpose that you understand, like investing for growth or income. Keep in mind that stocks are just a means to an end — figure out your desired end and then match the means. The following sections can help.

Even if an advisor pushes you to invest, be sure that advisor gives you an explanation of how each stock choice fits your purpose. I know of a very nice, elderly lady who had a portfolio brimming with aggressive-growth stocks because she had an overbearing broker. Her purpose should've been conservative, and she should've chosen investments that would preserve her wealth rather than grow it. Obviously, the broker's agenda got in the way. (To find out more about dealing with brokers, go to Chapter 7.)

Making loads of money quickly: Growth investing

When investors want their money to grow (versus just trying to preserve it), they look for investments that appreciate in value. *Appreciate* is just another way of saying *grow*. If you bought a stock for $8 per share and now its value is $30 per share, your investment has grown by $22 per share — that's appreciation. I know I would appreciate it.

Appreciation (also known as *capital gain*) is probably the number-one reason people invest in stocks. Few investments have the potential to grow your wealth as conveniently as stocks. If you want the stock market to make you loads of money (and you can assume some risk), head to Chapter 8, which takes an in-depth look at investing for growth.

Stocks are a great way to grow your wealth, but they're not the only way. Many investors seek alternative ways to make money, but many of these alternative ways are more aggressive than stocks and carry significantly more risk. You may have heard about people who made quick fortunes in areas such as commodities (like wheat, pork bellies, or precious metals), options, and other more-sophisticated investment vehicles. Keep in mind that you should limit these riskier investments to only a small portion of your portfolio, such as 5 or 10 percent of your investable funds. Experienced investors, however, can go higher.

Steadily making money: Income investing

Not all investors want to take on the risk that comes with making a killing. (Hey . . . no guts, no glory!) Some people just want to invest in the stock market as a means of providing a steady income. They don't need stock values to go through the ceiling. Instead, they need stocks that perform well consistently.

If your purpose for investing in stocks is to create income, you need to choose stocks that pay dividends. Dividends are typically paid quarterly to stockholders on record as of specific dates. How do you know if the dividend you're being paid is higher (or lower) than other vehicles (such as bonds)? The following sections help you figure it out.

Distinguishing between dividends and interest

Don't confuse dividends with interest. Most people are familiar with interest because that's how you grow your money over the years in the bank. The important difference is that *interest* is paid to creditors, and *dividends* are paid to owners (meaning *shareholders* — and if you own stock, you're a shareholder because shares of stock represent ownership in a publicly traded company).

When you buy stock, you buy a piece of that company. When you put money in a bank (or when you buy bonds), you basically loan your money. You become a creditor, and the bank or bond issuer is the debtor; as such, it must eventually pay your money back to you with interest.

Recognizing the importance of an income stock's yield

When you invest for income, you have to consider your investment's yield and compare it with the alternatives. The *yield* is an investment's payout expressed as a percentage of the investment amount. Looking at the yield is a way to compare the income you expect to receive from one investment with the expected income from others. Table 3-2 shows some comparative yields.

Table 3-2	Comparing the Yields of Various Investments				
Investment	**Type**	**Amount**	**Pay Type**	**Payout**	**Yield**
Smith Co.	Stock	$50/share	Dividend	$2.50	5.0%
Jones Co.	Stock	$100/share	Dividend	$4.00	4.0%
Acme Bank	Bank CD	$500	Interest	$25.00	5.0%
Acme Bank	Bank CD	$2,500	Interest	$131.25	5.25%
Acme Bank	Bank CD	$5,000	Interest	$287.50	5.75%
Brown Co.	Bond	$5,000	Interest	$300.00	6.0%

To calculate yield, use the following formula:

   yield = payout ÷ investment amount

For the sake of simplicity, the following exercise is based on an annual percentage yield basis (compounding would increase the yield).

Jones Co. and Smith Co. are typical dividend-paying stocks. Looking at Table 3-2 and presuming that both companies are similar in most respects except for their differing dividends, how can you tell whether the $50 stock with a $2.50 annual dividend is better (or worse) than the $100 stock with a $4.00 dividend? The yield tells you.

Even though Jones Co. pays a higher dividend ($4.00), Smith Co. has a higher yield (5 percent). Therefore, if you have to choose between those two stocks as an income investor, you should choose Smith Co. Of course, if you truly want to maximize your income and don't really need your investment to appreciate a lot, you should probably choose Brown Co.'s bond because it offers a yield of 6 percent.

Dividend-paying stocks do have the ability to increase in value. They may not have the same growth potential as growth stocks, but at the very least, they have a greater potential for capital gain than CDs or bonds. Dividend-paying stocks (good for investing for income) are covered in Chapter 9.

Investing for Your Personal Style

Your investing style isn't a blue-jeans-versus-three-piece-suit debate. It refers to your approach to stock investing. Do you want to be conservative or aggressive? Would you rather be the tortoise or the hare? Your investment personality greatly depends on your purpose and the term over which you're planning to invest (see the previous two sections). The following sections outline the two most general investment styles.

Conservative investing

Conservative investing means that you put your money in something proven, tried, and true. You invest your money in safe and secure places, such as banks and government-backed securities. But how does that apply to stocks? (Table 3-1 gives you suggestions.)

If you're a conservative stock investor, you want to place your money in companies that exhibit some of the following qualities:

- ✔ **Proven performance:** You want companies that have shown increasing sales and earnings year after year. You don't demand anything spectacular — just a strong and steady performance.

- ✔ **Large market size:** You want to invest in *large cap* companies (short for large capitalization). In other words, they should have a market value exceeding $5–$25 billion. Conservative investors surmise that bigger is safer.

- ✔ **Proven market leadership:** Look for companies that are leaders in their industries.

- ✔ **Perceived staying power:** You want companies with the financial clout and market position to weather uncertain market and economic conditions. What happens in the economy or who gets elected shouldn't matter.

As a conservative investor, you don't mind if the companies' share prices jump (who would?), but you're more concerned with steady growth over the long term.

Aggressive investing

Aggressive investors can plan long-term or look over only the intermediate term, but in any case, they want stocks that resemble jack rabbits — those that show the potential to break out of the pack.

If you're an aggressive stock investor, you want to invest your money in companies that exhibit some of the following qualities:

✔ **Great potential:** Choose companies that have superior goods, services, ideas, or ways of doing business compared to the competition.

✔ **Capital gains possibility:** Don't even consider dividends. If anything, you dislike dividends. You feel that the money dispensed in dividend form is better reinvested in the company. This, in turn, can spur greater growth.

✔ **Innovation:** Find companies that have innovative technologies, ideas, or methods that make them stand apart from other companies.

Aggressive investors usually seek out small capitalization stocks, known as *small caps,* because they can have plenty of potential for growth. Take the tree example, for instance: A giant redwood may be strong, but it may not grow much more, whereas a brand-new sapling has plenty of growth to look forward to. Why invest in big, stodgy companies when you can invest in smaller enterprises that may become the leaders of tomorrow? Aggressive investors have no problem buying stock in obscure businesses because they hope that such companies will become another Apple or McDonald's. Find out more about growth investing in Chapter 8.

Chapter 4

Recognizing Risk and Volatility

*I*nvestors face many risks, most of which I cover in this chapter. The simplest definition of risk for investors is "the possibility that your investment will lose some (or all) of its value." Yet you don't have to fear risk if you understand it and plan for it. You must understand the oldest equation in the world of investing — risk versus return. This equation states the following:

> If you want a greater return on your money, you need to tolerate more risk. If you don't want to tolerate more risk, you must tolerate a lower rate of return.

This point about risk is best illustrated from a moment in one of my investment seminars. One of the attendees told me that he had his money in the bank but was dissatisfied with the rate of return. He lamented, "The yield on my money is pitiful! I want to put my money somewhere where it can grow." I asked him, "How about investing in common stocks? Or what about growth mutual funds? They have a solid, long-term growth track record." He responded, "Stocks? I don't want to put my money there. It's too risky!" Okay, then. If you don't want to tolerate more risk, don't complain about earning less on your money. Risk (in all its forms) has a bearing on all your money concerns and goals. That's why understanding risk before you invest is so important.

This man — as well as the rest of us — needs to remember that risk is not a four-letter word. (Well, it is a four-letter word, but you know what I mean.) Risk is present no matter what you do with your money. Even if you simply stick your money in your mattress, risk is involved — several kinds of risk, in fact. You have the risk of fire. What if your house burns down? You have the risk of theft. What if burglars find your stash of cash? You also have relative risk. (In other words, what if your relatives find your money?)

Be aware of the different kinds of risk that I describe in this chapter, so you can easily plan around them to keep your money growing. And don't forget risk's kid brother . . . volatility! Volatility is about the rapid movement of buying or selling, which, in turn, causes stock prices to rise or fall rapidly. Technically, volatility is considered a "neutral" condition, but it's usually associated with rapid downward movement of stock because that means sudden loss for investors and causes anxiety.

Exploring Different Kinds of Risk

Think about all the ways that an investment can lose money. You can list all sorts of possibilities. So many that you may think, "Holy cow! Why invest at all?"

Don't let risk frighten you. After all, life itself is risky. Just make sure that you understand the different kinds of risk that I discuss in the following sections before you start navigating the investment world. Be mindful of risk and find out about the effects of risk on your investments and personal financial goals.

Financial risk

The financial risk of stock investing is that you can lose your money if the company whose stock you purchase loses money or goes belly up. This type of risk is the most obvious because companies do go bankrupt.

You can greatly enhance the chances of your financial risk paying off by doing an adequate amount of research and choosing your stocks carefully (which this book helps you do — see Part III for details). Financial risk is a real concern even when the economy is doing well. Some diligent research, a little planning, and a dose of common sense help you reduce your financial risk.

In the stock investing mania of the late 1990s, millions of investors (along with many well-known investment gurus) ignored some obvious financial risks of many then-popular stocks. Investors blindly plunked their money into stocks that were bad choices. Consider investors who put their money in DrKoop.com, a health information website, in 1999 and held on during 2000. This company had no profit and was overindebted. DrKoop.com went into cardiac arrest as it collapsed from $45 per share to $2 per share by mid-2000. By the time the stock was DOA, investors lost millions. RIP (risky investment play!).

Internet and tech stocks littered the graveyard of stock market catastrophes during 2000–2001 because investors didn't see (or didn't want to see?) the risks involved with companies that didn't offer a solid record of results (profits, sales, and so on). When you invest in companies that don't have a proven track record, you're not investing, you're speculating.

Fast forward to 2008. New risks abounded as the headlines railed on about the credit crisis on Wall Street and the subprime fiasco in the wake of the housing bubble popping. Think about how this crisis impacted investors as the market went through its stomach-churning roller-coaster ride. A good example of a casualty you didn't want to be a part of was Bear Stearns (BSC), which was caught in the subprime buzz saw. Bear Stearns was sky-high at $170 a share in early 2007, yet it crashed to $2 a share by March 2008. Yikes! Its problems arose from massive overexposure to bad debt, and investors could have done some research (the public data was revealing!) and avoided the stock entirely.

Investors who did their homework regarding the financial conditions of companies such as the Internet stocks (and Bear Stearns, among others) discovered that these companies had the hallmarks of financial risk — high debt, low (or no) earnings, and plenty of competition. They steered clear, avoiding tremendous financial loss. Investors who didn't do their homework were lured by the status of these companies and lost their shirts.

Of course, the individual investors who lost money by investing in these trendy, high-profile companies don't deserve all the responsibility for their tremendous financial losses; some high-profile analysts and media sources also should have known better. The late 1990s may someday be a case study of how euphoria and the herd mentality (rather than good, old-fashioned research and common sense) ruled the day (temporarily). The excitement of making potential fortunes gets the best of people sometimes, and they throw caution to the wind. Historians may look back at those days and say, "What *were* they thinking?" Achieving true wealth takes diligent work and careful analysis.

 In terms of financial risk, the bottom line is . . . well . . . the bottom line! A healthy bottom line means that a company is making money. And if a company is making money, then you can make money by investing in its stock. However, if a company isn't making money, you won't make money if you invest in it. Profit is the lifeblood of any company. See Chapter 11 for the scoop on determining whether a company's bottom line is healthy.

Interest rate risk

You can lose money in an apparently sound investment because of something that sounds as harmless as "interest rates have changed." Interest rate risk may sound like an odd type of risk, but in fact, it's a common consideration for investors. Be aware that interest rates change on a regular basis, causing some challenging moments. Banks set interest rates, and the primary institution to watch closely is the Federal Reserve (the Fed), which is, in effect, the country's central bank. The Fed raises or lowers its interest rates, actions that, in turn, cause banks to raise or lower their interest rates accordingly. Interest rate changes affect consumers, businesses, and, of course, investors.

Here's a generic introduction to the way fluctuating interest rate risk can affect investors in general: Suppose that you buy a long-term, high-quality corporate bond and get a yield of 6 percent. Your money is safe, and your return is locked in at 6 percent. Whew! That's 6 percent. Not bad, huh? But what happens if, after you commit your money, interest rates increase to 8 percent? You lose the opportunity to get that extra 2-percent interest. The only way to get out of your 6-percent bond is to sell it at current market values and use the money to reinvest at the higher rate.

The only problem with this scenario is that the 6-percent bond is likely to drop in value because interest rates rose. Why? Say that the investor is Bob and the bond yielding 6 percent is a corporate bond issued by Lucin-Muny (LM). According to the bond agreement, LM must pay 6 percent (called the *face rate* or *nominal rate*) during the life of the bond and then, upon maturity, pay the principal. If Bob buys $10,000 of LM bonds on the day they're issued, he gets $600 (of interest) every year for as long as he holds the bonds. If he holds on until maturity, he gets back his $10,000 (the principal). So far so good, right? The plot thickens, however.

Say that he decides to sell the bonds long before maturity and that, at the time of the sale, interest rates in the market have risen to 8 percent. Now what? The reality is that no one is going to want his 6-percent bonds if the market is offering bonds at 8 percent. What's Bob to do? He can't change the face rate of 6 percent, and he can't change the fact that only $600 is paid each year for the life of the bonds. What has to change so that current investors get the *equivalent* yield of 8 percent? If you said, "The bonds' value has to go down," . . . bingo! In this example, the bonds' market value needs to drop to $7,500 so that investors buying the bonds get an equivalent yield of 8 percent. (For simplicity's sake, I left out the time it takes for the bonds to mature.) Here's how that figures.

New investors still get $600 annually. However, $600 is equal to 8 percent of $7,500. Therefore, even though investors get the face rate of 6 percent, they get a yield of 8 percent because the actual investment amount is $7,500. In this example, little, if any, financial risk is present, but you see how interest rate risk presents itself. Bob finds out that you can have a good company with a good bond yet still lose $2,500 because of the change in the interest rate. Of course, if Bob doesn't sell, he doesn't realize that loss. (For more on the how and why of selling your stock, check out Chapter 17.)

Historically, rising interest rates have had an adverse effect on stock prices. I outline several reasons why in the following sections. Because our country is top-heavy in debt, rising interest rates are an obvious risk that threatens both stocks and fixed-income securities (such as bonds).

Hurting a company's financial condition

Rising interest rates have a negative impact on companies that carry a large current debt load or that need to take on more debt, because when interest rates rise, the cost of borrowing money rises, too. Ultimately, the company's profitability and ability to grow are reduced. When a company's profits (or earnings) drop, its stock becomes less desirable, and its stock price falls.

Affecting a company's customers

A company's success comes from selling its products or services. But what happens if increased interest rates negatively impact its customers (specifically, other companies that buy from it)? The financial health of its customers directly affects the company's ability to grow sales and earnings.

For a good example, consider Home Depot (HD) during 2005–2008. The company had soaring sales and earnings during 2005 and into early 2006 as the housing boom hit its high point (record sales, construction, and so on). As the housing bubble popped and the housing and construction industries went into an agonizing decline, the fortunes of Home Depot followed suit because its success is directly tied to home building, repair, and improvement. By late 2006, HD's sales were slipping, and earnings were dropping as the housing industry sunk deeper into its depression. This was bad news for stock investors. HD's stock went from more than $44 in 2005 to $21 by October 2008 (a drop of about 52 percent). Ouch! No "home improvement" there. The point to keep in mind is that because Home Depot's fortunes are tied to the housing industry, and this industry is very sensitive and vulnerable to rising interest rates, in an indirect — but significant — way, Home Depot is also vulnerable.

Impacting investors' decision-making considerations

When interest rates rise, investors start to rethink their investment strategies, resulting in one of two outcomes:

✔ Investors may sell any shares in interest-sensitive stocks that they hold. Interest-sensitive industries include electric utilities, real estate, and the financial sector. Although increased interest rates can hurt these sectors, the reverse is also generally true: Falling interest rates boost the same industries. Keep in mind that interest rate changes affect some industries more than others.

✔ Investors who favor increased current income (versus waiting for the investment to grow in value to sell for a gain later on) are definitely attracted to investment vehicles that offer a higher yield. Higher interest rates can cause investors to switch from stocks to bonds or bank certificates of deposit.

Hurting stock prices indirectly

High or rising interest rates can have a negative impact on any investor's total financial picture. What happens when an investor struggles with burdensome debt, such as a second mortgage, credit card debt, or *margin debt* (debt from borrowing against stock in a brokerage account)? He may sell some stock to pay off some of his high-interest debt. Selling stock to service debt is a common practice that, when taken collectively, can hurt stock prices.

As this book goes to press, the stock market and the U.S. economy face perhaps the greatest challenge since the Great Depression — a powerful recession mired in stagnation and lots of debt. In terms of gross domestic product (GDP), the size of the economy is about $14 trillion (give or take $100 billion), but the debt level is more than $50 trillion (this amount includes personal, corporate, mortgage, college, and government debt). This already enormous amount doesn't include more than $70 trillion of liabilities such as Social Security and Medicare. Additionally (Yikes! There's more?), some of our financial institutions hold more than 500 trillion dollars' worth of derivatives. These can be very complicated and sophisticated investment vehicles that can backfire. Derivatives have, in fact, sunk some large organizations (such as Enron and Bear Stearns), and investors should be aware of them. Just check out the company's financial reports. (Find out more in Chapter 12.)

Because of the effects of interest rates on stock portfolios, both direct and indirect, successful investors regularly monitor interest rates in both the general economy and in their personal situations. Although stocks have proven to be a superior long-term investment (the longer the term, the better), every investor should maintain a balanced portfolio that includes other investment vehicles. A diversified investor has some money in vehicles that do well when interest rates rise. These vehicles include money market funds, U.S. savings bonds (series I), and other variable-rate investments whose interest rates rise when market rates rise. These types of investments add a measure of safety from interest rate risk to your stock portfolio. (I discuss diversification in more detail later in this chapter.)

Market risk

People talk about *the market* and how it goes up or down, making it sound like a monolithic entity instead of what it really is — a group of millions of individuals making daily decisions to buy or sell stock. No matter how modern our society and economic system, you can't escape the laws of supply and demand. When masses of people want to buy a particular stock, it becomes in demand, and its price rises. That price rises higher if the supply is limited. Conversely, if no one's interested in buying a stock, its price falls. Supply and demand is the nature of market risk. The price of the stock you purchase can rise and fall on the fickle whim of market demand.

Millions of investors buying and selling each minute of every trading day affect the share price of your stock. This fact makes it impossible to judge which way your stock will move tomorrow or next week. This unpredictability and seeming irrationality is why stocks aren't appropriate for short-term financial growth.

Markets are volatile by nature; they go up and down, and investments need time to grow. Market volatility is an increasingly common condition that we have to live with (see the section "Getting the Scoop on Volatility" later in this chapter). Investors should be aware of the fact that stocks in general (especially in today's marketplace) aren't suitable for short-term (one year or less) goals (see Chapters 2 and 3 for more on short-term goals). Despite the fact that companies you're invested in may be fundamentally sound, all stock prices are subject to the gyrations of the marketplace and need time to trend upward.

Investing requires diligent work and research before putting your money in quality investments with a long-term perspective. Speculating is attempting to make a relatively quick profit by monitoring the short-term price movements of a particular investment. Investors seek to minimize risk, whereas speculators don't mind risk because it can also magnify profits. Speculating and investing have clear differences, but investors frequently become speculators and ultimately put themselves and their wealth at risk. Don't go there!

Consider the married couple nearing retirement who decided to play with their money in an attempt to make their pending retirement more comfortable. They borrowed a sizable sum by tapping in to their home equity to invest in the stock market. (Their home, which they had paid off, had enough equity to qualify for this loan.) What did they do with these funds? You guessed it; they invested in the high-flying stocks of the day, which were high-tech and Internet stocks. Within eight months, they lost almost all their money.

Understanding market risk is especially important for people who are tempted to put their nest eggs or emergency funds into volatile investments such as growth stocks (or mutual funds that invest in growth stocks or similar aggressive investment vehicles). Remember, you can lose everything.

Inflation risk

Inflation is the artificial expansion of the quantity of money so that too much money is used in exchange for goods and services. To consumers, inflation shows up in the form of higher prices for goods and services. Inflation risk is also referred to as *purchasing power risk.* This term just means that your money doesn't buy as much as it used to. For example, a dollar that bought you a sandwich in 1980 barely bought you a candy bar a few years later. For you, the investor, this risk means that the value of your investment (a stock that doesn't appreciate much, for example) may not keep up with inflation.

Say that you have money in a bank savings account currently earning 4 percent. This account has flexibility — if the market interest rate goes up, the rate you earn in your account goes up. Your account is safe from both financial risk and interest rate risk. But what if inflation is running at 5 percent? At that point you're losing money.

At the time of this writing, inflation is a very real and very serious concern, and it should not be ignored. I touch on inflation in Chapters 14 and 15.

Tax risk

Taxes (such as income tax or capital gains tax) don't affect your stock investment directly, but taxes can obviously affect how much of your money you get to keep. Because the entire point of stock investing is to build wealth, you need to understand that taxes take away a portion of the wealth that you're trying to build. Taxes can be risky because if you make the wrong move with your stocks (selling them at the wrong time, for example), you can end up paying higher taxes than you need to. Because tax laws change so frequently, tax risk is part of the risk-versus-return equation, as well.

It pays to gain knowledge about how taxes can impact your wealth-building program before you make your investment decisions. Chapter 21 covers the impact of taxes in greater detail.

Political and governmental risks

If companies were fish, politics and government policies (such as taxes, laws, and regulations) would be the pond. In the same way that fish die in a toxic or polluted pond, politics and government policies can kill companies. Of course, if you own stock in a company exposed to political and governmental risks, you need to be aware of these risks. For some companies, a single new regulation or law is enough to send them into bankruptcy. For other companies, a new law can help them increase sales and profits.

What if you invest in companies or industries that become political targets? You may want to consider selling them (you can always buy them back later) or consider putting in stop-loss orders on the stock (see Chapter 17). For example, tobacco companies were the targets of political firestorms that battered their stock prices. Whether you agree or disagree with the political machinations of today is not the issue. As an investor, you have to ask yourself, "How do politics affect the market value and the current and future prospects of my chosen investment?" (Chapter 15 gives some insights on how politics can affect the stock market.)

Taking the preceding point a step further, I'd like to remind you that politics and government have a direct and often negative impact on the economic environment. And one major pitfall for investors is that many misunderstand even basic economics. Considering all the examples I could find in recent years, I could write a book! Or . . . uh . . . simply add it to this book. Chapters 13 and 15 go into greater detail to help you make (and keep) stock market profits just by understanding rudimentary (and quite interesting) economics. (Don't worry; the dry stuff will be kept to a minimum!)

Personal risks

Frequently, the risk involved with investing in the stock market isn't directly related to the investment; rather, the risk is associated with the investor's circumstances.

Suppose that investor Ralph puts $15,000 into a portfolio of common stocks. Imagine that the market experiences a drop in prices that week and Ralph's stocks drop to a market value of $14,000. Because stocks are good for the long term, this type of decrease usually isn't an alarming incident. Odds are that this dip is temporary, especially if Ralph carefully chose high-quality companies. Incidentally, if a portfolio of high-quality stocks *does* experience a temporary drop in price, it can be a great opportunity to get more shares at a good price. (Chapter 17 covers orders you can place with your broker to help you do that.)

Over the long term, Ralph will probably see the value of his investment grow substantially. But what if Ralph experiences financial difficulty and needs quick cash during a period when his stocks are declining? He may have to sell his stock to get some money.

This problem occurs frequently for investors who don't have an emergency fund to handle large, sudden expenses. You never know when your company may lay you off or when your basement may flood, leaving you with a huge repair bill. Car accidents, medical emergencies, and other unforeseen events are part of life's bag of surprises — for anyone.

You probably won't get much comfort from knowing that stock losses are tax deductible — a loss is a loss (see Chapter 21 for more on taxes). However, you can avoid the kind of loss that results from prematurely having to sell your stocks if you maintain an emergency cash fund. A good place for your emergency cash fund is in either a bank savings account or a money market fund. Then you aren't forced to prematurely liquidate your stock investments to pay emergency bills. (Chapter 2 provides more guidance on having liquid assets for emergencies.)

Emotional risk

What does emotional risk have to do with stocks? Emotions are important risk considerations because investors are human beings. Logic and discipline are critical factors in investment success, but even the best investor can let emotions take over the reins of money management and cause loss. For stock investing, you're likely to be sidetracked by three main emotions: greed, fear, and love. You need to understand your emotions and what kinds of risk they can expose you to. If you get too attached to a sinking stock, you don't need a stock investing book — you need a therapist!

Paying the price for greed

In 1998–2000, millions of investors threw caution to the wind and chased highly dubious, risky dot-com stocks. The dollar signs popped up in their eyes (just like slot machines) when they saw that easy street was lined with dot-com stocks that were doubling and tripling in a very short time. Who cares about price/earnings (P/E) ratios when you can just buy stock, make a fortune, and get out with millions? (Of course, *you* care about making money with stocks, so you can flip to Chapter 11 and Appendix B to find out more about P/E ratios.)

Unfortunately, the lure of the easy buck can easily turn healthy attitudes about growing wealth into unhealthy greed that blinds investors and discards common sense. Avoid the temptation to invest for short-term gains in dubious hot stocks instead of doing your homework and buying stocks of solid companies with strong fundamentals and a long-term focus, as I explain in Part III.

Recognizing the role of fear

Greed can be a problem, but fear is the other extreme. People who are fearful of loss frequently avoid suitable investments and end up settling for a low rate of return. If you have to succumb to one of these emotions, at least fear exposes you to less loss.

Also, keep in mind that fear is frequently a symptom of lack of knowledge about what's going on. If you see your stocks falling and don't understand why, fear will take over, and you may act irrationally. When stock investors are affected by fear, they tend to sell their stocks and head for the exits and the lifeboats. When an investor sees his stock go down 20 percent, what goes through his head? Experienced, knowledgeable investors realize that no bull market goes straight up. Even the strongest bull goes up in a zigzag fashion. Conversely, even bear markets don't go straight down; they zigzag down. Out of fear, inexperienced investors sell good stocks when they see them go down temporarily (the *correction*), whereas experienced investors see that temporary downward move as a good buying opportunity to add to their positions. (Flip to Chapters 13 and 14 for details on dealing with bull and bear markets.)

Investment lessons from September 11

September 11, 2001, was a horrific day that is burned in our minds and won't be forgotten in our lifetime. The acts of terrorism that day took more than 3,000 lives and caused untold pain and grief. A much less important aftereffect was the hard lessons that investors learned that day. Terrorism reminds us that risk is more real than ever and that we should never let our guard down. What lessons can investors learn from the worst acts of terrorism to ever happen on U.S. soil? Here are a few pointers:

✔ **Diversify your portfolio.** Of course, the events of September 11 were certainly surreal and unexpected. But before the events occurred, investors should have made it a habit to assess their situations and see whether they had any vulnerabilities. Stock investors with no money outside the stock market are always more at risk. Keeping your portfolio diversified is a time-tested strategy that's more relevant than ever before. (I discuss diversification later in this chapter.)

✔ **Review and reallocate.** September 11 triggered declines in the overall market, but specific industries, such as airlines and hotels, were hit particularly hard. In addition, some industries, such as defense and food, saw stock prices rise. Monitor your portfolio and ask yourself whether it's overly reliant on or exposed to events in specific sectors. If so, reallocate your investments to decrease your risk exposure.

✔ **Check for signs of trouble.** Techniques such as trailing stops (which I explain in Chapter 17) come in very handy when your stocks plummet because of unexpected events. Even if you don't use these techniques, you can make it a regular habit to check your stocks for signs of trouble, such as debts or P/E ratios that are too high. If you see signs of trouble, consider selling.

Looking for love in all the wrong places

Stocks are dispassionate, inanimate vehicles, but people can look for love in the strangest places. Emotional risk occurs when investors fall in love with a stock and refuse to sell it, even when the stock is plummeting and shows all the symptoms of getting worse. Emotional risk also occurs when investors are drawn to bad investment choices just because they sound good, are popular, or are pushed by family or friends. Love and attachment are great in relationships with people but can be horrible with investments. To deal with this emotion, investors have to deploy techniques that take the emotion out. For example, you can use brokerage orders (such as trailing stops and limit orders; see Chapter 17), which can automatically trigger buy and sell transactions and leave out some of the agonizing. Hey, disciplined investing may just become your new passion!

Getting the Scoop on Volatility

How often have you heard a financial guy on TV say, "Well it looks like a volatile day as the markets plunge 700 points. . . ." Oh dear . . . pass me the antacid! Volatility has garnered a bad reputation because roller coasters and weak stomachs don't mix — especially when your financial future seems to be acting like a kite in a tornado.

Why more volatility?

People will always gasp at the occasional big up or down day, but volatility is more prevalent overall today than, say, 10 or 20 years ago. Why is that? There are several contributing factors:

- First of all, today's investor has the advantages of cheaper commissions and faster technology. Years ago, if an investor wanted to sell, he had to call the broker — usually during business hours. On top of that, the commission was usually $30 or higher. That discouraged a lot of rapid-fire trading. Today, trading is not only cheaper, but anyone can do it from home with a few clicks of a mouse on a website literally 24 hours a day, 7 days a week.

- In addition, large organizations — ranging from financial institutions to government-sponsored entities such as sovereign wealth funds — can make large trades or huge amounts of money either nationally or globally within seconds. The rapid movement of large amounts of money both in and out of a stock or an entire market means that volatility is high and likely to be with us for a long time to come.

- Lastly, the world is now more of a global marketplace, and our markets react more to international events than in the past. With new technology and the Internet, news travels farther and faster than ever before.

People may think of volatility as "risk on steroids," but you need to understand what volatility actually is. Technically, it isn't really good or bad (although it's usually associated with bad movements in the marketplace). *Volatility* is the movement of an asset (or the entire market) very quickly down (or up) in price due to large selling (or buying) in a very short period of time.

Volatility tends to be more associated with the negative due to crowd psychology. People are more likely to act quickly (sell!) due to fear than to other motivators (such as greed; see the earlier section "Emotional risk" for more info). More people are apt to run for the exits than they are to run to the entrance, so to speak.

Not all stocks are equal with regard to volatility. Some can be very volatile, whereas others can be quite stable. A good way to determine a stock's volatility is to look at the beta of the stock. *Beta* is a statistical measure that attempts to give the investor a clue as to how volatile a stock may be. It's determined by comparing the potential volatility of a particular stock to the market in general. The market (as represented by, say, the Standard & Poor 500) is assigned a beta of "1." Any stock with a beta greater than 1 is considered more volatile than the general stock market, whereas any stock with a beta of less than 1 is considered less volatile. If a stock has a beta of 1.5, for example, it's considered 50 percent more volatile than the general market. Meanwhile, a stock with a beta of 0.85 is considered 15 percent less volatile than the general stock market.

Therefore, if you don't want to keep gulping down more antacid, consider stocks that have a beta of less than 1. The beta can be found easily in the stock report pages that are usually provided by major financial websites such as Yahoo! Finance (`finance.yahoo.com`) and MarketWatch (`www.marketwatch.com`). (See Appendix A for more financial websites.)

Minimizing Your Risk

Now, before you go crazy thinking that stock investing carries so much risk that you may as well not get out of bed, take a breath. Minimizing your risk in stock investing is easier than you think. Although wealth-building through the stock market doesn't take place without some amount of risk, you can practice the following tips to maximize your profits and still keep your money secure.

Gaining knowledge

Some people spend more time analyzing a restaurant menu to choose a $10 entrée than analyzing where to put their next $5,000. Lack of knowledge constitutes the greatest risk for new investors, so diminishing that risk starts with gaining knowledge. The more familiar you are with the stock market — how it works, factors that affect stock value, and so on — the better you can navigate around its pitfalls and maximize your profits. The same knowledge that enables you to grow your wealth also enables you to minimize your risk. Before you put your money anywhere, you want to know as much as you can. This book is a great place to start — check out Chapter 6 for a rundown of the kinds of information you want to know before you buy stocks, as well as the resources that can give you the information you need to invest successfully.

Staying out until you get a little practice

If you don't understand stocks, don't invest! Yeah, I know this book is about stock investing, and I think that some measure of stock investing is a good idea for most people. But that doesn't mean you should be 100-percent invested 100 percent of the time. If you don't understand a particular stock (or don't understand stocks, period), stay away until you do. Instead, give yourself an imaginary sum of money, such as $100,000, give yourself reasons to invest, and just make believe (a practice called *simulated stock investing* or *trading*). Pick a few stocks that you think will increase in value, track them for a while, and see how they perform. Begin to understand how the price of a stock goes up and down, and watch what happens to the stocks you choose when various events take place. As you find out more about stock investing, you get better at picking individual stocks, without risking — or losing — any money during your learning period.

A good place to do your imaginary investing is at a website such as Investopedia's simulator (`simulator.investopedia.com`). You can design a stock portfolio and track its performance with thousands of other investors to see how well you do.

Putting your financial house in order

Advice on what to do before you invest could be a whole book all by itself. The bottom line is that you want to make sure that you are, first and foremost, financially secure before you take the plunge into the stock market. If you're not sure about your financial security, look over your situation with a financial planner. (You can find more on financial planners in Appendix A.)

Before you buy your first stock, here are a few things you can do to get your finances in order:

✔ **Have a cushion of money.** Set aside three to six months' worth of your gross living expenses somewhere safe, such as in a bank account or treasury money market fund, in case you suddenly need cash for an emergency (see Chapter 2 for details).

✔ **Reduce your debt.** Overindulging in debt was the worst personal economic problem for many Americans in the late 1990s, and this practice has continued in recent years. The year 2011 was another year where bankruptcies hovered near 1.5 million. In 2012, total college debt surpassed $1 trillion for the first time.

✔ **Make sure that your job is as secure as you can make it.** Are you keeping your skills up-to-date? Is the company you work for strong and growing? Is the industry that you work in strong and growing?

✔ **Make sure that you have adequate insurance.** You need enough insurance to cover your needs and those of your family in case of illness, death, disability, and so on.

Diversifying your investments

Diversification is a strategy for reducing risk by spreading your money across different investments. It's a fancy way of saying, "Don't put all your eggs in one basket." But how do you go about divvying up your money and distributing it among different investments? The easiest way to understand proper diversification may be to look at what you *shouldn't* do:

✔ **Don't put all your money in one stock.** Sure, if you choose wisely and select a hot stock, you may make a bundle, but the odds are tremendously against you. Unless you're a real expert on a particular company, it's a good idea to have small portions of your money in several different stocks. As a general rule, the money you tie up in a single stock should be money you can do without.

✔ **Don't put all your money in one industry.** I know people who own several stocks, but the stocks are all in the same industry. Again, if you're an expert in that particular industry, it can work out. But just understand that you're not properly diversified. If a problem hits an entire industry, you may get hurt.

Better luck next time!

A little knowledge can be very risky. Consider the true story of one "lucky" fellow who played the California lottery in 1987. He discovered that he had a winning ticket, with the first prize of $412,000. He immediately ordered a Porsche, booked a lavish trip to Hawaii for his family, and treated his wife and friends to a champagne dinner at a posh Hollywood restaurant. When he finally went to collect his prize, he found out that he had to share first prize with more than 9,000 other lottery players who also had the same winning numbers. His share of the prize was actually only $45! Hopefully, he invested that tidy sum based on his increased knowledge about risk. (That story always cracks me up.)

✔ **Don't put all your money in one type of investment.** Stocks may be a great investment, but you need to have money elsewhere. Bonds, bank accounts, treasury securities, real estate, and precious metals are perennial alternatives to complement your stock portfolio. Some of these alternatives can be found in mutual funds or exchange-traded funds (ETFs). An *exchange-traded fund* is a fund with a fixed portfolio of stocks or other securities that tracks a particular index but is traded like a stock. By the way, I love ETFs and I think that every serious investor should consider them; see Chapter 5 for more information.

Okay, now that you know what you *shouldn't* do, what *should* you do? Until you become more knowledgeable, follow this advice:

✔ **Keep only 5 to 10 percent (or less) of your investment money in a single stock.** Because you want adequate diversification, you don't want overexposure to a single stock. Aggressive investors can certainly go for 10 percent or even higher, but conservative investors are better off at 5 percent or less.

✔ **Invest in four or five (and no more than ten) different stocks that are in different industries.** Which industries? Choose industries that offer products and services that have shown strong, growing demand. To make this decision, use your common sense (which isn't as common as it used to be). Think about the industries that people need no matter what happens in the general economy, such as food, energy, and other consumer necessities. See Chapter 13 for more information about analyzing sectors and industries.

Weighing Risk against Return

How much risk is appropriate for you, and how do you handle it? Before you try to figure out what risks accompany your investment choices, analyze yourself. Here are some points to keep in mind when weighing risk versus return in your situation:

✔ **Your financial goal:** In five minutes with a financial calculator, you can easily see how much money you're going to need to become financially independent (presuming financial independence is your goal). Say that you need $500,000 in ten years for a worry-free retirement and that your financial assets (such as stocks, bonds, and so on) are currently worth $400,000. In this scenario, your assets need to grow by only 2.25 percent to hit your target. Getting investments that grow by 2.25 percent safely is easy to do because that's a relatively low rate of return.

The important point is that you don't have to knock yourself out trying to double your money with risky, high-flying investments; some run-of-the-mill bank investments will do just fine. All too often, investors take on more risk than is necessary. Figure out what your financial goal is so that you know what kind of return you realistically need. Flip to Chapters 2 and 3 for details on determining your financial goals.

✔ **Your investor profile:** Are you nearing retirement, or are you fresh out of college? Your life situation matters when it comes to looking at risk versus return.

  • If you're just beginning your working years, you can certainly tolerate greater risk than someone facing retirement. Even if you lose big-time, you still have a long time to recoup your money and get back on track.

  • However, if you're within five years of retirement, risky or aggressive investments can do much more harm than good. If you lose money, you don't have as much time to recoup your investment, and the odds are that you'll need the investment money (and its income-generating capacity) to cover your living expenses after you're no longer employed.

✔ **Asset allocation:** I never tell retirees to put a large portion of their retirement money into a high-tech stock or other volatile investment. But if they still want to speculate, I don't see a problem as long as they limit such investments to 5 percent of their total assets. As long as the bulk of their money is safe and sound in secure investments (such as U.S. Treasury bonds), I know I can sleep well (knowing that *they* can sleep well!).

Asset allocation beckons back to diversification, which I discuss earlier in this chapter. For people in their 20s and 30s, having 75 percent of their money in a diversified portfolio of growth stocks (such as mid cap and small cap stocks; see Chapter 1) is acceptable. For people in their 60s and 70s, it's not acceptable. They may, instead, consider investing no more than 20 percent of their money in stocks (mid caps and large caps are preferable). Check with your financial advisor to find the right mix for your particular situation.

Chapter 5

Stock Investing through Exchange-Traded Funds

*W*hen it comes to stock investing, there's more than one way to do it. Buying stocks directly is good; sometimes, buying stocks indirectly is equally good (or even better) — especially if you're risk-averse. Buying a great stock is every stock investor's dream, but sometimes you face investing environments that make finding a winning stock a hazardous pursuit. For 2013–14, prudent stock investors should consider adding exchange-traded funds (ETFs) to their wealth-building arsenal.

An exchange-traded fund (ETF) is basically a mutual fund that invests in a fixed basket of securities but with a few twists. In this chapter, I show you how ETFs are similar to (and different from) mutual funds, I provide some pointers on picking ETFs, and I note the fundamentals of stock indexes (which are connected to ETFs).

Comparing Exchange-Traded Funds and Mutual Funds

For many folks and for many years, the only choice besides investing directly in stocks was to invest indirectly through mutual funds. After all, why buy a single stock for roughly the same few thousand dollars that you can buy a mutual fund for and get benefits such as professional management and diversification?

For small investors, mutual fund investing isn't a bad way to go. Investors participate by pooling their money with others and get professional money management in an affordable manner. But mutual funds have their downsides too. Mutual fund fees, which include management fees and sales charges (referred to as *loads*), eat into gains, and investors have no choice about investments after they're in a mutual fund. Whatever the fund manager buys, sells, or holds on to is pretty much what the investors in the fund have to tolerate. Investment choice is limited to either being in the fund . . . or out.

But now, with the advent of ETFs, investors have greater choices than ever, a scenario that sets the stage for the inevitable comparison between mutual funds and ETFs. The following sections go over the differences and similarities between ETFs and mutual funds.

The differences

Simply stated, in a mutual fund, securities such as stocks and bonds are constantly bought, sold, and held (in other words, the fund is *actively managed*). An ETF holds similar securities, but the portfolio typically isn't actively managed. Instead, an ETF usually holds a fixed basket of securities that may reflect an index or a particular industry or sector (see Chapter 13). (An *index* is a method of measuring the value of a segment of the general stock market. It's a tool used by money managers and investors to compare the performance of a particular stock to a widely accepted standard; see the later section "Taking Note of Indexes" for more details.)

For example, an ETF that tries to reflect the S&P 500 will attempt to hold a securities portfolio that mirrors the composition of the S&P 500 as closely as possible. Here's another example: A water utilities ETF may hold the top 35 or 40 publicly held water companies. (You get the picture.)

Where ETFs are markedly different from mutual funds (and where they're really advantageous, in my opinion) is that they can be bought and sold like stocks. In addition, you can do with ETFs what you can generally do with stocks (but can't usually do with mutual funds): You can buy in share allotments, such as 1, 50, or 100 shares more. Mutual funds, on the other hand, are usually bought in dollar amounts, such as 1,000 or 5,000 dollars' worth. The dollar amount you can initially invest is set by the manager of the individual mutual fund.

Here are some other advantages: You can put various buy/sell brokerage orders on ETFs (see Chapter 17), and many ETFs are optionable (meaning you may be able to buy/sell put and call options on them; I discuss these options in Chapters 23 and 25). Mutual funds typically aren't optionable.

In addition, many ETFs are marginable (meaning that you can borrow against them with some limitations in your brokerage account). Mutual funds usually aren't marginable (although it is possible if they're within the confines of a stock brokerage account). To find out more about margin, check out Chapter 17.

Sometimes an investor can readily see the great potential of a given industry or sector but is hard-pressed to get that single really good stock that can take advantage of the profit possibilities of that particular segment of the market. The great thing about an ETF is that you can make that investment very easily, knowing that if you're unsure about it, you can put in place strategies that protect you from the downside (such as stop-loss orders or trailing stops). That way you can sleep easier!

The similarities

Even though ETFs and mutual funds have some major differences, they do share a few similarities:

- First and foremost, ETFs and mutual funds (MFs) are similar in that they aren't direct investments; they're "conduits" of investing, which means that they act like a connection between the investor and the investments.

- Both ETFs and MFs basically pool the money of investors and the pool becomes the "fund," which in turn invests in a portfolio of investments.

- Both ETFs and MFs offer the great advantage of diversification (although they accomplish it in different ways).

- Investors don't have any choice about what makes up the portfolio of either the ETF or the MF. The ETF has a fixed basket of securities (the money manager overseeing the portfolio makes those choices) and, of course, investors can't control the choices made in a mutual fund.

For those investors who want more active assistance in making choices and running a portfolio, the MF may very well be the way to go. For those who are more comfortable making their own choices in terms of the particular index or industry/sector they want to invest in, the ETF may be a better venue.

Choosing an Exchange-Traded Fund

Buying a stock is an investment in a particular company, but an ETF is an opportunity to invest in a block of stocks. In the same way a few mouse clicks can buy you a stock at a stock brokerage website, those same clicks can buy you virtually an entire industry or sector (or at least the top-tier stocks anyway).

For investors who are comfortable with their own choices and do their due diligence, a winning stock is a better (albeit more aggressive) way to go. For those investors who want to make their own choices but aren't that confident about picking winning stocks, an ETF is definitely a better way to go.

You had to figure that choosing an ETF wasn't going to be a coin flip. There are considerations that you should be aware of, some of which are tied more to your personal outlook and preferences than to the underlying portfolio of the ETF. I give you the info you need on bullish and bearish ETFs in the following sections.

Picking a winning industry or sector is easier than finding a great company to invest in. Therefore, ETF investing goes hand in hand with the guidance offered in Chapters 13 and 14.

Bullish ETFs

You may wake up one day and say "I think that the stock market will do very well going forward from today" and that's just fine if you think so. Maybe your research on the general economy, financial outlook, and political considerations make you feel happier than a starving man on a cruise ship. But you just don't know (or don't care to research) which stocks would best benefit from the good market moves yet to come. No problem!

In the following sections, I cover ETF strategies for bullish scenarios, but fortunately, ETF strategies for bearish scenarios exist too. I cover those later in this chapter.

Major market index ETFs

Why not invest in ETFs that mirror a general major market index such as the S&P 500? ETFs such as SPY construct their portfolios to track the composition of the S&P 500 as closely as possible. As they say, why try to beat the market when you can match it? It's a great way to go when the market is having a good rally. (See the later section "Taking Note of Indexes" for the basics on indexes.)

When the S&P 500 was battered in late 2008/early 2009, the ETF for the S&P 500, of course, mirrored that performance and hit the bottom in March 2009. But from that moment on and into late 2012, the S&P 500 (and the ETFs that tracked it) did extraordinarily well. It paid to buck the bearish sentiment of early 2009. Of course it did take some contrarian gumption to do so, but at least you had the benefit of the full S&P 500 stock portfolio, which at least had more diversification than a single stock or a single subsection of the market.

ETFs related to human need

Some ETFs cover industries such as food and beverage, water, energy, and other things that people will keep buying no matter how good or bad the economy is. Without needing a crystal ball or having an iron-will contrarian attitude, a stock investor can simply put money into stocks — or in this case, ETFs — tied to human need. Such ETFs may even do better than ETFs tied to major market indexes (see the preceding section).

Here's an example: At the end of 2007, what would have happened if you'd invested 50 percent of your money in an ETF that represented the S&P 500 and 50 percent in an ETF that was in consumer staples (such as food and beverage stocks)? I did such a comparison, and it was quite revealing to note that by the end of 2011, the consumer staples ETF (for the record I used "PBJ") actually beat out the S&P 500 ETF by about 20 percent (not including dividends). Very interesting!

ETFs that include dividend-paying stocks

ETFs don't necessarily have to be tied to a specific industry or sector; they can be tied to a specific type or subcategory of stock. All things being equal, what basic categories of stocks do you think would better weather bad times: stocks with no dividends or stocks that pay dividends? (I guess the question answers itself, pretty much like "What tastes better: apple pie or barbed wire?") Although some sectors are known for being good dividend payers, such as utilities (and there are some good ETFs that cover this industry), some ETFs cover stocks that meet a specific criteria.

You can find ETFs that include high-dividend income stocks (typically 4 percent or higher) as well as ETFs that include stocks of companies that don't necessarily pay high dividends, but do have a long track record of dividend increases that meet or exceed the rate of inflation.

Given these types of dividend-paying ETFs, it becomes clear which is good for what type of stock investor:

- ✔ If I were a stock investor who was currently retired, I'd choose the high-dividend stock ETF. Dividend-paying stock ETFs are generally more stable than those stock ETFs that don't pay dividends, and dividends are important for retirement income.

✔ If I were in "pre-retirement" (some years away from retirement but clearly planning for it), I'd choose the ETF with the stocks that had a strong record of growing the dividend payout. That way, those same dividend-paying stocks would grow in the short-term and provide better income down the road during retirement.

For more information on dividends, flip to Chapters 6 and 9.

Keep in mind that dividend-paying stocks generally fall within the criteria of "human need" investing because those companies tend to be large and stable, with good cash flows, giving them the ongoing wherewithal to pay good dividends.

To find out more about ETFs in general and to get more details on the ETFs I mention (SPY, PBJ, and SH), go to websites such as `www.etfdb.com` and `www.etfguide.com`. Many of the resources in Appendix A also cover ETFs.

Bearish ETFs

Most ETFs are bullish in nature because they invest in a portfolio of securities that they expect to go up in due course. But some ETFs have a bearish focus. Bearish ETFs (also called *short ETFs*) maintain a portfolio of securities and strategies that are designed to go the opposite way of the underlying or targeted securities. In other words, this type of ETF goes up when the underlying securities go down (and vice versa). Bearish ETFs employ securities such as put options (and similar derivatives) and/or employ strategies such as "going short" (see Chapter 17).

Take the S&P 500, for example. If you were bullish on that index, you might choose an ETF such as SPY. However, if you were bearish on that index and wanted to seek gains by betting that it would go down, you could choose an ETF such as SH.

You can take two approaches on bearish ETFs:

✔ **Hoping for a downfall:** If you're speculating on a pending market crash, a bearish ETF is a good consideration. In this approach, you're actually seeking to make a profit based on your expectations. Those folks who aggressively went into bearish ETFs during early or mid 2008 made some spectacular profits during the tumultuous downfall during late 2008 and early 2009.

✔ **Hedging against a downfall:** A more conservative approach is to use bearish ETFs to a more moderate extent, primarily as a form of hedging, whereby the bearish ETF acts like a form of insurance in the unwelcome event of a significant market pullback or crash. I say "unwelcome" because you're not really hoping for a crash; you're just trying to protect yourself with a modest form of diversification. In this context, diversification means that you have a mix of both bullish positions and, to a smaller extent, bearish positions.

Taking Note of Indexes

For stock investors, ETFs that are bullish or bearish are ultimately tied to major market indexes. You should take a quick look at indexes to better understand them (and the ETFs tied to them).

Whenever you hear the media commentary or the scuttlebutt at the local watering hole about "how the market is doing," it typically refers to a market proxy such as an index. You'll usually hear them mention "the Dow" or perhaps the "S&P 500." There are certainly other major market indexes, and there are many lesser, yet popular, measurements, such as the Dow Jones Transportation Average. Indexes and averages tend to be used interchangeably, but they're distinctly different entities of measurement.

Most people use these indexes basically as standards of market performance to see whether they're doing better or worse than a yardstick for comparison purposes. They want to know continuously whether their stocks, ETFs, mutual funds, or overall portfolios are performing well.

Appendix A gives you resources to help you gain a fuller understanding of indexes. You can also find great resources online, such as indexes.dowjones.com, that give you the history and composition of indexes. For your purposes, these are the main ones to keep an eye on:

✔ **Dow Jones Industrial Average (DJIA):** This is the most widely watched index (technically it's not an index, but it's utilized as one). It tracks 30 widely owned, large cap stocks, and it's occasionally re-balanced to drop (and replace) a stock that's not keeping up.

✔ **Nasdaq Composite:** This covers a cross-section of stocks from Nasdaq. It's generally considered a mix of stocks that are high-growth (riskier) companies with an over-representation of technology stocks.

- ✔ **S&P 500 index:** This index tracks 500 leading, publicly traded companies considered to be widely held. The publishing firm Standard & Poor's created this index (I bet you could've guessed that).

- ✔ **The Wilshire 5000:** This index is considered the widest sampling of stocks across the general stock market and, therefore, a more accurate measure of stock market movement.

If you don't want to go nuts trying to "beat the market," consider an ETF that closely correlates to any of the indexes mentioned in the preceding list. Sometimes it's better to join 'em than to beat 'em. The resources in Appendix A can help you find an index you believe is suitable for you.

Part II
Before You Start Buying

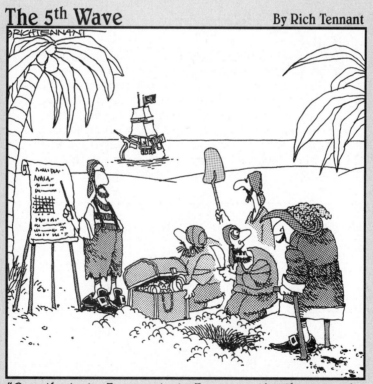

The 5th Wave   By Rich Tennant

"Growth stock? Income stock? I say we stick the money in the ground like always, and then feed this guy to the sharks."

In this part . . .

When you're about to begin investing in stocks, you should know that different types of stocks exist for different objectives. If you can at least get a stock that fits your situation, you're that much ahead in the game. In this part, you find out where to start gathering information, get the scoop on investing for growth and income, and discover what stockbrokers can do for you. In addition, you'll find a chapter on technical analysis that can help you time your stock purchases (or sales).

Chapter 6

Gathering Information

. . . .

In This Chapter

▶ Using stock exchanges to get investment information

▶ Applying accounting and economic know-how to your investments

▶ Deciphering stock tables

▶ Interpreting dividend news

▶ Recognizing good (and bad) investing advice

. . . .

Knowledge and information are two critical success factors in stock investing. (Isn't that true about most things in life?) People who plunge headlong into stocks without sufficient knowledge of the stock market in general, and current information in particular, quickly learn the lesson of the eager diver who didn't find out ahead of time that the pool was only an inch deep (ouch!). In their haste to avoid missing so-called golden investment opportunities, investors too often end up losing money.

Opportunities to *make* money in the stock market will always be there, no matter how well or how poorly the economy and the market are performing in general. There's no such thing as a single (and fleeting) magical moment, so don't feel that if you let an opportunity pass you by, you'll always regret that you missed your one big chance.

For the best approach to stock investing, build your knowledge and find quality information first so you can make your fortunes more assuredly. Before you buy, you need to know that the company you're investing in is

✔ Financially sound and growing

✔ Offering products and services that are in demand by consumers

✔ In a strong and growing industry (and general economy)

Where do you start and what kind of information do you want to acquire? Keep reading.

Looking to Stock Exchanges for Answers

Before you invest in stocks, you need to be completely familiar with the basics of stock investing. At its most fundamental, stock investing is about using your money to buy a piece of a company that will give you value in the form of appreciation or income (or both). Fortunately, many resources are available to help you find out about stock investing. Some of my favorite places are the stock exchanges themselves.

Stock exchanges are organized marketplaces for the buying and selling of stocks (and other securities). The New York Stock Exchange (NYSE; also referred to as "the Big Board"), the premier stock exchange, provides a framework for stock buyers and sellers to make their transactions. The NYSE makes money not only from a cut of every transaction but also from fees (such as listing fees) charged to companies and brokers that are members of its exchanges. In 2007, the NYSE merged with Euronext, a major European exchange, but no material differences exist for stock investors. In 2009, the American Stock Exchange (Amex) was taken over by (and completely merged into) the NYSE (Amex is no more!).

The main exchanges for most stock investors are the NYSE and Nasdaq. Technically, Nasdaq isn't an exchange, but it's a formal market that effectively acts as an exchange. Because the NYSE and Nasdaq benefit from increased popularity of stock investing and continued demand for stocks, they offer a wealth of free (or low-cost) resources and information for stock investors. Go to their websites to find useful resources such as:

- ✔ Tutorials on how to invest in stocks, common investment strategies, and so on

- ✔ Glossaries and free information to help you understand the language, practice, and purpose of stock investing

- ✔ A wealth of news, press releases, financial data, and other information about companies listed on the exchange or market, usually accessed through an on-site search engine

- ✔ Industry analysis and news

- ✔ Stock quotes and other market information related to the daily market movements of stocks, including data such as volume, new highs, new lows, and so on

- ✔ Free tracking of your stock selections (you can input a sample portfolio or the stocks you're following to see how well you're doing)

What each exchange/market offers keeps changing and is often updated, so explore them periodically at their respective websites:

- New York Stock Exchange: www.nyse.com
- Nasdaq: www.nasdaq.com

Grasping the Basics of Accounting and Economics

Stocks represent ownership in companies. Before you buy individual stocks, you want to understand the companies whose stock you're considering and find out about their operations. It may sound like a daunting task, but you'll digest the point more easily when you realize that companies work very similarly to the way you work. They make decisions on a daily basis just as you do.

Think about how you grow and prosper as an individual or as a family, and you see the same issues with businesses and how they grow and prosper. Low earnings and high debt are examples of financial difficulties that can affect both people and companies. You can better understand companies' finances by taking the time to pick up some information in two basic disciplines: accounting and economics. These two disciplines, which I discuss in the following sections, play a significant role in understanding the performance of a firm's stock.

Accounting for taste and a whole lot more

Accounting. Ugh! But face it: Accounting is the language of business, and believe it or not, you're already familiar with the most important accounting concepts! Just look at the following three essential principles:

- **Assets minus liabilities equals net worth.** In other words, take what you own (your *assets*), subtract what you owe (your *liabilities*), and the rest is yours (your *net worth*)! Your own personal finances work the same way as Microsoft's (except yours have fewer zeros at the end). See Chapter 2 to figure out how to calculate your own net worth.

  A company's balance sheet shows you its net worth at a specific point in time (such as December 31). The net worth of a company is the bottom line of its asset and liability picture, and it tells you whether the company is *solvent* (has the ability to pay its debts without going out of business). The net worth of a successful company grows regularly. To see whether your company is successful, compare its net worth with the net worth from the same point a year earlier. A firm that has a $4 million net worth on December 31, 2011, and a $5 million net worth on December 31, 2012, is doing well; its net worth has gone up 25 percent ($1 million) in one year.

✔ **Income minus expenses equals net income.** In other words, take what you make (your income), subtract what you spend (your expenses), and the remainder is your *net income* (or *net profit* or *net earnings* — your gain).

A company's profitability is the whole point of investing in its stock. As it profits, the business becomes more valuable, and in turn, its stock price becomes more valuable. To discover a firm's net income, look at its income statement. Try to determine whether the company uses its gains wisely, either by reinvesting them for continued growth or by paying down debt.

✔ **Do a comparative financial analysis.** That's a mouthful, but it's just a fancy way of saying how a company is doing now compared with something else (like a prior period or a similar company).

If you know that the company you're looking at had a net income of $50,000 for the year, you may ask, "Is that good or bad?" Obviously, making a net profit is good, but you also need to know whether it's good compared to something else. If the company had a net profit of $40,000 the year before, you know that the company's profitability is improving. But if a similar company had a net profit of $100,000 the year before and in the current year is making $50,000, then you may want to either avoid the company making the lesser profit or see what (if anything) went wrong with the company making less.

Accounting can be this simple. If you understand these three basic points, you're ahead of the curve (in stock investing as well as in your personal finances). For more information on how to use a company's financial statements to pick good stocks, see Chapters 11 and 12.

Understanding how economics affects stocks

Economics. Double ugh! No, you aren't required to understand "the inelasticity of demand aggregates" (thank heavens!) or "marginal utility" (say what?). But a working knowledge of basic economics is crucial (and I mean crucial) to your success and proficiency as a stock investor. The stock market and the economy are joined at the hip. The good (or bad) things that happen to one have a direct effect on the other. The following sections give you the lowdown.

Getting the hang of the basic concepts

Alas, many investors get lost on basic economic concepts (as do some so-called experts that you see on TV). I owe my personal investing success to my status as a student of economics. Understanding basic economics helps me (and will help you) filter the financial news to separate relevant information from the irrelevant in order to make better investment decisions. Be aware of these important economic concepts:

✔ **Supply and demand:** How can anyone possibly think about economics without thinking of the ageless concept of supply and demand? *Supply and demand* can be simply stated as the relationship between what's available (the supply) and what people want and are willing to pay for (the demand). This equation is the main engine of economic activity and is extremely important for your stock investing analysis and decision-making process. I mean, do you really want to buy stock in a company that makes elephant-foot umbrella stands if you find out that the company has an oversupply and nobody wants to buy them anyway?

✔ **Cause and effect:** If you pick up a prominent news report and read, "Companies in the table industry are expecting plummeting sales," do you rush out and invest in companies that sell chairs or manufacture table-cloths? Considering cause and effect is an exercise in logical thinking, and believe you me, logic is a major component of sound economic thought.

When you read business news, play it out in your mind. What good (or bad) can logically be expected given a certain event or situation? If you're looking for an effect ("I want a stock price that keeps increasing"), you also want to understand the cause. Here are some typical events that can cause a stock's price to rise:

  • **Positive news reports about a company:** The news may report that the company is enjoying success with increased sales or a new product.

  • **Positive news reports about a company's industry:** The media may be highlighting that the industry is poised to do well.

  • **Positive news reports about a company's customers:** Maybe your company is in industry A, but its customers are in industry B. If you see good news about industry B, that may be good news for your stock.

  • **Negative news reports about a company's competitors:** If the competitors are in trouble, their customers may seek alternatives to buy from, including your company.

✔ **Economic effects from government actions:** Political and governmental actions have economic consequences. As a matter of fact, nothing (and I mean nothing!) has a greater effect on investing and economics than government. Government actions usually manifest themselves as taxes, laws, or regulations. They also can take on a more ominous appearance, such as war or the threat of war. Government can willfully (or even accidentally) cause a company to go bankrupt, disrupt an entire industry, or even cause a depression. Government controls the money supply, credit, and all public securities markets. For more information on political effects, see Chapter 15.

Gaining insight from past mistakes

Because most investors ignored some basic observations about economics in the late 1990s, they subsequently lost trillions in their stock portfolios during 2000–2002. During 2000–2008, the U.S. experienced the greatest expansion of total debt in history, coupled with a record expansion of the money supply. The Federal Reserve (or "the Fed"), the U.S. government's central bank, controls both. This growth of debt and money supply resulted in more consumer (and corporate) borrowing, spending, and investing. The debt and spending that hyperstimulated the stock market during the late 1990s (stocks rose 25 percent per year for five straight years during that time period) came back with a vengeance afterwards. When the stock market bubble popped during 2000–2002, it was soon replaced with the housing bubble, which popped during 2005–2006. As of 2012, both the housing market and the general economy are still hobbled.

Of course, you should always be happy to earn 25 percent per year with your investments, but such a return can't be sustained and encourages speculation. This artificial stimulation by the Fed resulted in the following:

✔ More and more people depleted their savings. After all, why settle for 1–3 percent in the bank when you can get 25 percent in the stock market?

✔ More and more people bought on credit. If the economy is booming, why not buy now and pay later? Consumer credit hit record highs.

✔ More and more people borrowed against their homes. Why not borrow and get rich now? "I can pay off my debt later" was at the forefront of these folks' minds at the time.

✔ More and more companies sold more goods as consumers took more vacations and bought SUVs, electronics, and so on. Companies then borrowed to finance expansion, open new stores, and so on.

✔ More and more companies went public and offered stock to take advantage of the increase in money that was flowing to the markets from banks and other financial institutions.

In the end, spending started to slow down because consumers and businesses became too indebted. This slowdown in turn caused the sales of goods and services to taper off. Companies were left with too much overhead, capacity, and debt because they had expanded too eagerly. At this point, businesses were caught in a financial bind. Too much debt and too many expenses in a slowing economy mean one thing: Profits shrink or disappear. To stay in business, companies had to do the logical thing — cut expenses. What's usually the biggest expense for companies? People! Many companies started laying off employees. As a result, consumer spending dropped further because more people were either laid off or had second thoughts about their own job security.

As people had little in the way of savings and too much in the way of debt, they had to sell their stock to pay their bills. This trend was a major reason that stocks started to fall in 2000. Earnings started to drop because of shrinking sales from a sputtering economy. As earnings fell, stock prices also fell.

The lessons from the 1990s and 2000s are important ones for investors today:

✔ Stocks are not a replacement for savings accounts. Always have some money in the bank.

✔ Stocks should never occupy 100 percent of your investment funds.

✔ When anyone (including an expert) tells you that the economy will keep growing indefinitely, be skeptical and read diverse sources of information.

Know thyself before you invest in stocks

If you're reading this book, you're probably doing so because you want to become a successful investor. Granted, to be a successful investor, you have to select great stocks, but having a realistic understanding of your own financial situation and goals is equally important. I recall one investor who lost $10,000 in a speculative stock. The loss wasn't that bad because he had most of his money safely tucked away elsewhere. He also understood that his overall financial situation was secure and that the money he lost was "play" money — the loss wouldn't have a drastic effect on his life. But many investors often lose even more money, and the loss does have a major, negative effect on their lives. You may not be like the investor who can afford to lose $10,000. Take time to understand yourself, your own financial picture, and your personal investment goals before you decide to buy stocks. See Chapter 2 for guidance.

- If stocks do well in your portfolio, consider protecting your stocks (both your original investment and any gains) with stop-loss orders. (See Chapter 17 for more on these strategies.)

- Keep debt and expenses to a minimum.

- If the economy is booming, a decline is sure to follow as the ebb and flow of the economy's business cycle continues.

Staying on Top of Financial News

Reading the financial news can help you decide where or where not to invest. Many newspapers, magazines, and websites offer great coverage of the financial world. Obviously, the more informed you are, the better, but you don't have to read everything that's written. The information explosion in recent years has gone beyond overload, and you can easily spend so much time reading that you have little time left for investing. In the following sections, I describe the types of information you need to get from the financial news.

Appendix A of this book provides more information on the following resources, along with a treasure trove of some of the best publications, resources, and websites to assist you:

- The most obvious publications of interest to stock investors are *The Wall Street Journal* (www.wsj.com) and *Investor's Business Daily* (www.investors.com). These excellent publications report the news and stock data as of the prior trading day.

- Some of the more obvious websites are MarketWatch (www.marketwatch.com) and Bloomberg (www.bloomberg.com). These websites can actually give you news and stock data within 15 to 20 minutes after an event occurs.

- Don't forget the exchanges' websites that I list in the earlier section, "Looking to Stock Exchanges for Answers"!

Figuring out what a company's up to

Before you invest, you need to know what's going on with the company. When you read about the company, either from the firm's literature (its annual report, for example) or from media sources, be sure to get answers to some pertinent questions:

✔ **Is the company making more net income than it did last year?** You want to invest in a company that's growing.

✔ **Are the company's sales greater than they were the year before?** Keep in mind that you won't make money if the company isn't making money.

✔ **Is the company issuing press releases on new products, services, inventions, or business deals?** All these achievements indicate a strong, vital company.

Knowing how the company is doing, no matter what's happening with the general economy, is obviously important. To better understand how companies tick, see Chapters 11 and 12.

Discovering what's new with an industry

As you consider investing in a stock, make a point of knowing what's going on in that company's industry. If the industry is doing well, your stock is likely to do well, too. But then again, the reverse is also true.

Yes, I've seen investors pick successful stocks in a failing industry, but those cases are exceptional. By and large, it's easier to succeed with a stock when the entire industry is doing well. As you're watching the news, reading the financial pages, or viewing financial websites, check out the industry to ensure that it's strong and dynamic. See Chapter 13 for information on analyzing sectors and industries.

Knowing what's happening with the economy

No matter how well or how poorly the overall economy is performing, you want to stay informed about its general progress. It's easier for the value of stock to keep going up when the economy is stable or growing. The reverse is also true: If the economy is contracting or declining, the stock has a tougher time keeping its value. Some basic items to keep tabs on include the following:

✔ **Gross domestic product (GDP):** The GDP is roughly the total value of output for a particular nation, measured in the dollar amount of goods and services. It's reported quarterly, and a rising GDP bodes well for your stock. When the GDP is rising 3 percent or more on an annual basis, that's solid growth. If it rises but is less than 3 percent, that's generally considered less than stellar (or mediocre). A GDP under zero (a negative number) means that the economy is shrinking (heading into recession).

✔ **The index of leading economic indicators (LEI):** The LEI is a snapshot of a set of economic statistics covering activity that precedes what's happening in the economy. Each statistic helps you understand the economy in much the same way that barometers (and windows!) help you understand what's happening with the weather. Economists don't just look at an individual statistic; they look at a set of statistics to get a more complete picture of what's happening with the economy.

Chapter 15 goes into greater detail on economics and its effect on stock prices.

Seeing what politicians and government bureaucrats are doing

Being informed about what public officials are doing is vital to your success as a stock investor. Because federal, state, and local governments pass literally thousands of laws, rules, and regulations every year, monitoring the political landscape is critical to your success. The news media report what the president and Congress are doing, so always ask yourself, "How does a new law, tax, or regulation affect my stock investment?"

Laws being proposed or enacted by the federal government can be found through the Thomas legislative search engine, which is run by the Library of Congress (www.loc.gov). Also, some great organizations inform the public about tax laws and their impact, such as the National Taxpayers Union (www. ntu.org). Chapter 15 gives you more insights into politics and its effect on the stock market.

Checking for trends in society, culture, and entertainment

As odd as it sounds, trends in society, popular culture, and entertainment affect your investments, directly or indirectly. For example, a headline such as "The Graying of America — More People Than Ever Before Will Be Senior Citizens" gives you some important information that can make or break your stock portfolio. With that particular headline, you know that as more and more people age, companies that are well positioned to cater to that growing market's wants and needs will do well — meaning a successful stock for you.

Keep your eyes open to emerging trends in society at large by reading and viewing the media that cover such matters (*Time* magazine, CNN, Fox News, and so on). What trends are evident now? Can you anticipate the wants and needs of tomorrow's society? Being alert, staying a step ahead of the public, and choosing stocks appropriately gives you a profitable edge over other investors. If you own stock in a solid company with growing sales and earnings, other investors eventually notice. As more investors buy up your company's stocks, you're rewarded as the stock price increases.

Reading (And Understanding) Stock Tables

The stock tables in major business publications such as *The Wall Street Journal* and *Investor's Business Daily* are loaded with information that can help you become a savvy investor — *if* you know how to interpret them. You need the information in the stock tables for more than selecting promising investment opportunities. You also need to consult the tables after you invest to monitor how your stocks are doing.

Looking at the stock tables without knowing what you're looking for or why you're looking is the equivalent of reading *War and Peace* backwards through a kaleidoscope — nothing makes sense. But I can help you make sense of it all (well, at least the stock tables!). Table 6-1 shows a sample stock table. Each item gives you some clues about the current state of affairs for that particular company. The sections that follow describe each column to help you understand what you're looking at.

Table 6-1		A Sample Stock Table						
52-Wk High	52-Wk Low	Name (Symbol)	Div	Vol	Yld	P/E	Day Last	Net Chg
21.50	8.00	SkyHighCorp (SHC)		3,143		76	21.25	+.25
47.00	31.75	LowDownInc (LDI)	2.35	2,735	5.9	18	41.00	−.50
25.00	21.00	ValueNowInc (VNI)	1.00	1,894	4.5	12	22.00	+.10
83.00	33.00	DoinBadlyCorp (DBC)		7,601			33.50	−.75

Every newspaper's financial tables are a little different, but they give you basically the same information. Updated daily, these tables aren't the place to start your search for a good stock; they're usually where your search ends. The stock tables are the place to look when you own a stock or know what you want to buy and you're just checking to see the most recent price.

52-week high

The column in Table 6-1 labeled "52-Wk High" gives you the highest price that particular stock has reached in the most recent 52-week period. Knowing this price lets you gauge where the stock is now versus where it has been recently. SkyHighCorp's (SHC) stock has been as high as $21.50, whereas its last (most recent) price is $21.25, the number listed in the "Day Last" column. (Flip to the later section "Day last" for more on understanding this information.) SkyHighCorp's stock is trading very high right now because it's hovering right near its overall 52-week high figure.

Now, take a look at DoinBadlyCorp's (DBC) stock price. It seems to have tumbled big time. Its stock price has had a high in the past 52 weeks of $83, but it's currently trading at $33.50. Something just doesn't seem right here. During the past 52 weeks, DBC's stock price has fallen dramatically. If you're thinking about investing in DBC, find out why the stock price has fallen. If the company is strong, it may be a good opportunity to buy stock at a lower price. If the company is having tough times, avoid it. In any case, research the firm and find out why its stock has declined. (Chapters 11 and 12 provide the basics of researching companies.)

52-week low

The column labeled "52-Wk Low" gives you the lowest price that particular stock reached in the most recent 52-week period. Again, this information is crucial to your ability to analyze stock over a period of time. Look at DBC in Table 6-1, and you can see that its current trading price of $33.50 in the Day Last column is close to its 52-week low of $33.

Keep in mind that the high and low prices just give you a range of how far that particular stock's price has moved within the past 52 weeks. They can alert you that a stock has problems, or they can tell you that a stock's price has fallen enough to make it a bargain. Simply reading the 52-Wk High and 52-Wk Low columns isn't enough to determine which of those two scenarios is happening. They basically tell you to get more information before you commit your money.

Name and symbol

The "Name (Symbol)" column is the simplest in Table 6-1. It tells you the company name (usually abbreviated) and the stock symbol assigned to the company.

When you have your eye on a stock for potential purchase, get familiar with its symbol. Knowing the symbol makes it easier for you to find your stock in the financial tables, which list stocks in alphabetical order by the company's name (or symbol depending on the source). Stock symbols are the language of stock investing, and you need to use them in all stock communications, from getting a stock quote at your broker's office to buying stock over the Internet.

Dividend

Dividends (shown under the "Div" column in Table 6-1) are basically payments to owners (stockholders). If a company pays a dividend, it's shown in the dividend column. The amount you see is the annual dividend quoted for one share of that stock. If you look at LowDownInc (LDI) in Table 6-1, you can see that you get $2.35 as an annual dividend for each share of stock that you own. Companies usually pay the dividend in quarterly amounts. If I own 100 shares of LDI, the company pays me a quarterly dividend of $58.75 ($235 total per year). A healthy company strives to maintain or upgrade the dividend for stockholders from year to year. (I discuss additional dividend details later in this chapter.)

The dividend is very important to investors seeking income from their stock investments. For more about investing for income, see Chapter 9. Investors buy stocks in companies that don't pay dividends primarily for growth. For more information on growth stocks, see Chapter 8.

Volume

Normally, when you hear the word "volume" on the news, it refers to how much stock is bought and sold for the entire market: "Well, stocks were very active today. Trading volume at the New York Stock Exchange hit 2 billion shares." Volume is certainly important to watch because the stocks that you're investing in are somewhere in that activity. For the "Vol" column in Table 6-1, though, the volume refers to the individual stock.

Volume tells you how many shares of that particular stock were traded that day. If only 100 shares are traded in a day, then the trading volume is 100. SHC had 3,143 shares change hands on the trading day represented in Table 6-1. Is that good or bad? Neither, really. Usually the business news media only mention volume for a particular stock when it's unusually large. If a stock normally has volume in the 5,000 to 10,000 range and all of a sudden has a trading volume of 87,000, then it's time to sit up and take notice.

Keep in mind that a low trading volume for one stock may be a high trading volume for another stock. You can't necessarily compare one stock's volume against that of any other company. The large cap stocks like IBM or Microsoft typically have trading volumes in the millions of shares almost every day, whereas less active, smaller stocks may have average trading volumes in far, far smaller numbers.

The main point to remember is that trading volume that is far in excess of that stock's normal range is a sign that something is going on with that stock. It may be negative or positive, but something newsworthy is happening with that company. If the news is positive, the increased volume is a result of more people buying the stock. If the news is negative, the increased volume is probably a result of more people selling the stock. What are typical events that cause increased trading volume? Some positive reasons include the following:

- **Good earnings reports:** The company announces good (or better-than-expected) earnings.

- **A new business deal:** The firm announces a favorable business deal, such as a joint venture, or lands a big client.

- **A new product or service:** The company's research and development department creates a potentially profitable new product.

- **Indirect benefits:** The business may benefit from a new development in the economy or from a new law passed by Congress.

Some negative reasons for an unusually large fluctuation in trading volume for a particular stock include the following:

- **Bad earnings reports:** Profit is the lifeblood of a company. When its profits fall or disappear, you see more volume.

- **Governmental problems:** The stock is being targeted by government action, such as a lawsuit or a Securities and Exchange Commission (SEC) probe.

- **Liability issues:** The media report that the company has a defective product or similar problem.

- **Financial problems:** Independent analysts report that the company's financial health is deteriorating.

Check out what's happening when you hear about heavier-than-usual volume (especially if you already own the stock).

Yield

In general, yield is a return on the money you invest. However, in the stock tables, *yield* ("Yld" in Table 6-1) is a reference to what percentage that particular dividend is of the stock price. Yield is most important to income investors. It's calculated by dividing the annual dividend by the current stock price. In Table 6-1, you can see that the yield du jour of ValueNowInc (VNI) is 4.5 percent (a dividend of $1 divided by the company's stock price of $22). Notice that many companies report no yield; because they have no dividends, their yield is zero.

Keep in mind that the yield reported in the financial pages changes daily as the stock price changes. Yield is always reported as if you're buying the stock that day. If you buy VNI on the day represented in Table 6-1, your yield is 4.5 percent. But what if VNI's stock price rises to $30 the following day? Investors who buy stock at $30 per share obtain a yield of just 3.3 percent (the dividend of $1 divided by the new stock price, $30). Of course, because you bought the stock at $22, you essentially locked in the prior yield of 4.5 percent. Lucky you. Pat yourself on the back.

P/E

The *P/E ratio* is the ratio between the price of the stock and the company's earnings. P/E ratios are widely followed and are important barometers of value in the world of stock investing. The P/E ratio (also called the *earnings multiple* or just *multiple*) is frequently used to determine whether a stock is expensive (a good value). Value investors (such as yours truly) find P/E ratios to be essential to analyzing a stock as a potential investment. As a general rule, the P/E should be 10 to 20 for large cap or income stocks. For growth stocks, a P/E no greater than 30 to 40 is preferable. (See Chapter 11 for full details on P/E ratios.)

In the P/E ratios reported in stock tables, *price* refers to the cost of a single share of stock. *Earnings* refers to the company's reported earnings per share as of the most recent four quarters. The P/E ratio is the price divided by the earnings. In Table 6-1, VNI has a reported P/E of 12, which is considered a low P/E. Notice how SHC has a relatively high P/E (76). This stock is considered too pricey because you're paying a price equivalent to 76 times earnings. Also notice that DBC has no available P/E ratio. Usually this lack of a P/E ratio indicates that the company reported a loss in the most recent four quarters.

Day last

The "Day Last" column tells you how trading ended for a particular stock on the day represented by the table. In Table 6-1, LDI ended the most recent day of trading at $41. Some newspapers report the high and low for that day in addition to the stock's ending price for the day.

Net change

The information in the "Net Chg" column answers the question, "How did the stock price end today compared with its price at the end of the prior trading day?" Table 6-1 shows that SHC stock ended the trading day up 25 cents (at $21.25). This column tells you that SHC ended the prior day at $21. VNI ended the day at $22 (up 10 cents), so you can tell that the prior trading day it ended at $21.90.

Using News about Dividends

Reading and understanding the news about dividends is essential if you're an *income investor* (someone who invests in stocks as a means of generating regular income; see Chapter 9 for details). The following sections explain some basics you should know about dividends.

You can find news and information on dividends in newspapers such as *The Wall Street Journal, Investor's Business Daily,* and *Barron's* (you can find their websites online with your favorite search engine, or just check out Appendix A).

Looking at important dates

In order to understand how buying stocks that pay dividends can benefit you as an investor, you need to know how companies report and pay dividends. Some important dates in the life of a dividend are as follows:

✔ **Date of declaration:** This is the date when a company reports a quarterly dividend and the subsequent payment dates. On January 15, for example, a company may report that it "is pleased to announce a quarterly dividend of 50 cents per share to shareholders of record as of February 10." That was easy. The date of declaration is really just the announcement date. Whether you buy the stock before, on, or after the date of declaration doesn't matter in regard to receiving the stock's quarterly dividend. The date that matters is the date of record (see that bullet later in this list).

✔ **Date of execution:** This is the day you actually initiate the stock transaction (buying or selling). If you call up a broker (or contact her online) today to buy a particular stock, then today is the date of execution, or the date on which you execute the trade. You don't own the stock on the date of execution; it's just the day you put in the order. For an example, skip to the following section.

✔ **Closing date (settlement date):** This is the date on which the trade is finalized, which usually happens three business days after the date of execution. The closing date for stock is similar in concept to a real estate closing. On the closing date, you're officially the proud new owner (or happy seller) of the stock.

✔ **Ex-dividend date:** *Ex-dividend* means *without dividend.* Because it takes three days to process a stock purchase before you become an official owner of the stock, you have to qualify (that is, you have to own or buy the stock) *before* the three-day period. That three-day period is referred to as the "ex-dividend period." When you buy stock during this short time frame, you aren't on the books of record, because the closing (or settlement) date falls after the date of record. See the next section to see the effect that the ex-dividend date can have on an investor.

✔ **Date of record:** This is used to identify which stockholders qualify to receive the declared dividend. Because stock is bought and sold every day, how does the company know which investors to pay? The company establishes a cut-off date by declaring a date of record. All investors who are official stockholders as of the declared date of record receive the dividend on the payment date, even if they plan to sell the stock any time between the date of declaration and the date of record.

✔ **Payment date:** The date on which a company issues and mails its dividend checks to shareholders. Finally!

For typical dividends, the events in Table 6-2 happen four times per year.

Table 6-2	The Life of the Quarterly Dividend	
Event	**Sample Date**	**Comments**
Date of declaration	January 15	The date that the company declares the quarterly dividend
Ex-dividend date	February 7	Starts the three-day period during which, if you buy the stock, you don't qualify for the dividend
Date of record	February 10	The date by which you must be on the books of record to qualify for the dividend
Payment date	February 27	The date that payment is made (a dividend check is issued and mailed to stockholders who were on the books of record as of February 10)

Understanding why certain dates matter

Three business days pass between the date of execution and the closing date. Three business days also pass between the ex-dividend date and the date of record. This information is important to know if you want to qualify to receive an upcoming dividend. Timing is important, and if you understand these dates, you know when to purchase stock and whether you qualify for a dividend.

As an example, say that you want to buy ValueNowInc (VNI) in time to qualify for the quarterly dividend of 25 cents per share. Assume that the date of record (the date by which you have to be an official owner of the stock) is February 10. You have to execute the trade (buy the stock) no later than February 7 to be assured of the dividend. If you execute the trade right on February 7, the closing date occurs three days later, on February 10 — just in time for the date of record.

But what if you execute the trade on February 8, a day later? Well, the trade's closing date is February 11, which occurs *after* the date of record. Because you aren't on the books as an official stockholder on the date of record, you aren't getting that quarterly dividend. In this example, the February 7–10 period is called the *ex-dividend period*.

Fortunately, for those people who buy the stock during this brief ex-dividend period, the stock actually trades at a slightly lower price to reflect the amount of the dividend. If you can't get the dividend, you may as well save on the stock purchase. How's that for a silver lining?

Evaluating Investment Tips

Psssst. Have I got a stock tip for you! Come closer. You know what it is? Research! What I'm trying to tell you is to never automatically invest just because you get a hot tip from someone. Good investment selection means looking at several sources before you decide on a stock. No shortcut exists. That said, getting opinions from others never hurts — just be sure to carefully analyze the information you get. Here are some important points to bear in mind as you evaluate tips and advice from others:

- ✔ **Consider the source.** Frequently, people buy stock based on the views of some market strategist or market analyst. People may see an analyst being interviewed on a television financial show and take that person's opinions and advice as valid and good. The danger here is that the analyst may be biased because of some relationship that isn't disclosed on the show.

  It happens on TV all too often. The show's host interviews analyst U.R. Kiddingme from the investment firm Foollum & Sellum. The analyst says, "Implosion Corp. is a good buy with solid, long-term upside potential." You later find out that the analyst's employer gets investment banking fees from Implosion Corp. Do you really think that analyst would ever issue a negative report on a company that's helping to pay the bills? It's not likely.

- ✔ **Get multiple views.** Don't base your investment decisions on just one source unless you have the best reasons in the world for thinking that a particular, single source is outstanding and reliable. A better approach is to scour current issues of independent financial publications, such as *Barron's, Money* magazine, *SmartMoney,* and other publications (and websites) listed in Appendix A.

- ✔ **Gather data from the SEC.** When you want to get more objective information about a company, why not take a look at the reports that firms must file with the SEC? These reports are the same reports that the pundits and financial reporters read. Arguably, the most valuable report you can look at is the 10K. The 10K is a report that all publicly traded companies must file with the SEC. It provides valuable information on the company's operations and financial data for the most recent year, and it's likely to be less biased than the information a company includes in other corporate reports, such as an annual report. The next most important document from the SEC is the 10Q, which gives the investor similar detailed information but for a single quarter. (See Chapter 12 for more information about these documents.)

> To access 10K and 10Q reports, go to the SEC's website (`www.sec.gov`). From there, you can find the SEC's extensive database of public filings called EDGAR (Electronic Data Gathering, Analysis, and Retrieval system). By searching EDGAR, you can find companies' balance sheets, income statements, and other related information so that you can verify what others say and get a fuller picture of what a business is doing and what its financial condition is.

Chapter 7

Going for Brokers

*W*hen you're ready to dive in and start investing in stocks, you first have to choose a broker. It's kind of like buying a car: You can do all the research in the world and know exactly what kind of car you want, but you still need a venue to conduct the actual transaction. Similarly, when you want to buy stock, your task is to do all the research you can to select the company you want to invest in. Still, you need a broker to actually buy the stock, whether you buy over the phone or online. In this chapter, I introduce you to the intricacies of the investor/broker relationship.

For information on various types of orders you can place with a broker, such as market orders, stop-loss orders, and so on, flip to Chapter 17. To see how the latest technology (such as trade triggers) offers some cool possibilities for today's investor, check out Chapter 18.

Defining the Broker's Role

The broker's primary role is to serve as the vehicle through which you either buy or sell stock. When I talk about brokers, I'm referring to companies such as Charles Schwab, TD Ameritrade, E*TRADE, and many other organizations that can buy stock on your behalf. Brokers can also be individuals who work for such firms. Although you can buy some stocks directly from the company that issues them (I discuss direct purchase plans in Chapter 19), to purchase most stocks, you still need a broker.

The distinction between institutional stockbrokers and personal stockbrokers is important:

- **Institutional stockbrokers** make money from institutions and companies through investment banking and securities placement fees (such as initial public offerings and secondary offerings), advisory services, and other broker services.

- **Personal stockbrokers** generally offer the same services to individuals and small businesses.

Although the primary task of brokers is the buying and selling of securities (the word *securities* refers to the world of financial or paper investments, and stocks are only a small part of that world), they can perform other tasks for you, including the following:

- **Providing advisory services:** Investors pay brokers a fee for investment advice. Customers also get access to the firm's research.

- **Offering limited banking services:** Brokers can offer features such as interest-bearing accounts, check-writing, electronic deposits and withdrawals, and credit/debit cards.

- **Brokering other securities:** In addition to stocks, brokers can buy bonds, mutual funds, options, exchange-traded funds (ETFs), and other investments on your behalf.

Personal stockbrokers make their money from individual investors like you and me through various fees, including the following:

- **Brokerage commissions:** This fee is for buying and/or selling stocks and other securities.

- **Margin interest charges:** This interest is charged to investors for borrowing against their brokerage account for investment purposes. (I discuss margin accounts in more detail later in this chapter.)

- **Service charges:** These charges are for performing administrative tasks and other functions. Brokers charge fees to investors for Individual Retirement Accounts (IRAs) and for mailing stocks in certificate form.

Any broker (some brokers are now called *financial advisors*) you deal with should be registered with the Financial Industry Regulatory Authority (FINRA) and the Securities and Exchange Commission (SEC). In addition, to protect your money after you deposit it into a brokerage account, that broker should be a member of the Securities Investor Protection Corporation (SIPC). SIPC doesn't protect you from market losses; it protects your money in case the brokerage firm goes out of business or if your losses are due to brokerage fraud. To find out whether the broker is registered with these organizations, contact FINRA (`www.finra.org`), SEC (`www.sec.gov`), or SIPC (`www.sipc.org`). See Appendix A for more information on these organizations.

Distinguishing between Full-Service and Discount Brokers

Stockbrokers fall into two basic categories, which I discuss in the following sections: full-service and discount. The type you choose really depends on what type of investor you are. Here are the differences in a nutshell:

✔ **Full-service brokers** are suitable for investors who need some guidance and personal attention.

✔ **Discount brokers** are better for those investors who are sufficiently confident and knowledgeable about stock investing to manage with minimal help (usually through the broker's website).

Before you deal with any broker (either full-service or discount), get a free report on the broker from FINRA by calling 800-289-9999. Through its service called BrokerCheck, you can get a report on either a brokerage firm or an individual broker. More details on this and other services (such as investor education and so forth) can be found at `www.finra.org`. FINRA can tell you in its report whether any complaints or penalties have been filed against a brokerage firm or an individual rep.

At your disposal: Full-service brokers

Full-service brokers are just what the name indicates. They try to provide as many services as possible for investors who open accounts with them. When you open an account at a brokerage firm, a representative is assigned to your account. This representative is usually called an *account executive,* a *registered rep,* or a *financial advisor* by the brokerage firm. This person usually has a securities license (meaning that she's registered with the FINRA and the SEC) and is knowledgeable about stocks in particular and investing in general.

Examples of full-service brokers are Merrill Lynch and Morgan Stanley. Of course, all brokers now have full-featured websites to give you further information about their services. Get as informed as possible before you open your account. A full-service broker is there to help you build wealth, not make you . . . uh . . . broker.

What they can do for you

Your account executive is responsible for assisting you, answering questions about your account and the securities in your portfolio, and transacting your buy and sell orders. Here are some things that full-service brokers can do for you:

- **Offer guidance and advice:** The greatest distinction between full-service brokers and discount brokers is the personal attention you receive from your account rep. You get to be on a first-name basis with a full-service broker, and you disclose much information about your finances and financial goals. The rep is there to make recommendations about stocks and funds that are hopefully suitable for you.

- **Provide access to research:** Full-service brokers can give you access to their investment research department, which can give you in-depth information and analysis on a particular company. This information can be very valuable, but be aware of the pitfalls. (See the section "Judging Brokers' Recommendations," later in this chapter.)

- **Help you achieve your investment objectives:** A good rep gets to know you and your investment goals and *then* offers advice and answers your questions about how specific investments and strategies can help you accomplish your wealth-building goals.

- **Make investment decisions on your behalf:** Many investors don't want to be bothered when it comes to investment decisions. Full-service brokers can actually make decisions for your account with your authorization (this is also referred to as a *discretionary* account). This service is fine, but be sure to require brokers to explain their choices to you.

What to watch out for

Although full-service brokers, with their seemingly limitless assistance, can make life easy for an investor, you need to remember some important points to avoid problems:

- Brokers and account reps are salespeople. No matter how well they treat you, they're still compensated based on their ability to produce revenue for the brokerage firm. They generate commissions and fees from you on behalf of the company. (In other words, they're paid to sell you things.)

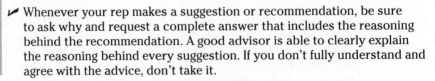

- Whenever your rep makes a suggestion or recommendation, be sure to ask why and request a complete answer that includes the reasoning behind the recommendation. A good advisor is able to clearly explain the reasoning behind every suggestion. If you don't fully understand and agree with the advice, don't take it.

✔ Working with a full-service broker costs more than working with a discount broker. Discount brokers are paid for simply buying or selling stocks for you. Full-service brokers do that and much more, like provide advice and guidance. Because of that, full-service brokers are more expensive (through higher brokerage commissions and advisory fees). Also, most full-service brokers expect you to invest at least $5,000 to $10,000 just to open an account, although many require higher minimums.

✔ Handing over decision-making authority to your rep can be a possible negative because letting others make financial decisions for you is always dicey — especially when they're using *your* money. If they make poor investment choices that lose you money, you may not have any recourse because you authorized them to act on your behalf.

✔ Some brokers engage in an activity called churning. *Churning* is basically buying and selling stocks for the sole purpose of generating commissions. Churning is great for brokers but bad for customers. If your account shows a lot of activity, ask for justification. Commissions, especially by full-service brokers, can take a big bite out of your wealth, so don't tolerate churning or other suspicious activity.

Just the basics: Discount brokers

Perhaps you don't need any hand-holding from a broker (that'd be kinda weird anyway). You know what you want, and you can make your own investment decisions. All you need is a convenient way to transact your buy/sell orders. In that case, go with a discount broker. They don't offer advice or premium services — just the basics required to perform your stock transactions.

Discount brokers, as the name implies, are cheaper to engage than full-service brokers. Because you're advising yourself (or getting advice and information from third parties such as newsletters, hotlines, or independent advisors), you can save on costs that you'd incur if you used a full-service broker.

If you choose to work with a discount broker, you must know as much as possible about your personal goals and needs. You have a greater responsibility for conducting adequate research to make good stock selections, and you must be prepared to accept the outcome, whatever that may be. (See Part III for details on researching stock selections.)

For a while, the regular investor had two types of discount brokers to choose from: conventional discount brokers and Internet discount brokers. But the two are basically synonymous now, so the differences are hardly worth mentioning. Through industry consolidation, most of the conventional discount brokers today have fully featured websites, while Internet discount brokers have adapted by adding more telephone and face-to-face services.

Charles Schwab and TD Ameritrade are examples of conventional discount brokers that have adapted well to the Internet era. Internet brokers such as E*TRADE.com (us.etrade.com), TradeKing.com (www.tradeking.com), Scottrade.com (www.scottrade.com), and thinkorswim.com (www.think orswim.com) have added more conventional services.

What they can do for you

Discount brokers offer some significant advantages over full-service brokers, such as:

- ✔ **Lower cost:** This lower cost is usually the result of lower commissions, and it's the primary benefit of using discount brokers.

- ✔ **Unbiased service:** Because they don't offer advice, discount brokers have no vested interest in trying to sell you any particular stock.

- ✔ **Access to information:** Established discount brokers offer extensive educational materials at their offices or on their websites.

What to watch out for

Of course, doing business with discount brokers also has its downsides, including the following:

- ✔ **No guidance:** Because you've chosen a discount broker, you *know* not to expect guidance, but the broker should make this fact clear to you anyway. If you're a knowledgeable investor, the lack of advice is considered a positive thing — no interference.

- ✔ **Hidden fees:** Discount brokers may shout about their lower commissions, but commissions aren't their only way of making money. Many discount brokers charge extra for services that you may think are included, such as issuing a stock certificate or mailing a statement. Ask whether they assess fees for maintaining IRAs or for transferring stocks and other securities (like bonds) in or out of your account, and find out what interest rates they charge for borrowing through brokerage accounts.

- ✔ **Minimal customer service:** If you deal with an Internet brokerage firm, find out about its customer service capability. If you can't transact business on its website, find out where you can call for assistance with your order.

Choosing a Broker

Before you choose a broker, you need to analyze your personal investing style (as I explain in Chapter 3), and then you can proceed to finding the kind of broker that fits your needs. It's almost like choosing shoes; if you don't know your size, you can't get a proper fit (and you can be in for a really uncomfortable future).

When it's time to choose a broker, keep the following points in mind:

- ✔ Match your investment style with a brokerage firm that charges the least amount of money for the services you're likely to use most frequently.

- ✔ Compare all the costs of buying, selling, and holding stocks and other securities through a broker. Don't compare only commissions; compare other costs, too, like margin interest and other service charges (see the earlier section "Defining the Broker's Role" for more about these costs).

- ✔ Use broker comparison services available in financial publications such as *SmartMoney* and *Barron's* (and, of course, their websites) and online sources such as www.comparebroker.com.

Finding brokers is easy. They're listed in the Yellow Pages (or on directory sites like www.superpages.com), in many investment publications, and on many financial websites. Start your search by using the sources in Appendix A, which includes a list of the major brokerage firms.

Discovering Various Types of Brokerage Accounts

When you start investing in the stock market, you have to somehow actually *pay* for the stocks you buy. Most brokerage firms offer investors several types of accounts, each serving a different purpose. I present three of the most common types in the following sections. The basic difference boils down to how particular brokers view your creditworthiness when it comes to buying and selling securities. If your credit isn't great, your only choice is a cash account. If your credit is good, you can open either a cash account or a margin account. After you qualify for a margin account, you can (with additional approval) upgrade it to do options trades.

To open an account, you have to fill out an application and submit a check or money order for at least the minimum amount required to establish an account.

Cash accounts

A *cash account* (also referred to as a *Type 1 account*) means just what you'd think. You must deposit a sum of money along with the new account application to begin trading. The amount of your initial deposit varies from broker to broker. Some brokers have a minimum of $10,000; others let you open an account for as little as $500. Once in a while you may see a broker offering cash accounts with no minimum deposit, usually as part of a promotion. Use the resources in Appendix A to help you shop around. Qualifying for a cash account is usually easy, as long as you have cash and a pulse.

With a cash account, your money has to be deposited in the account before the closing (or settlement) date for any trade you make. The closing occurs three business days after the date you make the trade (the date of execution). You may be required to have the money in the account even before the date of execution. See Chapter 6 for details on these and other important dates.

In other words, if you call your broker on Monday, October 10, and order 50 shares of CashLess Corp. at $20 per share, then on Thursday, October 13, you better have $1,000 in cash sitting in your account (plus commission). Otherwise, the purchase doesn't go through.

In addition, ask the broker how long it takes deposited cash (such as a check) to be available for investing. Some brokers put a hold on checks for up to ten business days (or longer), regardless of how soon that check clears your account (that would drive me crazy!).

See whether your broker will pay you interest on the uninvested cash in your brokerage account. Some brokers offer a service in which uninvested money earns money market rates, and you can even choose between a regular money market account and a tax-free municipal money market account.

Margin accounts

A *margin account* (also called a *Type 2 account*) allows you to borrow money against the securities in the account to buy more stock. Because you can borrow in a margin account, you have to be qualified and approved by the broker. After you're approved, this newfound credit gives you more leverage so you can buy more stock or do short-selling. (You can read more about buying on margin and short-selling in Chapter 17.)

For stock trading, the margin limit is 50 percent. For example, if you plan to buy $10,000 worth of stock on margin, you need at least $5,000 in cash (or securities owned) sitting in your account. The interest rate you pay varies depending on the broker, but most brokers generally charge a rate that's several points higher than their own borrowing rate.

Why use margin? Margin is to stocks what mortgage is to buying real estate. You can buy real estate with all cash, but using borrowed funds often makes sense because you may not have enough money to make a 100-percent cash purchase, or you may just prefer not to pay all cash. With margin, you can, for example, buy $10,000 worth of stock with as little as $5,000. The balance of the stock purchase is acquired using a loan (margin) from the brokerage firm.

Personally, I'm not a big fan of margin, and I use it sparingly. Margin is a form of leverage that can work out fine if you're correct but can be very danger-ous if the market moves against you. It's best applied with stocks that are generally stable and dividend-paying. That way, the dividends help pay off the margin interest.

Option accounts

An *option account* (also referred to as a *Type 3 account*) gives you all the capa-bilities of a margin account (which in turn also gives you the capabilities of a cash account) plus the ability to trade options on stocks and stock indexes. To upgrade your margin account to an option account, the broker usually asks you to sign a statement that you're knowledgeable about options and familiar with the risks associated with them.

Options can be a very effective addition to a stock investor's array of wealth-building investment tools. A more comprehensive review of options is avail-able in the book *Trading Options For Dummies* by George A. Fontanills (Wiley). I personally love to use options (as do my clients and students), and I think they can be a great tool in your wealth-building arsenal.

Judging Brokers' Recommendations

In recent years, Americans have become enamored with a new sport: the rating of stocks by brokers on TV financial shows. Frequently, these shows feature a dapper market strategist talking up a particular stock. Some stocks have been known to jump significantly right after an influential analyst issues a buy recommendation. Analysts' speculation and opinions make for great fun, and many people take their views very seriously. However, most inves-tors should be very wary when analysts, especially the glib ones on TV, make a recommendation. It's often just showbiz. In the following sections, I define basic broker recommendations and list a few important considerations for evaluating them.

Understanding basic recommendations

Brokers issue their recommendations (advice) as a general idea of how much regard they have for a particular stock. The following list presents the basic recommendations (or ratings) and what they mean to you:

✔ *Strong buy* **and** *buy:* Hot diggity dog! These ratings are the ones to get. The analyst loves this pick, and you would be very wise to get a bunch of shares. The thing to keep in mind, however, is that *buy* recommendations are probably the most common because (let's face it) brokers sell stocks.

✔ *Accumulate* **and** *market perform:* An analyst who issues these types of recommendations is positive, yet unexcited, about the pick. This rating is akin to asking a friend whether he likes your new suit and getting the response "It's nice" in a monotone voice. It's a polite reply, but you wish his opinion had been more definitive.

✔ *Hold* **or** *neutral:* Analysts use this language when their backs are to the wall, but they still don't want to say, "Sell that loser!" This recommendation reminds me of my mother telling me to be nice and either say something positive or keep my mouth shut. In this case, the rating is the analyst's way of keeping his mouth shut.

✔ *Sell:* Many analysts should have issued this recommendation during the bear markets of 2000–2002 and 2008 but didn't. What a shame. So many investors lost money because some analysts were too nice (or biased?) or just afraid to be honest, sound the alarm, and urge people to sell.

✔ *Avoid like the plague:* I'm just kidding about this one, but I wish this recommendation was available. I've seen plenty of stocks that I thought were dreadful investments — stocks of companies that made no money, were in terrible financial condition, and should never have been considered at all. Yet investors gobble up billions of dollars' worth of stocks that eventually become worthless.

Asking a few important questions

Don't get me wrong. An analyst's recommendation is certainly a better tip than what you'd get from your barber or your sister-in-law's neighbor, but you want to view recommendations from analysts with a healthy dose of reality. Analysts have biases because their employment depends on the very companies that are being presented. What investors need to listen to when a broker talks up a stock is the reasoning behind the recommendation. In other words, why is the broker making this recommendation?

Keep in mind that analysts' recommendations can play a useful role in your personal stock investing research. If you find a great stock and *then* you hear analysts give glowing reports on the same stock, you're on the right track! Here are some questions and points to keep in mind:

✔ **How does the analyst arrive at a rating?** The analyst's approach to evaluating a stock can help you round out your research as you consult other sources such as newsletters and independent advisory services.

✔ **What analytical approach is the analyst using?** Some analysts use *fundamental analysis* — looking at the company's financial condition and factors related to its success, such as its standing within the industry and the overall market. Other analysts use *technical analysis* — looking at the company's stock price history and judging past stock price movements to derive some insight regarding the stock's future price movement (see Chapter 10 for more about technical analysis). Many analysts use a combination of the two. Is this analyst's approach similar to your approach, or to those of sources that you respect or admire?

✔ **What is the analyst's track record?** Has the analyst had a consistently good record through both bull and bear markets? Major financial publications, such as *Barron's* and *Hulbert Financial Digest,* and websites, such as `MarketWatch.com`, regularly track recommendations from well-known analysts and stock pickers. Some resources for getting this type of info can be found in Appendix A.

✔ **How does the analyst treat important aspects of the company's performance, such as sales and earnings?** How about the company's balance sheet? The essence of a healthy company is growing sales and earnings coupled with strong assets and low debt. (See Chapter 11 for more details on these topics.)

✔ **Is the industry that the company's in doing well?** Do the analysts give you insight on this important information? A strong company in a weak industry can't stay strong for long. The right industry is a critical part of the stock selection process (for more information, see Chapter 13).

✔ **What research sources does the analyst cite?** Does the analyst quote the federal government or industry trade groups to support her thesis? These sources are important because they help give a more complete picture regarding the company's prospects for success. Imagine that you decide on the stock of a strong company. What if the federal government (through agencies like the SEC) is penalizing the company for fraudulent activity? Or what if the company's industry is shrinking or has ceased to grow (making it tougher for the company to continue growing)? The astute investor looks at a variety of sources before buying stock.

✔ **Is the analyst rational when citing a target price for a stock?** When he says, "We think the stock will hit $100 per share within 12 months," is he presenting a rational model, such as basing the share price on a projected price/earnings ratio (see Chapter 11)? The analyst must be able to provide a logical scenario explaining why the stock has a good chance of achieving the cited target price within the time frame mentioned. You may not necessarily agree with the analyst's conclusion, but the explanation can help you decide whether the stock choice is well thought out.

✔ **Does the company that's being recommended have any ties to the analyst or the analyst's firm?** During 2000–2002, the financial industry got bad publicity because many analysts gave positive recommendations on stocks of companies that were doing business with the very firms that employed those analysts. This conflict of interest is probably the biggest reason that analysts were so wrong in their recommendations during that period. Ask your broker to disclose any conflict of interest.

✔ **What school of economic thought does the analyst adhere to?** This may sound like an odd question, and it may not be readily answered, but it's a good thing to know. If I had to choose between two analysts that were very similar except that Analyst A adhered to the Keynesian school of economic thought and Analyst B adhered to the Austrian school, guess what? I'd choose Analyst B because those who embrace the Austrian school have a much better grasp of real-world economics (which means better stock investment choices).

The bottom line with brokerage recommendations is that you shouldn't use them to buy or sell a stock. Instead, use them to confirm your own research. I know that if I buy a stock based on my own research and later discover the same stock being talked up on the financial shows, that's just the icing on the cake. The experts may be great to listen to, and their recommendations can augment your own opinions, but they're no substitute for your own careful research. I devote Part III to researching and picking winning stocks.

Chapter 8

Investing for Long-Term Growth

In This Chapter

▶ Balancing growth and value

▶ Figuring out how to choose growth stocks

▶ Looking at small caps and other speculative investments

*W*hat's the number-one reason people invest in stocks? To grow their wealth (also referred to as *capital appreciation*). Yes, some people invest for income (in the form of dividends), but that's a different matter (I discuss investing for income in Chapter 9). Investors seeking growth would rather see the money that could have been distributed as dividends be reinvested in the company so that (hopefully) a greater gain is achieved when the stock's price rises or appreciates. People interested in growing their wealth see stocks as one of the convenient ways to do it. Growth stocks tend to be riskier than other categories of stocks, but they offer excellent long-term prospects for making the big bucks. If you don't believe me, just ask Warren Buffett, Peter Lynch, and other successful, long-term investors.

Although someone like Buffett is not considered a growth investor, his long-term, value-oriented approach has been a successful growth strategy. If you're the type of investor who has enough time to let somewhat risky stocks trend upward or who has enough money so that a loss won't devastate you financially, then growth stocks are definitely for you. As they say, no guts, no glory. The challenge is to figure out which stocks make you richer quicker; I give you tips on how to do so in this chapter.

Short of starting your own business, stock investing is the best way to profit from a business venture. I want to emphasize that to make money in stocks consistently over the long haul, you must remember that you're investing in a *company;* buying the stock is just a means for you to participate in the company's success (or failure). Why does it matter that you think of stock investing as buying a *company* versus buying a *stock?* Invest in a stock only if you're just as excited about it as you would be if you were the CEO in charge of running the company. If you're the sole owner of the company, do you act differently than one of a legion of obscure stockholders? Of course you do. As the firm's owner, you have a greater interest in the company. You have a strong desire to know how the enterprise is doing. As you invest in stocks, make believe that you're the owner, and take an active interest in the company's products, services, sales, earnings, and so on. This attitude and discipline can enhance your goals as a stock investor. This approach is especially important if your investment goal is growth.

Becoming a Value-Oriented Growth Investor

A stock is considered a *growth stock* when it's growing faster and higher than the overall stock market. Basically, a growth stock performs better than its peers in categories such as sales and earnings. *Value stocks* are stocks that are priced lower than the value of the company and its assets — you can identify a value stock by analyzing the company's fundamentals and looking at key financial ratios, such as the price-to-earnings (P/E) ratio. (Company finances are covered in Chapter 11, and ratios are covered in Chapter 11 and Appendix B.) Growth stocks tend to have better prospects for growth in the immediate future (from one to four years), but value stocks tend to have less risk and steadier growth over a longer term.

Over the years, a debate has quietly raged in the financial community about growth versus value investing. Some people believe that growth and value are mutually exclusive. They maintain that large numbers of people buying stock with growth as the expectation tend to drive up the stock price relative to the company's current value. Growth investors, for example, aren't put off by P/E ratios of 30, 40, or higher. Value investors, meanwhile, are too nervous to buy stocks at those P/E ratio levels.

However, you *can* have both. A value-oriented approach to growth investing serves you best. Long-term growth stock investors spend time analyzing the company's fundamentals to make sure that the company's growth prospects lie on a solid foundation. But what if you have to choose between a growth stock and a value stock? Which do you choose? Seek value when you're buying the stock and analyze the company's prospects for growth. Growth includes but is not limited to the health and growth of the company's specific industry, the economy at large, and the general political climate (see Chapters 13, 14 and 15).

The bottom line is that growth is much easier to achieve when you seek solid, value-oriented companies in growing industries. (To better understand industries and sectors and how they affect stock value, see Chapter 13.) It's also worth emphasizing that time, patience, and discipline are key factors in your success — especially in the tumultuous and uncertain stock investing environment of the current time (2013–2014).

Value-oriented growth investing probably has the longest history of success compared to most stock investing philosophies. The track record for those people who use value-oriented growth investing is enviable. Warren Buffett, Benjamin Graham, John Templeton, and Peter Lynch are a few of the more well-known practitioners. Each may have his own spin on the concepts, but all have successfully applied the basic principles of value-oriented growth investing over many years.

Choosing Growth Stocks with a Few Handy Tips

Although the information in the previous section can help you shrink your stock choices from thousands of stocks to maybe a few dozen or a few hundred (depending on how well the general stock market is doing), the purpose of this section is to help you cull the so-so growth stocks to unearth the go-go ones. It's time to dig deeper for the biggest potential winners. Keep in mind that you probably won't find a stock to satisfy all the criteria presented here. Just make sure that your selection meets as many criteria as realistically possible. But hey, if you do find a stock that meets all the criteria cited, *buy as much as you can!*

For the record, my approach to choosing a winning growth stock is probably almost the reverse method of . . . uh . . . that screaming money guy on TV (I won't mention his name!). People watch his show for "tips" on "hot stocks." The frenetic host seems to do a rapid-fire treatment of stocks in general. You get the impression that he looks over thousands of stocks and says "I like this one" and "I don't like that one." The viewer has to decide. Sheesh.

Verifiably, 80 to 90 percent of my stock picks are profitable. People ask me how I pick a winning stock. I tell them that I don't just pick a stock and hope that it does well. In fact, my personal stock-picking research doesn't even begin with stocks; I first look at the investing environment (politics, economics, demographics, and so on) and choose which industry will benefit. After I know which industry will prosper accordingly, *then* I start to analyze and choose my stock(s).

After I choose a stock, I wait. Patience is more than just a virtue; patience is to investing what time is to a seed that's planted in fertile soil. The legendary Jesse Livermore said that he didn't make his stock market fortunes by trading stocks; his fortunes were made "in the waiting." Why?

A case study in patience: Silver Wheaton

Talking about how to choose a growth stock is good, but even more instructive are real-life examples. Following is a case in point. In 2005, one of my favorite growth-stock choices was a small company that made money from silver: Silver Wheaton (stock symbol SLW). To me, it exhibited all the hallmarks of a good growth stock: It had good fundamentals (see the section "Checking out a company's fundamentals"), and my research indicated that it was in an appropriate industry that would benefit from a megatrend. SLW made its money by buying silver wholesale from the mining industry and selling it at retail. It benefited from silver without the traditional costs and risks of mining. At the time it was a $3 stock. If any stock rode the zigzags from 2005 to 2012, it's SLW. In the second half of 2008, when the market fell apart, SLW fell from more than $15 in July 2008 to less than $4 during November 2008. (Yikes! Talk about your volatility!) This precipitous drop of more than 70 percent was wretched to watch. Fortunately, if a company is fundamentally strong and the economy rebounds, recovery takes place. In 2012, SLW went to more than $30. Silver Wheaton's stock price not only recovered but went on to achieve all-time highs.

When I tell you to have patience and a long-term perspective, it isn't because I want you to wait years or decades for your stock portfolio to bear fruit. It's because you're waiting for a specific condition to occur: for the market to discover what you have! When you have a good stock in a good industry, it takes time for the market to discover it. When a stock has more buyers than sellers, it rises — it's as simple as that. As time passes, more buyers find your stock. As the stock rises, it attracts more attention and therefore more buyers. The more time that passes, the better your stock looks to the investing public.

When you're choosing growth stocks, you should consider investing in a company only *if* it makes a profit and *if* you understand *how* it makes that profit and from *where* it generates sales. Part of your research means looking at the industry and sector (see Chapter 13) and economic trends in general (which are covered in Chapter 14).

Looking for leaders in megatrends

A strong company in a growing industry is a common recipe for success. If you look at the history of stock investing, this point comes up constantly. Investors need to be on the alert for megatrends because they help ensure success.

A *megatrend* is a major development that has huge implications for much (if not all) of society for a long time to come. Good examples are the advent of the Internet and the aging of America. Both of these trends offer significant challenges and opportunities for our economy. Take the Internet, for example. Its potential for economic application is still being developed. Millions are flocking to it for many reasons. And census data tells us that senior citizens (over 65) will be the fastest-growing segment of the U.S. population during the next 20 years. How does the stock investor take advantage of a megatrend?

In this 4th edition, I plan to do what I did in the 3rd edition, which is to help you identify current megatrends to make it easier for you to pick winning stocks (you're welcome!). Find out more in Chapter 14.

Comparing a company's growth to an industry's growth

You have to measure the growth of a company against something to figure out whether its stock is a growth stock. Usually, you compare the growth of a company with growth from other companies in the same industry or with the stock market in general. In practical terms, when you measure the growth of a stock against the stock market, you're actually comparing it against a generally accepted benchmark, such as the Dow Jones Industrial Average (DJIA) or the Standard & Poor's 500 (S&P 500). For more on stock indexes, see Chapter 5.

If a company's earnings grow 15 percent per year over three years or more and the industry's average growth rate over the same time frame is 10 percent, then the stock qualifies as a growth stock. You can easily calculate the earnings growth rate by comparing a company's earnings in the current year to the preceding year and computing the difference as a percentage. For example, if a company's earnings (on a per-share basis) were $1 last year and $1.10 this year, then earnings grew by 10 percent. Many analysts also look at a current quarter and compare the earnings to the same quarter from the preceding year to see whether earnings are growing.

A growth stock is called that not only because the company is growing but also because the company is performing well with some consistency. Having a single year where your earnings do well versus the S&P 500's average doesn't cut it. Growth must be consistently accomplished.

Considering a company with a strong niche

Companies that have established a strong niche are consistently profitable. Look for a company with one or more of the following characteristics:

- **A strong brand:** Companies such as Coca-Cola and Microsoft come to mind. Yes, other companies out there can make soda or software, but a business needs a lot more than a similar product to topple companies that have established an almost irrevocable identity with the public.

- **High barriers to entry:** United Parcel Service and Federal Express have set up tremendous distribution and delivery networks that competitors can't easily duplicate. High barriers to entry offer an important edge to companies that are already established. Examples of high barriers include high capital requirements (needing lots of cash to start) or special technology that's not easily produced or acquired.

- **Research and development (R&D):** Companies such as Pfizer and Merck spend a lot of money researching and developing new pharmaceutical products. This investment becomes a new product with millions of consumers who become loyal purchasers, so the company's going to grow. You can find out what companies spend on R&D by checking their financial statements and their annual reports (more on this in Chapters 11 and 12).

Checking out a company's fundamentals

When you hear the word *fundamentals* in the world of stock investing, it refers to the company's financial condition and related data. When investors (especially value investors) do *fundamental analysis,* they look at the company's fundamentals — its balance sheet, income statement, cash flow, and other operational data, along with external factors such as the company's market position, industry, and economic prospects. Essentially, the fundamentals indicate the company's financial condition. Chapter 11 goes into greater detail about analyzing a company's financial condition. However, the main numbers you want to look at include the following:

- **Sales:** Are the company's sales this year surpassing last year's? As a decent benchmark, you want to see sales at least 10 percent higher than last year. Although it may differ depending on the industry, 10 percent is a reasonable, general yardstick.

- **Earnings:** Are earnings at least 10 percent higher than last year? Earnings should grow at the same rate as sales (or, hopefully, better).

- **Debt:** Is the company's total debt equal to or lower than the prior year? The death knell of many a company has been excessive debt.

A company's financial condition has more factors than I mention here, but these numbers are the most important. I also realize that using the 10-percent figure may seem like an oversimplification, but you don't need to complicate matters unnecessarily. I know someone's computerized financial model may come out to 9.675 percent or maybe 11.07 percent, but keep it simple for now.

Evaluating a company's management

The management of a company is crucial to its success. Before you buy stock in a company, you want to know that the company's management is doing a great job. But how do you do that? If you call up a company and ask, it may not even return your phone call. How do you know whether management is running the company properly? The best way is to check the numbers. The following sections tell you the numbers you need to check. If the company's management is running the business well, the ultimate result is a rising stock price.

Return on equity

Although you can measure how well management is doing in several ways, you can take a quick snapshot of a management team's competence by checking the company's return on equity (ROE). You calculate the ROE simply by dividing earnings by equity. The resulting percentage gives you a good idea whether the company is using its equity (or net assets) efficiently and profitably. Basically, the higher the percentage, the better, but you can consider the ROE solid if the percentage is 10 percent or higher. Keep in mind that not all industries have identical ROEs.

To find out a company's earnings, check out the company's income statement. The *income statement* is a simple financial statement that expresses this equation: sales (or revenue) minus expenses equals net earnings (or net income or net profit). You can see an example of an income statement in Table 8-1. (I give more details on income statements in Chapter 11.)

Table 8-1	Grobaby, Inc., Income Statement	
	2011 Income Statement	*2012 Income Statement*
Sales	$82,000	$90,000
Expenses	−$75,000	−$78,000
Net earnings	$7,000	$12,000

To find out a company's equity, check out that company's balance sheet. (See Chapter 11 for more details on balance sheets.) The *balance sheet* is actually a simple financial statement that illustrates this equation: total assets minus total liabilities equals net equity. For public stock companies, the net assets are called *shareholders' equity* or simply *equity*. Table 8-2 shows a balance sheet for Grobaby, Inc.

Table 8-2	Grobaby, Inc., Balance Sheet	
	Balance Sheet for December 31, 2011	*Balance Sheet for December 31, 2012*
Total assets (TA)	$55,000	$65,000
Total liabilities (TL)	–$20,000	–$25,000
Equity (TA minus TL)	$35,000	$40,000

Table 8-1 shows that Grobaby's earnings went from $7,000 to $12,000. In Table 8-2, you can see that Grobaby increased the equity from $35,000 to $40,000 in one year. The ROE for the year 2011 is 20 percent ($7,000 in earnings divided by $35,000 in equity), which is a solid number. The following year, the ROE is 30 percent ($12,000 in earnings divided by $40,000 equity), another solid number. A good minimum ROE is 10 percent, but 15 percent or more is preferred.

Equity and earnings growth

Two additional barometers of success are a company's growth in earnings and growth of equity.

✔ Look at the growth in earnings in Table 8-1. The earnings grew from $7,000 (in 2011) to $12,000 (in 2012), a percentage increase of 71 percent ($12,000 minus $7,000 equals $5,000, and $5,000 divided by $7,000 is 71 percent), which is excellent. At a minimum, earnings growth should be equal to or better than the rate of inflation, but because that's not always a reliable number, I like at least 10 percent.

✔ In Table 8-2, Grobaby's equity grew by $5,000 (from $35,000 to $40,000), or 14.3 percent ($5,000 divided by $35,000), which is very good — management is doing good things here. I like to see equity increasing by 10 percent or more.

Insider buying

Watching management as it manages the business is important, but another indicator of how well the company is doing is to see whether management is buying stock in the company as well. If a company is poised for growth, who knows better than management? And if management is buying up the company's stock en masse, that's a great indicator of the stock's potential. See Chapter 20 for more details on insider buying.

Noticing who's buying and/or recommending a company's stock

You can invest in a great company and still see its stock go nowhere. Why? Because what makes the stock go up is demand — having more buyers than sellers of the stock. If you pick a stock for all the right reasons and the market notices the stock as well, that attention causes the stock price to climb. The things to watch for include the following:

- **Institutional buying:** Are mutual funds and pension plans buying up the stock you're looking at? If so, this type of buying power can exert tremendous upward pressure on the stock's price. Some resources and publications track institutional buying and how that affects any particular stock. (You can find these resources in Appendix A.) Frequently, when a mutual fund buys a stock, others soon follow. In spite of all the talk about independent research, a herd mentality still exists.

- **Analysts' attention:** Are analysts talking about the stock on the financial shows? As much as you should be skeptical about an analyst's recommendation (given the stock market debacle of 2000–2002 and the market problems in 2008), it offers some positive reinforcement for your stock. Don't ever buy a stock solely on the basis of an analyst's recommendation. Just know that if you buy a stock based on your own research, and analysts subsequently rave about it, your stock price is likely to go up. A single recommendation by an influential analyst can be enough to send a stock skyward.

- **Newsletter recommendations:** Independent researchers usually publish newsletters. If influential newsletters are touting your choice, that praise is also good for your stock. Although some great newsletters are out there (find them in Appendix A) and they offer information that's as good as or better than that of some brokerage firms' research departments, don't base your investment decision on a single tip. However, seeing newsletters tout a stock that you've already chosen should make you feel good.

- **Consumer publications:** No, you won't find investment advice here. This one seems to come out of left field, but it's a source that you should notice. Publications such as *Consumer Reports* regularly look at products and services and rate them for consumer satisfaction. If a company's offerings are well received by consumers, that's a strong positive for the company. This kind of attention ultimately has a positive effect on that company's stock.

Making sure a company continues to do well

A company's financial situation does change, and you, as a diligent investor, need to continue to look at the numbers for as long as the stock is in your portfolio. You may have chosen a great stock from a great company with great numbers in 2009, but chances are pretty good that the numbers have changed since then.

Protecting your downside

I become a Johnny-one-note on one topic: trailing stops. (See Chapter 17 for a full explanation of trailing stops.) *Trailing stops* are stop losses that you regularly manage with the stock you invest in. I usually advocate using them, especially if you're new to the game of buying growth stocks. Trailing stops can help you, no matter how good or bad the economy is (or how good or bad the stock you're investing in is).

Suppose that you had invested in Enron, a classic example of a phenomenal growth stock that went bad. In 1999 and 2000, when its stock soared, investors were as happy as chocoholics at Hershey. Along with many investors who forgot that sound investing takes discipline and research, Enron investors thought, "Downside risk? What downside risk?"

Here's an example of how a stop-loss order would have worked if you had invested in Enron. Suppose that you had bought Enron in 2000 at $50 per share and put in a stop-loss order with your broker at $45. (Remember to make it a good-till-canceled, or GTC, order. If you do, the stop-loss order stays on indefinitely.) As a general rule, I like to place the stop-loss order at 10 percent below the market value. As the stock went up, you'd have kept the stop loss trailing upward like a tail. (Now you know why it's called a "trailing" stop; it trails the stock's

price.) When Enron hit $70, your stop loss would have changed to, say, $63, and so on. At $84, your new stop loss would have been at $76. Then what?

When Enron started its perilous descent, you'd have gotten out at $76. The new price of $76 would have triggered the stop loss, and the stock would have been automatically sold — you'd have stopped the loss! Actually, in this case, you could call it a "stop and cash in the gain" order. Because you'd have bought the stock at $50 and sold at $76, you'd have pocketed a nice capital gain of $26 (52 percent appreciation — a-do-en-ron, a-do-en-ron!). Then you would have safely stepped aside and watched the stock continue its plunge.

But what if the market is doing well? Are trailing stops a good idea? Because these stops are placed below the stock price, you're not stopping the stock from rising upward indefinitely. All you're doing is protecting your investment from loss. That's discipline! The stock market of 2004–2008 was fairly good to stock investors as the bear market that started in 2000 took a break. If a bear market continues, trailing stop strategies will again become very useful because a potential decline in the stock price will become a greater risk.

Great stocks don't always stay that way. A great selection that you're drawn to today may become tomorrow's pariah. Information, both good and bad, moves like lightning. Keep an eye on your stock company's numbers! To help minimize the downside risk, see the nearby sidebar "Protecting your downside" for an example. For more information on a company's financial data, check out Chapter 11.

Heeding investing lessons from history

A growth stock isn't a creature like the Loch Ness monster — always talked about but rarely seen. Growth stocks have been part of the financial scene for nearly a century. Examples abound that offer rich information that you can apply to today's stock market environment. Look at past market winners, especially those during the bull market of the late 1990s and the bearish markets of 2000–2010, and ask yourself, "What made them profitable stocks?" I mention these two time frames because they offer a stark contrast to each other. The 1990s were booming times for stocks, whereas more recent years were very tough and bearish. (See Chapter 14 for info about bullish and bearish megatrends that will affect stocks in the coming years.)

Being aware and acting logically are as vital to successful stock investing as they are to any other pursuit. Over and over again, history gives you the formula for successful stock investing:

- Pick a company that has strong fundamentals, including signs such as rising sales and earnings and low debt. (See Chapter 11.)

- Make sure that the company is in a growing industry. (See Chapter 13.)

- Fully participate in stocks that are benefiting from bullish market developments in the general economy. (See Chapter 14.)

- During a bear market or in bearish trends, switch more of your money out of growth stocks (such as technology) and into defensive stocks (such as utilities).

- Monitor your stocks. Hold on to stocks that continue to have growth potential, and sell those stocks with declining prospects. (See Chapters 22 and 23 for tips on what to do if the stocks in your portfolio are up or down.)

Exploring Small Caps and Speculative Stocks

Everyone wants to get in early on a hot new stock. Why not? You buy Shlobotky, Inc., at $1 per share and hope it zooms to $98 before lunchtime.

Who doesn't want to buy a cheapy-deepy stock today that could become the next Apple or Walmart? This possibility is why investors are attracted to small cap stocks.

Small cap (or small capitalization) is a reference to the company's market size, as I explain in Chapter 1. *Small cap stocks* are stocks that have a market value under $1 billion. Investors may face more risk with small caps, but they also have the chance for greater gains.

Out of all the types of stocks, small cap stocks continue to exhibit the greatest amount of growth. In the same way that a tree planted last year has more opportunity for growth than a mature 100-year-old redwood, small caps have greater growth potential than established large cap stocks. Of course, a small cap doesn't exhibit spectacular growth just because it's small. It grows when it does the right things, such as increasing sales and earnings by producing goods and services that customers want.

For every small company that becomes a Fortune 500 firm, hundreds of companies don't grow at all or go out of business. When you try to guess the next great stock before any evidence of growth, you're not investing — you're speculating. Have you heard that one before? (If not, flip to Chapter 16 on speculating, trading, and investing for details.) Of course you have, and you'll hear it again. Don't get me wrong — there's nothing wrong with speculating. But it's important to *know* that you're speculating when you're doing it. If you're going to speculate in small stocks hoping for the next Google, use the guidelines I present in the following sections to increase your chances of success.

Knowing when to avoid IPOs

Initial public offerings (IPOs) are the birthplaces of public stocks, or the proverbial ground floor. The *IPO* is the first offering to the public of a company's stock. The IPO is also referred to as "going public." Because a company going public is frequently an unproven enterprise, investing in an IPO can be risky. Here are the two types of IPOs:

- **Start-up IPO:** This is a company that didn't exist before the IPO. In other words, the entrepreneurs get together and create a business plan. To get the financing they need for the company, they decide to go public immediately by approaching an investment banker. If the investment banker thinks that it's a good concept, the banker will seek funding (selling the stock to investors) via the IPO.

- **A private company that decides to go public:** In many cases, the IPO is done for a company that already exists and is seeking expansion capital. The company may have been around for a long time as a smaller private concern, but now decides to seek funding through an IPO to grow even larger (or to fund a new product, promotional expenses, and so on).

Which of the two IPOs do you think is less risky? That's right — the private company going public. Why? Because it's already a proven business, which is a safer bet than a brand-new start-up. Some great examples of successful IPOs in recent years are United Parcel Service and Google (they were established companies *before* they went public).

Great stocks started as small companies going public. You may be able to recount the stories of Federal Express, Dell, AOL, Home Depot, and hundreds of other great successes. But do you remember an IPO by the company Lipschitz & Farquar? No? I didn't think so. It's among the majority of IPOs that don't succeed.

IPOs have a dubious track record of success in their first year. Studies periodically done by the brokerage industry have revealed that IPOs actually decline in price 60 percent of the time (more often than not) during the first 12 months. In other words, an IPO has a better-than-even chance of dropping in price. For investors, the lesson is clear: Wait until a track record appears before you invest in a company. If you don't, you're simply rolling the dice (in other words, you're speculating, not investing!). Don't worry about missing that great opportunity; if it's a bona fide opportunity, you'll still do well after the IPO.

Making sure a small cap stock is making money

I emphasize two points when investing in stocks:

- **Make sure that a company is established.** Being in business for at least three years is a good minimum.

- **Make sure that a company is profitable.** It should show net profits of 10 percent or more over two years or longer.

These points are especially important for investors in small stocks. Plenty of start-up ventures lose money but hope to make a fortune down the road. A good example is a company in the biotechnology industry. Biotech is an exciting area, but it's esoteric, and at this early stage, companies are finding it difficult to use the technology in profitable ways. You may say, "But shouldn't I jump in now in anticipation of future profits?" You may get lucky, but understand that when you invest in unproven, small cap stocks, you're speculating.

Analyzing small cap stocks before you invest

The only difference between a small cap stock and a large cap stock is a few zeros in their numbers and the fact that you need to do more research with small caps. By sheer dint of size, small caps are riskier than large caps, so you offset the risk by accruing more information on yourself and the stock in question. Plenty of information is available on large cap stocks because they're widely followed. Small cap stocks don't get as much press, and fewer analysts issue reports on them. Here are a few points to keep in mind:

- ✔ **Understand your investment style.** Small cap stocks may have more potential rewards, but they also carry more risk. No investor should devote a large portion of his capital to small cap stocks. If you're considering retirement money, you're better off investing in large cap stocks, exchange-traded funds (ETFs; see Chapter 5), investment-grade bonds, bank accounts, and/or mutual funds. For example, retirement money should be in investments that are either very safe or have proven track records of steady growth over an extended period of time (five years or longer).

- ✔ **Check with the Securities and Exchange Commission (SEC).** Get the financial reports that the company must file with the SEC (such as its 10Ks and 10Qs — see Chapter 12 for more details). These reports offer more complete information on the company's activities and finances. Go to the SEC website at www.sec.gov and check its massive database of company filings at EDGAR (Electronic Data Gathering, Analysis, and Retrieval system). You can also check to see whether any complaints have been filed against the company.

- ✔ **Check other sources.** See whether brokers and independent research services, such as Value Line, follow the stock. If two or more different sources like the stock, it's worth further investigation. Check the resources in Appendix A for further sources of information before you invest.

Chapter 9

Investing for Income

In This Chapter

▶ Familiarizing yourself with income stock fundamentals

▶ Selecting income stocks with a few criteria in mind

▶ Checking out utilities, REITs, and royalty trusts

*I*nvesting for income means investing in stocks that provide you with regular cash payments (dividends). Income stocks may not be known to offer stellar growth potential, but they're good for a steady infusion of cash. If you have a low tolerance for risk, or if your investment goal is anything less than long-term, income stocks are a better bet than growth stocks. Long-term, conservative investors who need income in their situations can also benefit from income stocks because they have a good track record of keeping pace with inflation (versus fixed-income investments, such as bonds).

The bottom line is that I like dividend-paying stocks, and they deserve a spot in a variety of portfolios. In this chapter, I explain the basics of income stocks, show you how to analyze income stocks with a few handy formulas, and describe several typical income stocks.

Getting your stock portfolio to yield more income is easier than you think. Many investors increase income using proven techniques such as covered call writing. Covered call writing is beyond the scope of this book, but I encourage you to find out more about this technique and whether it applies to your situation. Talk to your financial advisor or read up on it — it's covered more fully in *Trading Options For Dummies* by George A. Fontanills (Wiley). You can also find great educational material on this option strategy (and many others) at the Chicago Board Options Exchange (www.cboe.com).

Understanding the Basics of Income Stocks

I certainly think that dividend-paying stocks are a great consideration for those investors seeking greater income in their portfolios. I especially like stocks with higher-than-average dividends that are known as *income stocks*. Income stocks take on a dual role in that they can not only appreciate but also provide regular income. The following sections take a closer look at dividends and income stocks.

Getting a grip on dividends and dividend rates

When people talk about gaining income from stocks, they're usually talking about dividends. A *dividend* is nothing more than money paid out to the owner of stock. You purchase dividend stocks primarily for income — not for spectacular growth potential.

Dividends are sometimes confused with interest. However, dividends are payouts to owners, whereas interest is a payment to a creditor. A stock investor is considered a part owner of the company he invests in and is entitled to dividends when they're issued. A bank, on the other hand, considers you a creditor when you open an account. The bank borrows your money and pays you interest on it.

A dividend is quoted as an annual number but is usually paid on a quarterly basis. For example, if a stock pays a dividend of $4, you're probably paid $1 every quarter. If, in this example, you have 200 shares, you're paid $800 every year (if the dividend doesn't change during that period), or $200 per quarter. Getting that regular dividend check every three months (for as long as you hold the stock) can be a nice perk.

A good income stock has a higher-than-average dividend (typically 4 percent or higher).

Dividend rates aren't guaranteed — they can go up or down, or in some extreme cases, the dividend can be discontinued. Fortunately, most companies that issue dividends continue them indefinitely and actually increase dividend payments from time to time. Historically, dividend increases have equaled (or exceeded) the rate of inflation.

Recognizing who's well-suited for income stocks

What type of person is best suited to income stocks? Income stocks can be appropriate for many investors, but they're especially well-suited for the following individuals:

- ✔ **Conservative and novice investors:** Conservative investors like to see a slow-but-steady approach to growing their money while getting regular dividend checks. Novice investors who want to start slowly also benefit from income stocks.

- ✔ **Retirees:** Growth investing (which I describe in Chapter 8) is best suited for long-term needs, whereas income investing is best suited to current needs. Retirees may want some growth in their portfolios, but they're more concerned with regular income that can keep pace with inflation.

- ✔ **Dividend reinvestment plan (DRP) investors:** For those investors who like to compound their money with DRPs, income stocks are perfect. For more information on DRPs, see Chapter 19.

Assessing the advantages of income stocks

Income stocks tend to be among the least volatile of all stocks, and many investors view them as defensive stocks. *Defensive stocks* are stocks of companies that sell goods and services that are generally needed no matter what shape the economy is in. (Don't confuse defensive stocks with *defense stocks,* which specialize in goods and equipment for the military.) Food, beverage, and utility companies are great examples of defensive stocks. Even when the economy is experiencing tough times, people still need to eat, drink, and turn on the lights. Companies that offer relatively high dividends also tend to be large firms in established, stable industries.

Some industries in particular are known for high-dividend stocks. Utilities (such as electric, gas, and water), real estate investment trusts (REITs), and the energy sector (oil and gas royalty trusts) are places where you definitely find income stocks. Yes, you can find high-dividend stocks in other industries, but you find a higher concentration of them in these industries. For more details, see the sections highlighting these industries later in this chapter.

Watching out for the disadvantages of income stocks

Before you say, "Income stocks are great! I'll get my checkbook and buy a batch right now," take a look at the following potential disadvantages (ugh!). Income stocks do come with some fine print.

What goes up . . .

Income stocks can go down as well as up, just as any stock can. The factors that affect stocks in general — politics (Chapter 15), economic trends (Chapter 14), industry changes (Chapter 13), and so on — affect income stocks, too. Fortunately, income stocks don't get hit as hard as other stocks when the market is declining, because high dividends tend to act as a support to the stock price. Therefore, income stocks' prices usually fall less dramatically than other stocks' prices in a declining market.

Interest-rate sensitivity

Income stocks can be sensitive to rising interest rates. When interest rates go up, other investments (such as corporate bonds, U.S. Treasury securities, and bank certificates of deposit) are more attractive. When your income stock yields 4 percent and interest rates go up to 5 percent, 6 percent, or higher, you may think, "Hmm. Why settle for a 4 percent yield when I can get 5 percent or better elsewhere?" As more and more investors sell their low-yield stocks, the prices for those stocks fall.

Another point to note is that rising interest rates may hurt the company's financial strength. If the company has to pay more interest, that may affect the company's earnings, which in turn may affect the company's ability to continue paying dividends.

Dividend-paying companies that experience consistent falling revenues tend to cut dividends. In this case, *consistent* means two or more years.

The effect of inflation

Although many companies raise their dividends on a regular basis, some don't. Or if they do raise their dividends, the increases may be small. If income is your primary consideration, you want to be aware of this fact. If you're getting the same dividend year after year and this income is important to you, rising inflation becomes a problem.

Say that you have XYZ stock at $10 per share with an annual dividend of 30 cents (the yield is 30 cents divided by $10, or 3 percent). If you have a yield of 3 percent two years in a row, how do you feel when inflation rises 6 percent one year and 7 percent the next year? Because inflation means your costs are rising, inflation shrinks the value of the dividend income you receive.

Playing it safe with alternatives for generating income

If you're an investor seeking income and you're nervous about potential risks with income stocks, here are some nonstock alternatives:

✔ **U.S. Treasury securities:** Issued by the federal government, these securities are considered the safest investments in the world. Examples of treasury securities are U.S. savings bonds and treasury bonds. They pay interest and are an ideal addition to any income investor's portfolio.

✔ **Bank certificates of deposit (CDs):** These investments are backed by the Federal Deposit Insurance Corporation (FDIC) and are considered very safe.

✔ **Income mutual funds:** Many mutual funds, such as treasury bond mutual funds and corporate bond funds, are designed for income investors. They offer investors diversification and professional management, and you can invest with as little as $1,000. For more details, refer to *Mutual Funds For Dummies* by Eric Tyson (published by Wiley).

Fortunately, studies show that in general, dividends do better in inflationary environments than bonds and other fixed-rate investments. Usually, the dividends of companies that provide consumer staples (food, energy, and so on) meet or exceed the rate of inflation.

Uncle Sam's cut

The government usually taxes dividends as ordinary income. As I write this, higher tax rates on dividends are being considered so find out from your tax person whether this is (or will be) an issue for you. See Chapter 21 for more information on taxes for stock investors.

Analyzing Income Stocks

As I explain in the preceding section, even conservative income investors can be confronted with different types of risk. (Chapter 4 covers risk and volatility in greater detail.) Fortunately, this section helps you carefully choose income stocks so that you can minimize potential disadvantages.

Look at income stocks in the same way you do growth stocks when assessing the financial strength of a company. Getting nice dividends comes to a screeching halt if the company can't afford to pay them. If your budget depends on dividend income, then monitoring the company's financial strength is that much more important. You can apply the same techniques I list in Chapters 8 and 11 for assessing the financial strength of growth stocks to your assessment of income stocks.

Pinpointing your needs first

You choose income stocks primarily because you want or need income now. As a secondary point, income stocks have the potential for steady, long-term appreciation. So if you're investing for retirement needs that won't occur for another 20 years, maybe income stocks aren't suitable for you — a better choice may be to invest in growth stocks because they're more likely to grow your money faster over a lengthier investment term. (I explain who's best suited to income stocks earlier in this chapter.)

If you're certain you want income stocks, do a rough calculation to figure out how big a portion of your portfolio you want income stocks to occupy. Suppose that you need $25,000 in investment income to satisfy your current financial needs. If you have bonds that give you $20,000 in interest income and you want the rest to come from dividends from income stocks, you need to choose stocks that pay you $5,000 in annual dividends. If you have $80,000 left to invest, you need a portfolio of income stocks that yields 6.25 percent ($5,000 divided by $80,000 equals a yield of 6.25 percent; I explain yield in more detail in the following section).

You may ask, "Why not just buy $80,000 of bonds (for instance) that yield at least 6.25 percent?" Well, if you're satisfied with that $5,000 and inflation for the foreseeable future is 0 or considerably less than 6.25 percent, then you have a point. Unfortunately, inflation will probably be with us for a long time. Fortunately, the steady growth that income stocks provide is a benefit to you.

If you have income stocks and don't have any immediate need for the dividends, consider reinvesting the dividends in the company's stock. For more details on this kind of reinvesting, see Chapter 19.

Every investor is different. If you're not sure about your current or future needs, your best choice is to consult with a financial planner. Flip to Appendix A for helpful financial planning and investing resources.

Checking out yield

Because income stocks pay out dividends — income — you need to assess which stocks can give you the highest income. How do you do that? The main thing to look for is *yield*, which is the percentage rate of return paid on a stock in the form of dividends. Looking at a stock's dividend yield is the quickest way to find out how much money you'll earn versus other dividend-paying stocks (or even other investments, such as a bank account). Table 9-1 illustrates this point. Dividend yield is calculated in the following way:

Dividend yield = Dividend income ÷ Stock investment

The next two sections use the information in Table 9-1 to compare the yields from different investments and to show how evaluating yield helps you choose the stock that earns you the most money.

Table 9-1		Comparing Yields		
Investment	*Type*	*Investment Amount*	*Annual Investment Income (Dividend)*	*Yield (Annual Investment Income ÷ Investment Amount)*
Smith Co.	Common stock	$20 per share	$1.00 per share	5%
Jones Co.	Common stock	$30 per share	$1.50 per share	5%
Wilson Bank	Savings account	$1,000 deposit	$40 (interest)	4%

Don't stop scrutinizing stocks after you acquire them. You may make a great choice that gives you a great dividend, but that doesn't mean the stock will stay that way indefinitely. Monitor the company's progress for as long as it's in your portfolio by using resources such as www.bloomberg.com and www.marketwatch.com (see Appendix A for more resources).

Examining changes in yield

Most people have no problem understanding yield when it comes to bank accounts. If I tell you that my bank certificate of deposit (CD) has an annual yield of 3.5 percent, you can easily figure out that if I deposit $1,000 in that account, a year later I'll have $1,035 (slightly more if you include compounding). The CD's market value in this example is the same as the deposit amount — $1,000. That makes it easy to calculate.

How about stocks? When you see a stock listed in the financial pages, the dividend yield is provided, along with the stock's price and annual dividend. The dividend yield in the financial pages is always calculated as if you bought the stock on that given day. Just keep in mind that based on supply and demand, stock prices change every business day (virtually every minute!) that the market's open, so the yield changes daily as well. So keep the following two things in mind when examining yield:

✔ **The yield listed in the financial pages may not represent the yield you're receiving.** What if you bought stock in Smith Co. (see Table 9-1) a month ago at $20 per share? With an annual dividend of $1, you know your yield is 5 percent. But what if today Smith Co. is selling for $40 per share? If you look in the financial pages, the yield quoted is 2.5 percent. Gasp! Did the dividend get cut in half?! No, not really. You're still getting 5 percent because you bought the stock at $20 rather than the current $40 price; the quoted yield is for investors who purchase Smith Co. today. They pay $40 and get the $1 dividend, and they're locked into the current yield of 2.5 percent. Although Smith Co. may have been a good income investment for you a month ago, it's not such a hot pick today because the price of the stock has doubled, cutting the yield in half. Even though the dividend hasn't changed, the yield has changed dramatically because of the stock price change.

✔ **Stock price affects how good of an investment the stock may be.** Another way to look at yield is by looking at the investment amount. Using Smith Co. in Table 9-1 as the example, the investor who bought, say, 100 shares of Smith Co. when they were $20 per share only paid $2,000 (100 shares × $20 — leave out commissions to make the example simple). If the same stock is purchased later at $40 per share, the total investment amount is $4,000 (100 shares × $40). In either case, the investor gets a total dividend income of $100 (100 shares × $1 dividend per share). Which investment is yielding more — the $2,000 investment or the $4,000 investment? Of course, it's better to get the income ($100 in this case) with the smaller investment (a 5 percent yield is better than a 2.5 percent yield).

Comparing yield between different stocks

All things being equal, choosing Smith Co. or Jones Co. is a coin toss. It's looking at your situation and each company's fundamentals and prospects that will sway you. What if Smith Co. is an auto stock (similar to General Motors in 2008) and Jones Co. is a utility serving the Las Vegas metro area? Now what? In 2008, the automotive industry struggled tremendously, but utilities were generally in much better shape. In that scenario, Smith Co.'s dividend is in jeopardy, whereas Jones Co.'s dividend is more secure. Another issue is the payout ratio (see the next section). Therefore, companies whose dividends have the same yield may still have different risks.

Looking at a stock's payout ratio

You can use the payout ratio to figure out what percentage of a company's earnings is being paid out in the form of dividends (earnings = sales – expenses). Keep in mind that companies pay dividends from their net earnings. Therefore, the company's earnings should always be higher than the dividends the company pays out. Here's how to figure a payout ratio:

Dividend (per share) ÷ Earnings (per share) = Payout ratio

Say that the company CashFlow Now, Inc. (CFN), has annual earnings (or net income) of $1 million. Total dividends are to be paid out of $500,000, and the company has 1 million outstanding shares. Using those numbers, you know that CFN's earnings per share (EPS) is $1 ($1 million in earnings ÷ 1 million shares) and that it pays an annual dividend of 50 cents per share ($500,000 ÷ 1 million shares). The dividend payout ratio is 50 percent (the 50-cent dividend is 50 percent of the $1 EPS). This number is a healthy dividend payout ratio because even if CFN's earnings fall by 10 percent or 20 percent, plenty of room still exists to pay dividends.

If you're concerned about your dividend income's safety, regularly watch the payout ratio. The maximum acceptable payout ratio should be 80 percent, and a good range is 50 to 70 percent. A payout ratio of 60 percent or lower is considered very safe (the lower the percentage, the safer the dividend).

When a company suffers significant financial difficulties, its ability to pay dividends is compromised. (Good examples of stocks that have had their dividends cut in recent years due to financial difficulties are mortgage companies in the wake of the housing bubble bursting and the fallout from the subprime debt fiasco. Mortgage companies received less and less income due to mortgage defaults, which forced the lowering of dividends as cash inflow shrunk.) So if you need dividend income to help you pay your bills, you better be aware of the dividend payout ratio.

Studying a company's bond rating

Bond rating? Huh? What's that got to do with dividend-paying stocks? Actually, a company's bond rating is very important to income stock investors. The bond rating offers insight into the company's financial strength. Bonds get rated for quality for the same reasons that consumer agencies rate products like cars or toasters. Standard & Poor's (S&P) is the major independent rating agency that looks into bond issuers. S&P looks at the bond issuer and asks, "Does this bond issuer have the financial strength to pay back the bond and the interest as stipulated in the bond indenture?"

To understand why this rating is important, consider the following:

✓ **A good bond rating means that the company is strong enough to pay its obligations.** These obligations include expenses, payments on debts, and declared dividends. If a bond rating agency gives the company a high rating (or if it raises the rating), that's a great sign for anyone holding the company's debt or receiving dividends.

- ✔ **If a bond rating agency lowers the rating, that means the company's financial strength is deteriorating** — a red flag for anyone who owns the company's bonds or stock. A lower bond rating today may mean trouble for the dividend later on.

- ✔ **A poor bond rating means that the company is having difficulty paying its obligations.** If the company can't pay all its obligations, it has to choose which ones to pay. More times than not, a financially troubled company chooses to cut dividends or (in a worst-case scenario) not pay dividends at all.

The highest rating issued by S&P is AAA. The grades AAA, AA, and A are considered *investment grade,* or of high quality. Bs and Cs indicate a poor grade, and anything lower than that is considered very risky (the bonds are referred to as *junk bonds*). So if you see a XXX rating, then . . . gee . . . you better stay away! (You may even get an infection.)

Diversifying your stocks

If most of your dividend income is from stock in a single company or single industry, consider reallocating your investment to avoid having all your eggs in one basket. Concerns about diversification apply to income stocks as well as growth stocks. If all your income stocks are in the electric utility industry, then any problems in that industry are potential problems for your portfolio as well. See Chapter 4 for more on risk.

Exploring Some Typical Income Stocks

Although virtually every industry has stocks that pay dividends, some industries have more dividend-paying stocks than others. You won't find too many dividend-paying income stocks in the computer or biotech industries, for instance. The reason is that these types of companies need a lot of money to finance expensive research and development (R&D) projects to create new products. Without R&D, the company can't create new products to fuel sales, growth, and future earnings. Computer, biotech, and other innovative industries are better for growth investors. Keep reading for the scoop on stocks that work well for income investors.

It's electric! Utilities

Utilities generate a large cash flow. (If you don't believe me, look at your gas and electric bills!) Cash flow includes money from income (sales of products and/or services) and other items (such as the selling of assets, for example).

This cash flow is needed to cover expenses, loan payments, and dividends. Utilities are considered the most common type of income stocks, and many investors have at least one utility company in their portfolio. Investing in your own local utility isn't a bad idea — at least it makes paying the utility bill less painful.

Before you invest in a public utility, consider the following:

- ✔ **The utility company's financial condition:** Is the company making money, and are its sales and earnings growing from year to year? Make sure the utility's bonds are rated A or higher (I cover bond ratings in the earlier section "Studying a company's bond rating").

- ✔ **The company's dividend payout ratio:** Because utilities tend to have a good cash flow, don't be too concerned if the ratio reaches 70 percent. From a safety point of view, however, the lower the rate, the better. See the earlier section "Looking at a stock's payout ratio" for more on payout ratios.

- ✔ **The company's geographic location:** If the utility covers an area that's doing well and offers an increasing population base and business expansion, that bodes well for your stock. A good resource for researching population and business data is the U.S. Census Bureau (www.census.gov).

An interesting mix: Real estate investment trusts (REITs)

Real estate investment trusts (REITs) are a special breed of stock. A *REIT* is an investment that has elements of both a stock and a *mutual fund* (a pool of money received from investors that's managed by an investment company).

- ✔ A REIT resembles a stock in that it's a company whose stock is publicly traded on the major stock exchanges, and it has the usual features that you expect from a stock — it can be bought and sold easily through a broker, income is given to investors as dividends, and so on.

- ✔ A REIT resembles a mutual fund in that it doesn't make its money selling goods and services; it makes its money by buying, selling, and managing an investment portfolio of real estate investments. It generates revenue from rents and property leases, as any landlord does. In addition, some REITs own mortgages, and they gain income from the interest.

REITs are called trusts only because they meet the requirements of the Real Estate Investment Trust Act of 1960. This act exempts REITs from corporate income tax and capital gains taxes as long as they meet certain criteria, such as dispensing 95 percent of their net income to shareholders. This provision is the reason why REITs generally issue generous dividends. Beyond this status, REITs are, in a practical sense, like any other publicly traded company.

The main advantages to investing in REITs include the following:

✔ Unlike other types of real estate investing, REITs are easy to buy and sell. You can buy a REIT by making a phone call to a broker or visiting a broker's website, just as you can to purchase any stock.

✔ REITs have higher-than-average yields. Because they must distribute at least 95 percent of their income to shareholders, their dividends usually yield a return of 5 to 12 percent.

✔ REITs involve a lower risk than the direct purchase of real estate because they use a portfolio approach diversified among many properties. Because you're investing in a company that buys the real estate, you don't have to worry about managing the properties — the company's management does that on a full-time basis. Usually, the REIT doesn't just manage one property; it's diversified in a portfolio of different properties.

✔ Investing in a REIT is affordable for small investors. REIT shares usually trade in the $10 to $40 range, meaning that you can invest with very little money.

REITs do have disadvantages. Although they tend to be diversified with various properties, they're still susceptible to risks tied to the general real estate sector. Real estate investing reached manic, record-high levels during 2000–2007, which meant that a downturn was likely. Whenever you invest in an asset (like real estate or REITs in recent years) that has already skyrocketed due to artificial stimulants (in the case of real estate, very low interest rates and too much credit and debt), the potential losses can offset any potential (unrealized) income.

When you're looking for a REIT to invest in, analyze it the way you'd analyze a property. Look at the location and type of property. If shopping malls are booming in California and your REIT buys and sells shopping malls in California, then you'll probably do well. However, if your REIT invests in office buildings across the country and the office building market is overbuilt and having tough times, you'll have a tough time, too.

As I write this, the real estate market has generally bottomed although weakness should remain for a few more years before a strong rise in real estate values appears. Many of the dangers of the "housing bubble" have passed, and investors can start looking at real estate investments (such as REITs) with less anxiety. However, choosing REITs with a view toward quality and strong fundamentals (location, potential rents, and so forth) is still a good idea.

Good energy: Royalty trusts

In recent years, the oil and gas sector has generated much interest as people and businesses experience much higher energy prices. Due to a variety of bullish factors, such as increased international demand from China and other emerging industrialized nations, oil and gas prices have zoomed to record highs. Some income investors have capitalized on this price increase by investing in energy stocks called royalty trusts.

Royalty trusts are companies that hold assets such as oil-rich and/or natural gas–rich land and generate high fees from companies that seek access to these properties for exploration. The fees paid to the royalty trusts are then disbursed as high dividends to their shareholders. During early 2012, royalty trusts sported yields in the 7 to 12 percent range, which is very enticing given how low the yields have been in this decade for other investments like bank accounts and bonds. See Appendix A for resources on royalty trusts and other income investments.

Although energy has been a hot field in recent years and royalty trusts have done well, keep in mind that their payout ratios are very high (often in the 90 to 100 percent range), so dividends will suffer should their cash flow shrink. (I discuss payout ratios in detail earlier in this chapter.)

Chapter 10

Understanding Technical Analysis for Stock Investors

*1*n my early days as a stock investor, I rarely used technical analysis, but in my later years, I came to see it as a useful part of my overall investing approach. Yes, technical analysis is . . . well . . . technical, but it can help you time your decision about when you want to buy, sell, or hold a particular stock. In short, fundamental analysis (what the rest of this book discusses) tells you *what* to buy, and technical analysis tells you *when* to buy. I won't make this chapter an exhaustive treatment of this topic (I bet you just said "Whew!"), but I do want to alert you to techniques and resources that will give you a leg up in today's volatile and uncertain markets.

I'd like to mention some resources right out of the starting gate. Use the following resources to discover more information about technical analysis:

- ✔ Big Charts (www.bigcharts.com)
- ✔ Incredible Charts (www.incrediblecharts.com)
- ✔ International Federation of Technical Analysts (www.ifta.org)
- ✔ Online Trading Concepts (www.onlinetradingconcepts.com)
- ✔ StockCharts (www.stockcharts.com)
- ✔ *Stocks & Commodities* magazine (www.traders.com)
- ✔ TraderPlanet (www.traderplanet.com)
- ✔ *Technical Analysis For Dummies,* 2nd Edition, by Barbara Rockefeller (Wiley) (www.dummies.com)

Comparing Technical Analysis and Fundamental Analysis

When figuring out what to do in the investment world, most professionals use one of two basic approaches: fundamental analysis and technical analysis (many use some combination of the two). Both approaches are used in a number of markets ranging from the stock market to commodities, but I limit this chapter to stock investing. The main differences between fundamental analysis and technical analysis are pretty easy to understand:

- **Fundamental analysis** goes into the economics of the company itself, such as sales and profit data, as well as external factors affecting it, such as politics, regulations, and industry trends.

- **Technical analysis** tries to understand where a stock's price is going based on market behavior as evidenced in its market statistics (presented in charts, price, and trading volume data). Technical analysis doesn't try to figure out the worth of an investment; it's used to figure out where the price of that stock or investment is trending.

In the following sections, I talk about the main principles of technical analysis, and I note its pros and cons as compared to fundamental analysis. I also explain how to combine technical analysis with fundamental analysis, and I list some tools of the trade.

Looking under the hood of technical analysis

To get the most benefit from using technical analysis, you need to understand how it operates and what it is that you're looking at. Technical analysis, for the purposes of this book, is based on the following assumptions.

The price is the be-all and end-all

The premise of technical analysis is that the stock's market price provides enough information to render a trading decision. Those who criticize technical analysis point out that it considers the price and its movement without paying adequate attention to the fundamental factors of the company. The argument made favoring technical analysis is that the price is a snapshot that, in fact, does reflect the basic factors affecting the company, including the company's (or investment's) fundamentals.

Technical analysts (also called technicians or chartists) believe that the company's fundamentals, along with broader economic factors and market psychology, are all priced into the stock, removing the need to actually consider these factors separately. The bottom line is that technicians look at the price and its movement to extract a forecast for where the stock is going.

The trend is your friend

The price of a stock tends to move in trends. In the world of technical analysis, the phrase "the trend is your friend" is as ubiquitous as the phrase "you spoiled the broth, now you lie in it!" is in the restaurant industry. Maybe even more so. Following the trend is a bedrock principle in technical analysis, and the data either supports the trend, or it doesn't. When a trend in the stock's price is established, its tendency is to continue. The three types of trends are up, down, and sideways (but you knew that). (See the later section "Staying on Top of Trends" for more information.)

If it happened before, it will happen again

Another foundational idea in technical analysis is that history tends to repeat itself, mainly in terms of price movement. The repetitive nature of price movements is attributed to market psychology; in other words, market participants tend to provide a consistent reaction to similar market stimuli over time.

Technical analysis uses chart patterns to analyze market movements and understand trends. Although many of these charts have been used for more than 100 years, they're still believed to be relevant because they illustrate patterns in price movements that often repeat themselves. (I talk about chart patterns in more detail later in this chapter.)

Examining the good and bad of technical analysis

Although technical analysis is the "star" of this chapter, it does have its shortcomings. The major drawback of technical analysis is that it's a human approach that tracks human behavior in a particular market. In other words, just because it's called technical analysis doesn't mean that it's technical à la the laws of physics. It's called technical analysis because the data you look at is technical. But the movement of the price of the underlying stock or investment is due to the cumulative decisions of many buyers and sellers who are human — and therefore fallible.

Why mention this? Everyone is looking to make money, and many trading systems and approaches are based on technical analysis. Unfortunately, making profitable investments isn't a matter of 2 + 2 = 4. If technical analysis made things so easy that mere computer models or trading systems could give you a voilà-moneymaking decision, everyone could — and would — do it. Yet, that's not the case.

Here's my take on it. I favor fundamental analysis for long-term investing. I shun technical analysis for choosing individual stocks because I don't see the long-term value in it. Long-term investors don't have to bother with things such as triangles, pennants, cup-and-handles, or other paraphernalia. Long-term investors just ask questions like "Is the company making money?" or "Are financial and economic conditions still favorable for my investment?" When the fundamentals are in your favor, any short-term move against you is a buying opportunity (provided that you choose wisely from the start). But unfortunately, too many investors aren't patient, and they get too busy with the short-term trees to be bothered by the long-term forest. Yet that long-term forest has a lot more green, if you know what I mean (I hope I'm not meandering here).

If you were to do a nose count of successful investors in stock market history and what approaches they used, you'd find that those long-term investors who used some variation of fundamental analysis (such as those who used a value-investing approach) overwhelmingly comprise the larger category. Legendary investors like Warren Buffett and Peter Lynch rarely looked at a chart. Think about it: Warren Buffett is obviously one of history's greatest success stories in the world of stock investing. His track record and multibillion-dollar net worth attest to this. Yet, he rarely (if ever) looks at any technical analysis. He isn't concerned with short-term squiggles and fluctuations. He is indeed a long-term investor, and one of his greatest assets is *patience.* He has held some stocks for decades. The point makes for an interesting observation into human nature. Everyone wants to succeed like Warren Buffett, but few are willing to go the distance.

The short term is a different animal. It requires more attention and discipline. You need to monitor all the indicators to see whether you're on track or whether the signals are warning a change in course. The technicals can be bearish one month and bullish the next. And the month after that, the signals can be mixed and give no clear warnings at all. Being a proficient technician ultimately requires more monitoring, more trading, and more hedging.

Note that all this activity also means more taxes, more transaction costs (commissions and the like), and more administrative work (tax reporting and so on). After all, who do you think will pay more in taxes: someone who buys and holds for a year or longer or someone who makes the same profit by jumping in and out based on which way the technical winds are blowing? Short-term gains don't have the same favorable rates as long-term gains. Sometimes the issue isn't what you make but what you keep (taxes are covered in Chapter 21).

But before you throw out technical analysis with the bath water, read on. Those who use technical analysis in short-term trading or speculating in larger-scope investments tend to do better than those who don't use it. That means that if you apply technical analysis to something larger than a company, such as an index or a commodity, you'll tend to do better. If you're getting into trading stocks and/or stock-related exchange-traded funds (ETFs; see Chapter 5), then understanding the basics of technical analysis will make you, overall, a better (and hence more profitable) trader. Because short-term market behavior and psychology can be very mercurial and irrational (human), technical analysis has its usefulness. It's most useful for those folks who are trading and/or speculating during a relatively short time frame measured in days, weeks, or months. It isn't that useful when you're trying to forecast where a stock's price will be a year or more down the road.

Combining the best of both worlds

I think that a useful way to combine both fundamental analysis and technical analysis is to take advantage of the strength of each. Fundamental analysis helps you understand *what* to invest (or trade or speculate) in, whereas technical analysis guides you as to *when* to do it. Because markets ebb and flow, zig and zag, technical analysis can help you spot low-risk points to either enter or exit a trade. Technical analysis, therefore, helps you stack the deck a little more in your favor. Considering how markets have been going lately, every little bit helps.

Blending the two approaches to some extent has been done with success. Obviously, if the fundamental and the technical factors support your decision, then the chance for a profitable trade has more going for it. How does this blend occur?

For an example, look at the concepts of oversold and overbought (see the section "The Relative Strength Index," later in this chapter). If you're looking at buying a stock (or other investment) because you think it's a strong investment but you're not sure about when to buy, you want to look at the technical data. If the data tells you that it has been oversold, it's a good time to buy. *Oversold* just means that the market was a little too extreme in selling that particular investment during a particular period of time.

By the way, I like to think that the technical terms *oversold* and *overbought* have a parallel to fundamental terms such as *undervalued* and *overvalued*. Because fundamental analysis is a major part of a school of thought referred to as value investing, the concepts make sense (yes, I'm into value investing). Just as investing in an undervalued stock is usually a good idea, so is buying a stock that has been oversold. It's logical to presume that an oversold stock is undervalued (all things being equal). Of course, the other terms (overbought and overvalued) can also run in tandem. I may as well finish here before you're overwhelmed and underinterested.

On the other hand, the fundamentals can help a technical analyst make a better trading decision. Say that a technical analyst has a profitable position in a particular stock called Getting Near a Cliff Corp. (GNAC). If the technical indicators are turning bearish and the new quarterly earnings report for GNAC indicates a significantly lower profit, then selling GNAC's stock is probably a good idea. (Of course, because you're reading this book, you're doing something better like immediately putting on a trailing stop, right? See Chapter 17 for details on trailing stops.)

Using the technician's tools

When you roll up your sleeves and get into technical analysis, what will you be dealing with? It depends on what type of technical analyst you are. In technical analysis, there are two subcategories: those who predominantly use charts (these technicians are called . . . chartists!) and those who predominantly use data (such as price and volume data). Of course, many technicians use a combination of both (and I discuss both later in this chapter):

- ✔ **Charts:** Charts are the neat pictures that graph price movements (such as chart patterns).
- ✔ **Data:** Data includes price and volume information (along with technical and behavioral indicators derived from it).

Technical analysts don't look at the fundamentals because they believe that the marketplace (as depicted in the charts, price, and volume data) already take into account the fundamentals.

Staying on Top of Trends

Identifying trends is a crucial part of technical analysis. A trend is just the overall direction of a stock (or another security or a commodity); you can see trends in technical charts (I provide details about charts later in this chapter). Which way is the price headed? In the following sections, I describe different types of trends, talk about trend length, and discuss trend lines and channel lines.

Distinguishing different trends

Three basic trends exist:

- ✔ **An uptrend or bullish trend** is when each successive high is higher than the previous high and each successive low is higher than the previous low.

✔ **A downtrend or bearish trend** is when each successive high is lower that the previous high and each successive low is lower than the previous low.

✔ **A sideways trend or horizontal trend** shows that the highs and the lows are both in a generally sideways pattern with no clear indication of trending up or down (at least not yet).

It's easy to see which way the stock is headed in Figure 10-1. Unless you're a skier, that's not a pretty picture. The bearish trend is obvious.

Figure 10-1: Generic chart sloping in a definite downward direction.

What do you do with a chart like Figure 10-2? Yup . . . looks like somebody's heart monitor while he's watching a horror movie. A sideways or horizontal trend just shows a consolidation pattern that means that the stock will break out into an up or down trend.

Figure 10-2: Generic chart showing a sideways pattern.

Regardless of whether a trend is up, down, or sideways, you'll notice that it's rarely (closer to never) in a straight line. The line is usually jagged and bumpy because it's really a summary of all the buyers and sellers making their trades. Some days the buyers have more impact, and some days it's the sellers' turn. Figure 10-3 shows all three trends.

Figure 10-3:
Chart that
simultane-
ously shows
an up,
down, and
sideways
trend.

Illustration by Wiley, Composition Services Graphics

Technical analysts call the highs *peaks* and the lows *troughs*. In other words, if the peaks and troughs keep going up, that's bullish. If the peaks and troughs keep going down, it's bearish. And if the peaks and troughs are horizontal, you're probably in California (just kidding).

Looking at a trend's length

With trends, you're not just looking at the direction; you're also looking at the trend's duration, or the length of time that it goes along. Trend durations can be (you guessed it) short-term, intermediate-term, or long-term.

- ✔ **A short-term (or near-term) trend** is generally less than a month.

- ✔ **An intermediate-term trend** is up to a quarter (three months) long.

- ✔ **A long-term trend** can last up to a year. And to muddy the water a bit, the long-term trend may have several trends inside it (don't worry; the quiz has been cancelled).

Using trendlines

A *trendline* is a simple feature added to a chart: a straight line designating a clear path for a particular trend. Trendlines simply follow the peaks and troughs to show a distinctive direction. They can also be used to identify a trend reversal, or a change in the opposite direction. Figure 10-4 shows two trendlines: the two straight lines that follow the tops and bottoms of the jagged line (which shows the actual price movement of the asset in question).

Figure 10-4: Chart that shows the jagged edge going upward along with the trendlines.

Watching the channel for resistance and support

The concepts of resistance and support are critical to technical analysis the way tires are to cars. When the rubber meets the road, you want to know where the price is going.

- *Resistance* is like the proverbial glass ceiling in the market's world of price movement. As a price keeps moving up, how high can or will it go? That's the $64,000 question, and technical analysts watch this closely. Breaking through resistance is considered a positive sign for the price, and the expectation is definitely bullish.

- *Support* is the lowest point or level that a price is trading at. When the price goes down and hits this level, it's expected to bounce back, but what happens when it goes below the support level? It's then considered a bearish sign, and technical analysts watch closely for a potential reversal even though they expect the price to head down.

Channel lines are lines that are added to show both the peaks and troughs of the primary trend. The top line indicates resistance (of the price movement), and the lower line indicates support. Resistance and support form the trading range for the stock's price. The channel can slope or point upward or downward, or go sideways. Technical traders view the channel with interest because the assumption is that that the price will continue in the direction of the channel (between resistance and support) until technical indicators signal a change. (To me, this tells me to change to a cable channel, but that's just me. Please continue reading. . . .) Check out the channel in Figure 10-5; it shows you how the price is range-bound. The emphasis on trends is to help you make more profitable decisions because you're better off trading with the trend than not.

10-Apr-2000 **Open** 80.91 **High** 82.80 **Low** 80.61 **Close** 81.50 **Volume** 1.3M **Chg** –0.36 (–0.43%)

Figure 10-5:
Chart
showing a
channel.

Illustration by Wiley, Composition Services Graphics

In Figure 10-5, you see a good example of a channel for a particular stock. In this case, the stock is zigzagging downward, and toward the end of the channel, it indicates that the stock is getting more volatile as the stock's price movement is outside the original channel lines. This tells the trader/investor to be cautious and on the lookout for opportunities or pitfalls (depending on your outlook for the stock).

Getting the Scoop on Technical Charts

Charts are to technical analysis what pictures are to photography. You can't avoid them 'cause you're not supposed to. If you're serious about trading stocks (or ETFs, commodities, or whatever), charts and the related technical data come in handy. In the following sections, I describe different types of charts and chart patterns.

Checking out types of charts

Technical analysts use charts to "diagnose" an investment's situation the same way any analyst uses different tools and approaches. Different charts provide fresh angles for viewing the data. In terms of visualization and utility, the following are the four most common charts used in technical analysis.

Line charts

A chart simply shows a series of prices plotted in a graph that displays how the price has moved over a period of time. The period of time can be a day, week, month, year, or longer. The prices that are usually chosen for a line chart are the closing prices for those market days.

With a yearlong line chart (like those that appear earlier in this chapter), you can see how the stock has progressed during the 12-month period, and you can do some simple analysis. When were the peaks? How about the troughs? What were the strongest seasons for this stock's price movement?

I prefer to use five-year charts; I like to encourage my clients, students, and readers to focus on the longer term because positive results can be easier to achieve.

Bar charts

Bar charts are a little fancier. Whereas the line chart only gives you the closing prices for each market day, the bar chart gives you the range of trading prices for each day during the chosen time period. Each trading day is a vertical line that represents the price movements, and you see the stock's high, low, and closing prices.

In a bar chart, the vertical line has two notches. The notch on the left indicates the opening price, and the notch on the right indicates the closing price. If the opening price notch is higher than the closing price notch, the line is in red to indicate that the closing price of the stock declined versus the opening price. An up day is in black, and the closing price notch is higher than the opening price notch.

Candlestick charts

Candlestick charts have been all the rage in recent years. They're basically bar charts, but they're a little more complex. A candlestick chart provides a more complete picture by adding a visualization of other data that simple charts don't contain, such as the high, low, and closing price of the security the chart is tracking. It stands to reason that because candlestick charts provide more information in a visual form than bar charts, they can provide more guidance in trading. Candlestick charting is too involved to adequately describe in this space, so please continue your research with the resources provided at the start of this chapter.

The full name for these charts is Japanese candlestick charts because they originated as a form of technical analysis in the 17th century, when the Japanese were trading in rice markets. You know, they do look like candlesticks (but I'm waxing eloquent here).

Point-and-figure charts

A more obscure chart that chartists use is the point-and-figure chart. When you look at it, you'll notice a series of X's and O's. The X's represent upward price trends, and the O's represent downward price trends. This type of chart enables the stock trader to easily determine which prices are "support levels" and which are "resistance levels" to better judge buy and sell prices.

Picking out chart patterns

Chart patterns are the graphical language of technical analysis, and a very interesting language at that. For technical analysts, the pattern is important because it provides a potential harbinger for what is to come. It's not 100 percent accurate, but it's usually accurate better than 50 percent of the time as odds go. In the world of trading, being right more than 50 percent of the time can be enough. Usually a proficient technician is better than that. The following sections cover common chart patterns.

Technical analysts don't say that the next step after a particular pattern is a certainty; it's a probability. Probable outcomes, more times than not, tend to materialize. Increasing the probability of success for more profitable decision-making (entering or exiting a trade) is the bottom-line mission of technical analysis.

Above the rest: The head and shoulders

The head and shoulders pattern is essentially bearish. It's usually a signal that an uptrend has ended and the pattern is set to reverse and head downward. Technical analysts consider this to be one of the most reliable patterns.

The pattern shows three peaks and two troughs. The three peaks break down into the tall center peak (the head) and the shorter peaks (the shoulders) that are on either side of the center peak. The two troughs form the neckline.

The head and shoulders pattern tells technical analysts that the preceding trend basically ran out of gas. The selling pressures build up and overpower the buyers. Hence, the price starts to come down. The shoulder on the right is like a last effort for the bullish trend to regain its traction, but to no avail. Keep in mind that the neckline in this pattern is the support (which I discuss in the earlier section "Watching the channel for resistance and support"). As support is broken, the tendency is a bearish expectation.

In reverse: The reverse head and shoulders

As you can infer, this pattern is the opposite of the prior chart pattern, and it's essentially bullish. This pattern signals that a downtrend has ended and is set to reverse and head upward. In this pattern, you have three troughs and two peaks. The middle trough is usually the deepest one. The small trough on the right is an interim low, which is higher than the middle trough low and typically indicates the trend is moving upward.

In this pattern, buying pressures build up and form a base from which to spring upward. Note that a bullish pattern is a series of higher highs and higher lows. In the reverse head and shoulders pattern, the neckline is resistance (which I discuss earlier in this chapter). Once resistance is broken, the expectation is for an upward move.

Wake up and smell the coffee: The cup and handle

This pattern is generally bullish. In the pattern, the price first peaks and then craters into a bowl-shaped trough (the cup). It peaks again at the end with a small downward move (the handle) before it moves up.

This pattern basically tells the technician that the stock's price took a breather to build support and then continued its bullish pattern.

Twice as nice: The double top and the double bottom

Both the double top and the double bottom chart patterns indicate a trend reversal.

- ✔ **The double top** is essentially a bearish pattern wherein the price makes two attempts (the double top) to break through resistance but fails to do so. The bottom of the trough between the two peaks indicates support. However, the two failed attempts at the resistance level are more significant than the support at the trough, so this pattern signals a potential downturn for that stock's price.

- ✔ **The double bottom** is the opposite reversal pattern. It's a bullish pattern because the support level indicators are stronger than the resistance. This pattern signals a potential upturn in the stock's price. Because this indicates a support level, bullish traders tend to look at it as a generally safe entry point to get positioned for the next potential up-move in the stock.

Triple tops and triple bottoms are variations of double tops and double bottoms. These are sideways or horizontal patterns that do portend a trend reversal. Don't even ask about quadruple tops and bottoms!

Triangles (And I don't mean Bermuda!)

A triangle is formed when the resistance line and the support line converge to form the triangle point that shows a general direction in the stock's price movement. There are three types of triangles: symmetrical, ascending, and descending.

> ✔ **Symmetrical:** The symmetrical triangle points sideways, which tells you it's a horizontal pattern that becomes a setup for a move upward or downward once more price movement provides a bullish or bearish indicator.
>
> ✔ **Ascending:** The ascending triangle is a bullish pattern.
>
> ✔ **Descending:** The descending triangle is bearish.

Of course, if you see a divergent trapezoidal and octagonal candlestick formation supported in a bowl-shaped isosceles triangle, do nothing! Just take two aspirin and try again tomorrow.

Time to cheer: Flags and pennants

Flags and pennants are familiar chart patterns that are short-term in nature (usually not longer than a few weeks). They're continuation patterns that are formed immediately after a sharp price movement, which is usually followed by a sideways price movement. Both the flag and the pennant are similar except that the flag is triangular whereas the pennant is in a channel formation (I talk about channels earlier in this chapter).

Cut it up: Wedges

The wedge pattern can be either a continuation or reversal pattern. It seems to be much like a symmetrical triangle, but it slants (up or down), whereas the symmetrical triangle generally shows a sideways movement. In addition, the wedge forms over a longer period of time (typically three to six months).

Watch your step: Gaps

A gap in a chart is an empty space between two trading periods. This pattern occurs when the difference in the price between those two periods is substantial. Say that in the first period, the trading range is $10 to $15. The next trading session opens at $20. That $5 discrepancy will appear as a large gap between those two periods on the chart. These gaps are typically found on bar and candlestick charts. Gaps may happen when positive (or negative) news comes out about the company, and initial buying pressure causes the price to jump in the subsequent period as soon as trading commences.

There are three types of gaps: breakaway, runaway, and exhaustion. The breakaway gap forms at the start of a trend, and the runaway gap forms during the middle of the trend. So what obviously happens when the trend gets tired at the end? Why, the exhaustion gap of course! See, this stuff isn't that hard to grasp.

Surveying Technical Indicators for Stock Investors

An *indicator* is a mathematical calculation that can be used with the stock's price and/or volume. The end result is a value that's used to anticipate future changes in price. There are two types of indicators: leading and lagging.

- ✔ *Leading* indicators help you profit by attempting to forecast what prices will do next. Leading indicators provide greater rewards at the expense of increased risk. They perform best in sideways or trading markets. They work by measuring how overbought or oversold a stock is.

- ✔ *Lagging* (or trend-following) indicators are best suited to price movements in relatively long trends. They don't warn you of any potential changes in price. Lagging indicators have you buy and sell in a mature trend, when the risk is reduced.

The following sections describe a variety of leading and lagging indicators.

The Relative Strength Index

As noted in the earlier section "Combining the best of both worlds," the technical conditions of overbought and oversold are important to be aware of. They're good warning flags to help you time a trade, whether that means getting in or getting out of a position. The Relative Strength Index (RSI) is a convenient metric for measuring the overbought/oversold condition. Generally, the RSI quantifies the condition and gives you a number that acts like a barometer. On a reading of 0 to 100, the RSI becomes oversold at about the 30 level and overbought at about the 70 level.

The RSI is a metric usually calculated and quoted by most charting sources and technical analysis websites. It's generally considered a leading indicator because it forewarns potential price movements.

For stock investors, I think the RSI is particularly useful for timing the purchase or sale of a particular stock. I know when I'm looking at a favorite stock that I like and notice that its RSI is below 30, I check to see whether anything is wrong with the stock (did the fundamentals change?). If nothing is wrong and it's merely a temporary, market-driven event, I consider buying more of the stock. After all, if I loved a great stock at $40 and it's now cheaper at $35, all things being equal, I have a great buying opportunity. Conversely, if I'm not crazy about a stock and I see that it's overbought, I consider either selling it outright or at least putting a stop-loss order on the stock (see Chapter 17).

Part II: Before You Start Buying

Moving averages

In terms of price data, a favorite tool of the technical analyst is the moving average. A *moving average* is the average price of a stock over a set period of time (which can range from 5 days to six months — or sometimes longer). It's considered a lagging indicator. Frequently a chart shows price movements as too jumpy and haphazard, so the moving average smoothes out the price movements to show a clearer path. This technique helps to decipher the stock's trend and plot out the support and resistance levels. Moving averages are also very helpful in identifying all the various peaks and troughs necessary to analyze the trend's direction. There are three types of moving averages: simple, linear, and exponential.

A snapshot: Simple moving averages (SMA)

The first (and most common) type of average is referred to as a simple moving average (SMA). You calculate it by simply taking the sum of all the past closing prices over the chosen time period and dividing the result by the number of prices used in the calculation. For example, in a ten-day simple moving average, the last ten closing prices are added together and then divided by ten.

Say that the prices for the last ten trading days (in order) are $20, $21, $22, $20, $21, $23, $24, $22, $22, and $24. It's hard to derive a trend from that data, but a moving average can help. First you add up all the prices; in this case the total is $219. Then you take the total of $219 and divide it by ten (the total number of trading days). You get an average price of $21.90. As you do this with more and more price data (in ten-day chronological sets), you can see a trend unfolding.

Say that on the 11th day, the closing price is $26. At this point, the next ten-day trading period starts with $21 (the closing price from the second day in the example from the preceding paragraph) and ends with a new closing price for the 10th day, $26. Now when you add up this new ten-day range, you get a total of $225. When you divide that number by ten, you get the average of $22.50 ($225 total divided by 10 days). In this brief and simple example, the 10-day moving average tells you that the price trend is up (from $21.90 to $22.50).

Of course, you need to see a much longer string of ten-day sets to ascertain a useful ten-day moving average, but you get the point. These averages can also be plotted on a graph to depict the trend and help render a trading decision. The more time periods you graph, the easier it is to see how strong (or weak) the trend is.

Technical analysts most frequently use 10-day, 20-day, and 50-day averages for short-term trading. To confirm longer-term trends, they also watch the 100-day and 200-day moving averages. Of course, other time frames are used as well, but these are the most common.

The longer-period moving averages help to put the short terms in perspective so that the trader can still view the big picture. In other words, you may have a stock "correct" or pull back and see its price fall significantly, but does it mean that a trend has reversed? If the stock is in a long-term bull market, it's common for it to violate (or go below) its short-term (such as 10-, 20- or 50-day) moving averages temporarily. The more serious red flags start to appear when it violates the longer-term averages, such as the 200-day moving average. And if it violates the ten-year moving average . . . hey . . . watch out!

More complex tactics: Linear and exponential averages

Some critics believe that the SMA is too limited in its scope and therefore not as useful as it should be. Therefore, they use more involved variants of the SMA such as the linear weighted average (LWA) and the exponential moving average (EMA). These averages are too involved to adequately cover in this book. You can get more details on them through the resources at the start of this chapter. For beginners, though, the SMA is sufficient.

Moving average convergence/divergence

The moving average convergence/divergence (MACD) is a lagging indicator that shows the relationship between two moving averages of prices. The MACD is calculated by subtracting the 26-day exponential moving average (EMA) from the 12-day EMA. A nine-day EMA of the MACD, called the *signal line,* is then plotted on top of the MACD, which acts as a trigger for making buy and sell orders.

That's the technical definition of the MACD but don't worry if you didn't understand it on the first go-round. Fortunately, it's not something that you have to calculate on your own; the MACD indicator is usually provided by the technical analysis software or trading service that you may use.

Crossovers and divergence

A *crossover* is the point when the stock's price and an indicator intersect (or cross over). It's used as a signal to make a buy or sell order. Say that a stock, for example, falls past $20 per share to $19, and the 20-day moving average is $19.50. That would be a bearish crossover, and it would indicate a good time to sell or risk further downward movement. The opposite is true as well; some crossovers indicate a good time to buy.

Divergence occurs when the price of a stock and an indicator (or index or other related security) part company and head off in opposite directions. Divergence is considered either positive or negative, both of which are signals of changes in the price trend.

- ✒ **Positive divergence** occurs when the price of a stock makes a new low while a bullish indicator starts to climb upward.

- ✒ **Negative divergence** happens when the price of a stock makes a new high, but bearish indicators signal the opposite, and instead the closing price at the end of the trading day is lower than the previous high.

Crossovers and divergence are usually leading indicators.

Oscillators

Oscillators are indicators that are used when you're analyzing charts that have no clear trend. Moving averages and other indicators are certainly important when the trend is clear, but oscillators are more beneficial under either of the following circumstances:

- ✒ When the stock is in a horizontal or sideways trading pattern

- ✒ When a definite trend can't be established because the market is volatile and the price action is very uneven

Oscillators may be either leading or lagging indicators, depending on what type they are. Momentum oscillators, for example, are considered leading indicators because they're used to track the momentum of price and volume. Use the resources I mention earlier in this chapter to do your homework on oscillators.

Bollinger bands

Bollinger bands have nothing to do with musical groups. A *band* is plotted two standard deviations away from a simple moving average. The bollinger band (a lagging indicator) works like a channel and moves along with the simple moving average.

Bollinger bands help the technical analyst watch out for overbought and oversold conditions. Basically, if the price moves closer to the upper band, it indicates an overbought condition. If the price moves closer to the lower band, it indicates an oversold condition.

Part III
Picking Winners

The 5th Wave   By Rich Tennant

"Oh Martin, you scared me half to death! Next time let me know when you're picking a new stock."

In this part . . .

After you have the basics down, it's time to become a pro at picking individual stocks. When you consider investing in a company, you need to gain insight into what makes a particular stock's price rise. And because the stock market doesn't operate in a vacuum, I introduce political and governmental factors that can have a huge effect on the stock market. I also include megatrends that can help your choices do better over the long haul. The chapters in this part steer you to key financial information and important company documents and show you how to interpret the information you find.

Chapter 11

Using Basic Accounting to Choose Winning Stocks

*T*oo often, the only number investors look at when they look at a stock is the stock's price. Yet what determines the stock price is the company behind that single number. To make a truly good choice in the world of stocks, you have to consider the company's financial information. What does it take to see these important numbers?

This book in your hands and a little work on your part are all you need to succeed. This chapter takes the mystery out of the numbers behind the stock. The most tried-and-true method for picking a good stock starts with picking a good company. Picking a company means looking at its products, services, industry, and financial strength. Considering the problems that the market has witnessed in recent years — such as subprime debt problems and derivative meltdowns wreaking havoc on public companies and financial firms — this chapter is more important than ever. Understanding the basics behind the numbers can save your portfolio.

Recognizing Value When You See It

If you pick a stock based on the value of the underlying company that issues it, you're a *value investor* — an investor who looks at a company's value to judge whether you can purchase the stock at a good price. Companies have value the same way many things have value, such as eggs or elephant-foot umbrella stands. And there's a fair price to buy them at, too. Take eggs, for example. You can eat them and have a tasty treat while getting nutrition as well. But would you buy an egg for $1,000 (and no, you're not a starving millionaire on a deserted island)? Of course not. But what if you could buy an egg for 5 cents? At that point, it has value *and* a good price. This kind of deal is a value investor's dream.

Value investors analyze a company's *fundamentals* (earnings, assets, and so on) to see whether the information justifies purchasing the stock. They see whether the stock price is low relative to these verifiable, quantifiable factors. Therefore, value investors use *fundamental analysis,* whereas other investors may use technical analysis. *Technical analysis* looks at stock charts and statistical data, such as trading volume and historical stock prices (I take a closer look at technical analysis for investors in Chapter 10). Some investors use a combination of both strategies.

History has shown that the most successful long-term investors have typically been value investors using fundamental analysis as their primary investing approach. The most consistently successful long-term investors were — and are — predominately value investors (yes, I count myself in this crowd as well).

In the following sections, I describe different kinds of value and explain how to spot a company's value in several places.

Understanding different types of value

Value may seem like a murky or subjective term, but it's the essence of good stock-picking. You can measure value in different ways (as you discover in the following sections), so you need to know the differences and understand the impact that value has on your investment decisions.

Market value

When you hear someone quoting a stock at $47 per share, that price reflects the stock's market value. The total market valuation of a company's stock is also referred to as its *market cap* or *market capitalization.* How do you determine a company's market cap? With the following simple formula:

Market capitalization = Share price × Number of shares outstanding

If Bolshevik Corp.'s stock is $35 per share and it has 10 million shares outstanding (or shares available for purchase), its market cap is $350 million. Granted, $350 million may sound like a lot of money, but Bolshevik Corp. is considered a small cap stock. (For more information about small cap stocks, dip into Chapter 8.)

Who sets the market value of stock? The market, of course! Millions of investors buying and selling directly and through intermediaries such as mutual funds determine the market value of any particular stock. If the market perceives that the company is desirable, investor demand for the company's stock pushes up the share price.

The problem with market valuation is that it's not always a good indicator of a good investment. In recent years, plenty of companies have had astronomical market values, yet they've proven to be very risky investments. For example, think about Bear Stearns. During 2007, it hit a stock price of $170; its market cap was measured in billions. Yet its stock price plunged to only $2 per share in the spring of 2008. Yikes! Because market value is a direct result of the buying and selling of stock investors, it can be a fleeting thing. This precariousness is why investors must understand the company behind the stock price.

Book value and intrinsic value

Book value (also referred to as *accounting value*) looks at a company from a balance sheet perspective (assets – liabilities = net worth, or *stockholders' equity*). It's a way of judging a firm by its net worth to see whether the stock's market value is reasonable compared to the company's intrinsic value. *Intrinsic value* is tied to what the market price of a company's assets — both tangible (such as equipment) and intangible (such as patents) — would be if they were sold.

Generally, market value tends to be higher than book value. If market value is substantially higher than book value, the value investor becomes more reluctant to buy that particular stock because it's overvalued. The closer the stock's market capitalization is to the book value, the safer the investment.

I like to be cautious with a stock whose market value is more than twice its book value. If the market value is $1 billion or more and the book value is $500 million or less, that's a good indicator that the business may be *overvalued,* or valued at a higher price than its book value and ability to generate a profit. Just understand that the farther the market value is from the company's book value, the more you'll pay for the company's real potential value. And the more you pay for the company's real value, the greater the risk that the company's market value (the stock price, that is) can decrease.

Sales value and earnings value

A company's intrinsic value is directly tied to its ability to make money. For this reason, many analysts like to value stocks from the perspective of the company's income statement. Two common barometers of value are expressed in ratios: the price-to-sales ratio (PSR) and the price-to-earnings (P/E) ratio. In both instances, the price is a reference to the company's market value (as reflected in its share price). Sales and earnings are references to the firm's ability to make money. These two ratios are covered more fully in the section "Tooling around with ratios," later in this chapter.

For investors, the general approach is clear. The closer the market value is to the company's intrinsic value, the better. And, of course, if the market value is lower than the company's intrinsic value, you have a potential bargain worthy of a closer look. Part of looking closer means examining the company's income statement (which I discuss later in this chapter), also called the *profit and loss statement,* or simply the *P&L.* A low price-to-sales ratio is 1, a medium PSR is between 1 and 2, and a high PSR is 3 or higher.

Putting the pieces together

When you look at a company from a value-oriented perspective, here are some of the most important items to consider (see the later section "Accounting for Value" for more information):

- ✔ **The balance sheet, to figure out the company's net worth:** A value investor doesn't buy a company's stock because it's cheap; she buys it because it's *undervalued* (the company is worth more than the price its stock reflects — its market value is as close as possible to its book value).

- ✔ **The income statement, to figure out the company's profitability:** A company may be undervalued from a simple comparison of the book value and the market value, but that doesn't mean it's a screaming buy. For example, what if you find out that a company is in trouble and losing money this year? Do you buy its stock then? No, you don't. Why invest in the stock of a losing company? (If you do, you aren't investing — you're gambling or speculating.) The heart of a firm's value, besides its net worth, is its ability to generate profit.

- ✔ **Ratios that let you analyze just how well (or not so well) the company is doing:** Value investors basically look for a bargain. That being the case, they generally don't look at companies that everyone is talking about, because by that point, the stock of those companies ceases to be a bargain. The value investor searches for a stock that will eventually be discovered by the market and then watches as the stock price goes up. But before you bother digging into the fundamentals to find that bargain stock, first make sure that the company is making money.

The more ways that you can look at a company and see value, the better.

- ✔ **Examine the P/E ratio.** The first thing I look at is the P/E ratio. Does the company have one? (This question may sound dumb, but if the company's losing money, it may not have one.) Does the P/E ratio look reasonable, or is it in triple-digit, nosebleed territory?

- ✔ **Check out the debt load.** Next, look at the company's debt load (the total amount of liabilities). Is it less than the company's equity? Are sales healthy and increasing from the prior year? Does the firm compare favorably in these categories versus other companies in the same industry?

✔ **Think in terms of 10s.** Simplicity to me is best. You'll notice that the number 10 comes up frequently as I measure a company's performance, juxtaposing all the numbers that you need to be aware of. If net income is rising by 10 percent or more, that's fine. If the company is in the top 10 percent of its industry, that's great. If the industry is growing by 10 percent or better (sales and so on), that's terrific. If sales are up 10 percent or more from the prior year, that's wonderful. A great company doesn't have to have all these things going for it, but it should have as many of these things happening as possible to ensure greater potential success.

Does every company/industry have to neatly fit these criteria? No, of course not. But it doesn't hurt you to be as picky as possible. You need to find only a handful of stocks from thousands of choices. (Hey, this approach has worked for me, my clients, and my students for nearly 2½ decades — 'nuff said.)

Value investors can find thousands of companies that have value, but they can probably buy only a handful at a truly good price. The number of stocks that can be bought at a good price is relative to the market. In mature *bull markets* (markets in a prolonged period of rising prices), a good price is hard to find because most stocks have probably seen significant price increases, but in *bear markets* (markets in a prolonged period of falling prices), good companies at bargain prices are easier to come by.

Accounting for Value

Profit is to a company what oxygen is to you and me. Without profit, a company can't survive, much less thrive. Without profit, it can't provide jobs, pay taxes, and invest in new products, equipment, or innovation. Without profit, the company eventually goes bankrupt, and the price of its stock plummets toward zero.

In the heady days leading up to the bear market of 2000–2002, many investors lost a lot of money simply because they invested in stocks of companies that weren't making a profit. Lots of public companies ended up like bugs that just didn't see the windshield coming their way. Companies such as Enron, WorldCom, and Global Crossing entered the graveyard of rather-be-forgotten stocks. Stock investors as a group lost trillions of dollars investing in glitzy companies that sounded good but weren't making money. When their brokers were saying, "buy, buy, buy," their hard-earned money was saying, "bye, bye, bye!" What were they thinking?

Stock investors need to pick up some rudimentary knowledge of accounting to round out their stock-picking prowess and to be sure that they're getting a good value for their investment dollars. Accounting is the language of business. If you don't understand basic accounting, you'll have difficulty being a successful investor. Investing without accounting knowledge is like traveling without a map. However, if you can run a household budget, using accounting analysis to evaluate stocks is easier than you think, as you find out in the following sections.

Finding the relevant financial data on a company isn't difficult in the age of information and 24-hour Internet access. Websites such as `www.nasdaq.com` can give you the most recent balance sheets and income statements of most public companies. You can find out more about public information and company research in Chapter 6.

Breaking down the balance sheet

A company's balance sheet gives you a financial snapshot of what the company looks like in terms of the following equation:

Assets – liabilities = Net worth (or net equity)

In the following sections, I list the questions that a balance sheet can answer and explain how to judge a company's strength over time from a balance sheet.

Answering a few balance sheet questions

Analyze the following items that you find on the balance sheet:

- ✔ **Total assets:** Have they increased from the prior year? If not, was it because of the sale of an asset or a write-off (uncollectable accounts receivable, for example)?

- ✔ **Financial assets:** In recent years, many companies (especially banks and brokerage firms) had questionable financial assets (such as subprime mortgages and specialized bonds) that went bad, and they had to write them off as unrecoverable losses. Does the company you're analyzing have a large exposure to financial assets that are low-quality (and hence, risky) debt?

- ✔ **Inventory:** Is inventory higher or lower than last year? If sales are flat but inventory is growing, that may be a problem.

- ✔ **Debt:** Debt is the biggest weakness on the corporate balance sheet. Make sure that debt isn't a growing item and that it's under control. In recent years, debt has become a huge problem.

- ✔ **Derivatives:** A *derivative* is a speculative and complex financial instrument that doesn't constitute ownership of an asset (such as a stock, bond, or commodity) but is a promise to convey ownership. Some derivatives are quite acceptable because they're used as protective or hedging vehicles (this use isn't my primary concern). However, they're frequently used to generate income and can then carry risks that can increase liabilities. Standard options and futures are examples of derivatives on a regulated exchange, but the derivatives I'm talking about here are a different animal and in an unregulated part of the financial world. They have a book value exceeding $600 trillion and can easily devastate a company, sector, or market (as the credit crisis of 2008 showed).

Find out whether the company dabbles in these complicated, dicey, leveraged financial instruments. Find out (from the company's 10K report; see Chapter 12) whether it has derivatives and, if so, the total amount. Having derivatives that are valued higher than the company's net equity may cause tremendous problems. Derivatives problems sank many organizations ranging from stodgy banks (Barings Bank of England) to affluent counties (Orange County, California) to once-respected hedge funds (LTCM) to infamous corporations (Enron).

✔ **Equity:** Equity is the company's net worth (what's left in the event that all the assets are used to pay off all the company debts). The stockholders' equity should be increasing steadily by at least 10 percent per year. If not, find out why.

Crash-test dummy candidate?

From 2001–2003, consumers were buying up SUVs . . . uh . . . ASAP. Demand was very high for those popular gas-guzzling vehicles, and auto giant General Motors (GM) was racking up record sales. Investors noticed GM's success, and its stock surpassed $76 in 2001. However, the numbers (and the times) were catching up with GM. Its zero-interest financing program started to sputter. Debts and human resource liabilities (such as employee health and retirement commitments) started accelerating. Energy costs rose, making SUVs less attractive. The red flags came out. GM's 2004 year-end balance sheet showed debt of more than $451 billion, while total shareholder equity was only $27.7 billion. GM's net income fell to just 1 percent of net sales, and its price-to-earnings (P/E) ratio ballooned to a lofty 39. The stock price hit $25 by April 2005. Although the price rebounded to the mid-$30s by July 2005, investors had skid marks on their portfolio as the stock lost nearly two-thirds of its value during that time frame. By September 2005, GM reported a net loss

(goodbye P/E ratio). In my reckoning, GM was no longer an investment; it was a speculation.

As a contrasting point, look at Exxon Mobil (XOM) during that same time frame. Its stock price went from about $35 in early 2001 to $60 in July 2005 (it had a 2-for-1 stock split in mid-2001; in other words, investors who previously had 100 shares of stock at, say, $100 had 200 shares at $50 after the split). XOM's net income was a healthy 8 percent of sales, and the P/E ratio was only 14. In its 2004 year-end balance sheet, total shareholder equity of $101.7 billion comfortably exceeded its total liabilities of $89.5 billion. A sound company with sound numbers. (Ya hear me?)

The point here is that the stock price ultimately reflects the financial health and vitality of the company, and you can easily find and evaluate that information. You don't need luck or a crystal ball. Again, just a little work in the form of fundamental analysis is sufficient.

Table 11-1 shows you a brief example of a balance sheet.

Table 11-1	XYZ Balance Sheet — December 31, 2012
Assets (What the Company Owns)	**Amount**
1. Cash and inventory	$5,000
2. Equipment and other assets	$7,000
3. TOTAL ASSETS (Item 1 + Item 2)	$12,000
Liabilities (What the Company Owes)	
4. Short-term debt	$1,500
5. Other debt	$2,500
6. TOTAL LIABILITIES (Item 4 + Item 5)	$4,000
7. NET EQUITY (Item 3 – Item 6)	$8,000

By looking at a company's balance sheet, you can address the following questions:

- **What does the company own (assets)?** The company can own assets, which can be financial, tangible, and/or intangible. An *asset* is anything that has value or that can be converted to or sold for cash. Financial assets can be cash, investments (such as stocks or bonds of other companies), or accounts receivable. Assets can be tangible items such as inventory, equipment, and/or buildings. They can also be intangible things such as licenses, trademarks, or copyrights.

- **What does the company owe (liabilities)?** A *liability* is anything of value that the company must ultimately pay someone else for. Liabilities can be invoices (accounts payable) or short-term or long-term debt.

- **What is the company's net equity (net worth)?** After you subtract the liabilities from the assets, the remainder is called *net worth, net equity,* or *net stockholders' equity.* This number is critical when calculating a company's book value.

Assessing a company's financial strength over time

The logic behind the assets/liabilities relationship of a company is the same as that of your own household. When you look at a snapshot of your own finances (your personal balance sheet), how can you tell whether you're doing well? Odds are that you start by comparing some numbers. If your net worth is $5,000, you may say, "That's great!" But a more appropriate remark is something like, "That's great compared to, say, a year ago."

Compare a company's balance sheet at a recent point in time to a past time. You should do this comparative analysis with all the key items on the balance sheet, which I list in the preceding section, to see the company's progress (or lack thereof). Is it growing its assets and/or shrinking its debt? Most important, is the company's net worth growing? Has it grown by at least 10 percent since a year ago? All too often, investors stop doing their homework after they make an initial investment. You should continue to look at the firm's numbers regularly so that you can be ahead of the curve. If the business starts having problems, you can get out before the rest of the market starts getting out (which causes the stock price to fall).

To judge the financial strength of a company, ask yourself the following questions:

- ✔ **Are the company's assets greater in value than they were three months ago, a year ago, or two years ago?** Compare current asset size to the most recent two years to make sure that the company is growing in size and financial strength.

- ✔ **How do the individual items compare with prior periods?** Some particular assets that you want to take note of are cash, inventory, and accounts receivable.

- ✔ **Are liabilities such as accounts payable and debt about the same, lower, or higher compared to prior periods? Are they growing at a similar, faster, or slower rate than the company's assets?** Debt that rises faster and higher than items on the other side of the balance sheet is a warning sign of pending financial problems.

- ✔ **Is the company's net worth or equity greater than the preceding year? And is that year's equity greater than the year before?** In a healthy company, the net worth is constantly rising. As a general rule, in good economic times, net worth should be at least 10 percent higher than the preceding year. In tough economic times (such as a recession), 5 percent is acceptable. Seeing the net worth grow at a rate of 15 percent or higher is great.

Looking at the income statement

Where do you look if you want to find out what a company's profit is? Check out the firm's income statement. It reports, in detail, a simple accounting equation that you probably already know:

Sales – expenses = Net profit (or net earnings, or net income)

Look at the following figures found on the income statement:

- ✔ **Sales:** Are they increasing? If not, why not? By what percentage are sales increasing? Preferably, they should be 10 percent higher than the year before. Sales are, after all, where the money comes from to pay for all the company's activities (such as expenses) and create subsequent profits.

- ✔ **Expenses:** Do you see any unusual items? Are total expenses reported higher than the prior year, and if so, by how much? If the total is significantly higher, why? A company with large, rising expenses will see profits suffer, which isn't good for the stock price.

- ✔ **Research and development (R&D):** How much is the company spending on R&D? Companies that rely on new product development (such as pharmaceuticals or biotech firms) should spend at least as much as they did the year before (preferably more) because new products mean future earnings and growth.

- ✔ **Earnings:** This figure reflects the bottom line. Are total earnings higher than the year before? How about earnings from operations (leaving out expenses such as taxes and interest)? The earnings section is the heart and soul of the income statement and of the company itself. Out of all the numbers in the financial statements, earnings have the greatest single impact on the company's stock price.

Table 11-2 shows you a brief example of an income statement.

Table 11-2 XYZ Income Statement for Year Ending 12/31/2012	
Total Sales (Or Revenue)	*Amount*
1. Sales of products	$11,000
2. Sales of services	$3,000
3. TOTAL SALES (Item 1 + Item 2)	$14,000
Expenses	
4. Marketing and promotion	$2,000
5. Payroll costs	$9,000
6. Other costs	$1,500
7. TOTAL EXPENSES (Item 4 + Item 5 + Item 6)	$12,500
8. NET INCOME (Item 3 – Item 7) (In this case, it's a net profit)	$1,500

Looking at the income statement, an investor can try to answer the following questions:

- ✔ **What sales did the company make?** Businesses sell products and services that generate revenue (known as *sales* or *gross sales*). Sales also are referred to as the *top line*.

- ✔ **What expenses did the company incur?** In generating sales, companies pay expenses such as payroll, utilities, advertising, administration, and so on.

- ✔ **What is the net profit?** Also called net earnings or net income, net profit is the *bottom line*. After paying for all expenses, what profit did the company make?

The information you glean should give you a strong idea about a firm's current financial strength and whether it's successfully increasing sales, holding down expenses, and ultimately maintaining profitability. You can find out more about sales, expenses, and profits in the sections that follow.

Sales

Sales refers to the money that a company receives as customers buy its goods and/or services. It's a simple item on the income statement and a useful number to look at. Analyzing a business by looking at its sales is called *top line analysis*.

As an investor, you should take into consideration the following points about sales:

- ✔ **Sales should be increasing.** A healthy, growing company has growing sales. They should grow at least 10 percent from the prior year, and you should look at the most recent three years.

- ✔ **Core sales (sales of those products or services that the company specializes in) should be increasing.** Frequently, the sales figure has a lot of stuff lumped into it. Maybe the company sells widgets (what the heck is a widget, anyway?), but the core sales shouldn't include other things, such as the sale of a building or other unusual items. Take a close look. Isolate the firm's primary offerings and ask whether these sales are growing at a reasonable rate (such as 10 percent).

- ✔ **Does the company have odd items or odd ways of calculating sales?** In the late 1990s, many companies boosted their sales by aggressively offering affordable financing with easy repayment terms. Say you find out that Suspicious Sales Inc. (SSI) had annual sales of $50 million, reflecting a 25 percent increase from the year before. Looks great! But what if you find out that $20 million of that sales number comes from sales made on credit that the company extended to buyers? Some companies that use this approach later have to write off losses as uncollectable debt because the customers ultimately can't pay for the goods.

If you want to get a good clue as to whether a company is artificially boosting sales, check its *accounts receivable* (listed in the asset section of its balance sheet). Accounts receivable refers to money that is owed to the company for goods that customers have purchased on credit. If you find out that sales went up by $10 million (great!) but accounts receivable went up by $20 million (uh-oh), something just isn't right. That may be a sign that the financing terms were too easy, and the company may have a problem collecting payment (especially in a recession).

Expenses

How much a company spends has a direct relationship to its profitability. If spending isn't controlled or held at a sustainable level, it may spell trouble for the business.

When you look at a company's expense items, consider the following:

- **Compare expense items to the prior period.** Are expenses higher than, lower than, or about the same as those from the prior period? If the difference is significant, you should see commensurate benefits elsewhere. In other words, if overall expenses are 10 percent higher compared to the prior period, are sales at least 10 percent more during the same period?

- **Are some expenses too high?** Look at the individual expense items. Are they significantly higher than the year before? If so, why?

- **Have any unusual items been expensed?** An unusual expense isn't necessarily a negative. Expenses may be higher than usual if a company writes off uncollectable accounts receivable as a bad debt expense. Doing so inflates the total expenses and subsequently results in lower earnings. Pay attention to nonrecurring charges that show up on the income statement and determine whether they make sense.

Profit

Earnings or profit is the single most important item on the income statement. It's also the one that receives the most attention in the financial media. When a company makes a profit, it's usually reported as earnings per share (EPS). So if you hear that XYZ Corporation (yes, the infamous XYZ Corp.!) beat last quarter's earnings by a penny, here's how to translate that news. Suppose that the company made $1 per share this quarter and 99 cents per share last quarter. If that company had 100 million shares of stock outstanding, its profit this quarter is $100 million (the EPS times the number of shares outstanding), which is $1 million more than it made in the prior quarter ($1 million is 1 cent per share times 100 million shares).

Don't simply look at current earnings as an isolated figure. Always compare current earnings to earnings in past periods (usually a year). For example, if you're looking at a retailer's fourth-quarter results, don't compare them with the retailer's third-quarter outcome. Doing so is like comparing apples to oranges. What if the company usually does well during the December holidays but poorly in the fall? In that case, you don't get a fair comparison.

A strong company should show consistent earnings growth from the period before (such as the prior year or the same quarter from the prior year), and you should check the period before that, too, so that you can determine whether earnings are consistently rising over time. Earnings growth is an important barometer of the company's potential growth and bodes well for the stock price.

When you look at earnings, here are some things to consider:

- **Total earnings:** This item is the most watched. Total earnings should grow year to year by at least 10 percent.

- **Operational earnings:** Break down the total earnings and look at a key subset — that portion of earnings derived from the company's core activity. Is the company continuing to make money from its primary goods and services?

- **Nonrecurring items:** Are earnings higher (or lower) than usual or than expected, and if so, why? Frequently, the difference results from items such as the sale of an asset or a large depreciation write-off.

I like to keep percentages as simple as possible. Ten percent is a good number because it's easy to calculate and it's a good benchmark. However, 5 percent isn't unacceptable if you're talking about tough times, such as a recession. Obviously, if sales, earnings, and/or net worth are hitting or surpassing 15 percent, that's great.

Tooling around with ratios

A ratio is a helpful numerical tool that you can use to find out the relationship between two or more figures found in a company's financial data. A ratio can add meaning to a number or put it in perspective. Ratios sound complicated, but they're easier to understand than you may think.

Say that you're considering a stock investment and the company you're looking at has earnings of $1 million this year. You may think that's a nice profit, but in order for this amount to be meaningful, you have to compare it to something. What if you find out that the other companies in the industry (of similar size and scope) had earnings of $500 million? Does that change your thinking? Or what if the same company had earnings of $75 million in the prior period? Does that change your mind?

Two key ratios to be aware of are

- Price-to-earnings (P/E) ratio
- Price-to-sales ratio (PSR)

Every investor wants to find stocks that have a 20 percent average growth rate over the past five years and have a low P/E ratio (sounds like a dream). Use stock screening tools available for free on the Internet to do your research. A *stock screening tool* lets you plug in numbers, such as sales or earnings, and ratios, such as the P/E ratio or the debt to equity ratio, and then click! — up come stocks that fit your criteria. These tools are a good starting point for serious investors. Many brokers have them at their websites (such as Charles Schwab at www.schwab.com and E*TRADE at www.etrade.com). Some excellent stock screening tools can also be found at Yahoo! (finance.yahoo.com), Bloomberg (www.bloomberg.com), Nasdaq (www.nasdaq.com), and MarketWatch (www.marketwatch.com). Check out Appendix B for even more on ratios.

The P/E ratio

The *price-to-earnings (P/E) ratio* is very important in analyzing a potential stock investment because it's one of the most widely regarded barometers of a company's value, and it's usually reported along with the company's stock price in the financial page listing. The major significance of the P/E ratio is that it establishes a direct relationship between the bottom line of a company's operations — the earnings (or net profit) — and the stock price.

The *P* in P/E stands for the stock's current price. The *E* is for earnings per share (typically the most recent 12 months of earnings). The P/E ratio is also referred to as the *earnings multiple* or just *multiple*.

You calculate the P/E ratio by dividing the price of the stock by the earnings per share. If the price of a single share of stock is $10 and the earnings (on a per-share basis) are $1, then the P/E is 10. If the stock price goes to $35 per share and the earnings are unchanged, then the P/E is 35. Basically, the higher the P/E, the more you pay for the company's earnings.

Why would you buy stock in one company with a relatively high P/E ratio instead of investing in another company with a lower P/E ratio? Keep in mind that investors buy stocks based on expectations. They may bid up the price of the stock (subsequently raising the stock's P/E ratio) because they feel that the company will have increased earnings in the near future. Perhaps they feel that the company has great potential (a pending new invention or lucrative business deal) that will eventually make it more profitable. More profitability in turn has a beneficial impact on the firm's stock price. The danger with a high P/E is that if the company doesn't achieve the hoped-for results, the stock price can fall.

You should look at two types of P/E ratios to get a balanced picture of the company's value:

- ✔ **Trailing P/E:** This P/E is the most frequently quoted because it deals with existing data. The trailing P/E uses the most recent 12 months of earnings in its calculation.

- ✔ **Forward P/E:** This P/E is based on projections or expectations of earnings in the coming 12-month period. Although this P/E may seem preferable because it looks into the near future, it's still considered an estimate that may or may not prove to be accurate.

The following example illustrates the importance of the P/E ratio. Say that you want to buy a business and I'm selling a business. You come to me and say, "What do you have to offer?" I say, "Have I got a deal for you! I operate a retail business downtown that sells spatulas. The business nets a cool $2,000 profit per year." You reluctantly say, "Uh, okay, what's the asking price for the business?" I reply, "You can have it for only $1 million! What do you say?"

If you're sane, odds are that you politely turn down that offer. Even though the business is profitable (a cool $2,000 a year), you'd be crazy to pay a million bucks for it. In other words, the business is way overvalued (too expensive for what you're getting in return for your investment dollars). The million dollars would generate a better rate of return elsewhere and probably with less risk. As for the business, the P/E ratio of 500 ($1 million divided by $2,000) is outrageous. This is definitely a case of an overvalued company — and a lousy investment.

What if I offered the business for $12,000? Does that price make more sense? Yes. The P/E ratio is a more reasonable 6 ($12,000 divided by $2,000). In other words, the business pays for itself in about 6 years (versus 500 years in the prior example).

Looking at the P/E ratio offers a shortcut for investors asking the question, "Is this stock overvalued?" As a general rule, the lower the P/E, the safer (or more conservative) the stock is. The reverse is more noteworthy: The higher the P/E, the greater the risk.

When someone refers to a P/E as high or low, you have to ask the question, "Compared to what?" A P/E of 30 is considered very high for a large cap electric utility but quite reasonable for a small cap, high-technology firm. Keep in mind that phrases such as *large cap* and *small cap* are just a reference to the company's market value or size (see Chapter 1 for details on these terms). *Cap* is short for *capitalization* (the total number of shares of stock outstanding × the share price).

The following basic points can help you evaluate P/E ratios:

✔ **Compare a company's P/E ratio with its industry.** Electric utility industry stocks, for example, generally have a P/E that hovers in the 9–14 range. Therefore, an electric utility with a P/E of 45 indicates that something is wrong with that utility. (I touch on how to analyze industries in Chapter 13.)

✔ **Compare a company's P/E with the general market.** If you're looking at a small cap stock on the Nasdaq that has a P/E of 100 but the average P/E for established companies on the Nasdaq is 40, find out why. You should also compare the stock's P/E ratio with the P/E ratio for major indexes such as the Dow Jones Industrial Average (DJIA), the Standard & Poor's 500 (S&P 500), and the Nasdaq Composite. Stock indexes are useful for getting the big picture, and I include them in Chapter 5 and Appendix A.

✔ **Compare a company's current P/E with recent periods** (such as this year versus last year). If it currently has a P/E ratio of 20 and it previously had a P/E ratio of 30, you know that either the stock price has declined or that earnings have risen. In this case, the stock is less likely to fall. That bodes well for the stock.

✔ **Low P/E ratios aren't necessarily a sign of a bargain,** but if you're looking at a stock for many other reasons that seem positive (solid sales, strong industry, and so on) and it also has a low P/E, that's a good sign.

✔ **High P/E ratios aren't necessarily bad,** but they do mean that you should investigate further. If a company is weak and the industry is shaky, heed the high P/E as a warning sign. Frequently, a high P/E ratio means that investors have bid up a stock price, anticipating future income. The problem is that if the anticipated income doesn't materialize, the stock price can fall.

✔ **Watch out for a stock that doesn't have a P/E ratio.** In other words, it may have a price (the *P*), but it doesn't have earnings (the *E*). No earnings means no P/E, meaning that you're better off avoiding the stock. Can you still make money buying a stock with no earnings? You can, but you aren't investing; you're speculating.

The PSR

The *price-to-sales ratio (PSR)* is a company's stock price divided by its sales. Because the sales number is rarely expressed as a per-share figure, it's easier to divide a company's total market value (I explain market value earlier in this chapter) by its total sales for the last 12 months.

As a general rule, stock trading at a PSR of 1 or less is a reasonably priced stock worthy of your attention. For example, say that a company has sales of $1 billion and the stock has a total market value of $950 million. In that case, the PSR is 0.95. In other words, you can buy $1 of the company's sales for only 95 cents. All things being equal, that stock may be a bargain.

Analysts frequently use the PSR as an evaluation tool in the following circumstances:

- ✔ In tandem with other ratios to get a more well-rounded picture of the company and the stock.

- ✔ When they want an alternate way to value a business that doesn't have earnings.

- ✔ When they want a true picture of the company's financial health, because sales are tougher for companies to manipulate than earnings.

- ✔ When they're considering a company offering products (versus services). PSR is more suitable for companies that sell items that are easily counted (such as products). Firms that make their money through loans, such as banks, aren't usually valued with a PSR because deriving a usable PSR for them is more difficult.

Compare the company's PSR with other companies in the same industry, along with the industry average, so that you get a better idea of the company's relative value.

Chapter 12

Decoding Company Documents

· ·

In This Chapter

▶ Paging through an annual report

▶ Reviewing other information sources for a second opinion

▶ Organizing your own research library

· ·

*F*inancial documents — good grief! Some people would rather suck a hospital mop than read some dry corporate or government report. Yet if you're serious about choosing stocks, you should be serious about your research. Fortunately, it's not as bad as you think (put away that disgusting mop). When you see that some basic research helps you build wealth, it gets easier.

In this chapter, I discuss the basic documents that you come across (or should come across) most often in your investing life. These documents include essential information that all investors need to know, not only at the time of the initial investment decision, but also for as long as that stock remains in their portfolio.

If you plan to hold a stock for the long haul, reading the annual report and other reports covered in this chapter will be very helpful. If you intend to get rid of the stock soon or plan to hold it only for the short term, reading these reports diligently isn't that important.

A Message from the Bigwigs: Reading the Annual Report

When you're a regular stockholder, the company sends you its annual report. If you're not already a stockholder, contact the company's shareholder service department for a hard copy or to get a copy e-mailed to you, or look for a link to it on the company's website.

You can often view a company's annual report at its website. Any major search engine can help you find it. Downloading or printing the annual report is easy.

The following resources also provide access to annual reports:

- **Check out the Public Register's Annual Report Service.** Go to www. prars.com to order a hard copy or to www.annualreportservice. com to view reports online. This organization maintains an extensive collection of annual reports.

- **Use the free annual report service of *The Wall Street Journal*.** If you read this newspaper's financial pages and see a company with the club symbol (like the one you see on a playing card), then you can order that company's annual report by calling 800-654-2582 or visiting the website (www.wsj.com).

You need to carefully analyze an annual report to find out the following:

- **How well the company is doing:** Are earnings higher, lower, or the same as the year before? How are sales doing? You can find these numbers clearly presented in the annual report's financial section.

- **Whether the company is making more money than it's spending:** How does the balance sheet look? Are assets higher or lower than the year before? Is debt growing, shrinking, or about the same as the year before? For more details on balance sheets, see Chapter 11.

- **What management's strategic plan is for the coming year:** How will management build on the company's success? This plan is usually covered in the beginning of the annual report — frequently in the letter from the chairman of the board.

Your task boils down to figuring out where the company has been, where it is now, and where it's going. As an investor, you don't need to read the annual report like a novel — from cover to cover. Instead, approach it like a newspaper and jump around to the relevant sections to get the answers you need to decide whether you should buy or hold on to the stock. I describe the makeup of the annual report and proxy materials in the following sections.

Analyzing the annual report's anatomy

Not every company puts its annual report together in exactly the same way — the style of presentation varies. Some annual reports have gorgeous graphics or coupons for the company's products, whereas others are in a standard black-and-white typeface with no cosmetic frills at all. But every annual report does include common basic content, such as the income statement and the balance sheet. The following sections present typical components of an average annual report. (Keep in mind that not every annual report presents the sections in the same order.)

The letter from the chairman of the board

The first thing you see is usually the letter from the chairman of the board. It's the "Dear Stockholder" letter that communicates views from the head muckety-muck. The chairman's letter is designed to put the best possible perspective on the company's operations during the past year. Be aware of this bias; no one in upper management wants to panic stockholders. If the company is doing well, the letter will certainly point it out. If the company is having hard times, the letter will probably put a positive spin on the company's difficulties. If the *Titanic* had had an annual report, odds are that the last letter would have reported, "Great news! A record number of our customers participated in our spontaneous moonlight swimming program. In addition, we confidently project no operating expenses whatsoever for the subsequent fiscal quarter." You get the point.

To get a good idea of what issues the company's management team feels are important and what goals it wants to accomplish, keep the following questions in mind:

✔ What does the letter say about changing conditions in the company's business? How about in the industry?

✔ If any difficulties exist, does the letter communicate a clear and logical action plan (cutting costs, closing money-losing plants, and so on) to get the company back on a positive track?

✔ What's being highlighted and why? For example, is the firm focusing on research and development for new products or on a new deal with China?

✔ Does the letter offer apologies for anything the company did? If, for example, it fell short of sales expectations, does the letter offer a reason for the shortcoming?

✔ Did the company make (or will it make) new acquisitions or major developments (say, selling products to China, or a new marketing agreement with a Fortune 500 company)?

Read an annual report (or any messages from upper management) in the same way you read or hear anything from a politician — be more concerned with means than ends. In other words, don't tell me what the goal is (greater profitability, or peace on earth), tell me how you're going to get there. Executives may say "we will increase sales and profits," but saying "we will increase sales and profits by doing X, Y, and Z" is a better message, because you can then decide for yourself whether the road map makes sense.

The company's offerings

This section of an annual report can have various titles (such as "Sales and Marketing"), but it generally covers what the company sells. You should understand the products or services (or both) that the business sells and why customers purchase them. If you don't understand what the company offers, then understanding how it earns money, which is the driving force behind its stock, is more difficult.

Are the company's core or primary offerings selling well? If, for example, the earnings of McDonald's are holding steady but earnings strictly from burgers and fries are fizzling, that's a cause for concern. If a business ceases making money from its specialty, you should become cautious. Here are some other questions to ask:

- ✔ **How does the company distribute its offerings?** Through a website, malls, representatives, or some other means? Does it sell only to the U.S. market, or is its distribution international? Generally, the greater the distribution, the greater the potential sales and, ultimately, the higher the stock price.

- ✔ **Are most of the company's sales to a definable marketplace?** For example, if most of the sales are to a war-torn or politically unstable country, you should worry. If the company's customers aren't doing well, that has a direct impact on the company and, eventually, its stock.

- ✔ **How are sales doing versus market standards?** In other words, is the company doing better than the industry average? Is it a market leader in what it offers? The firm should be doing better than (or as well as) its peers in the industry. If the company is falling behind its competitors, that doesn't bode well for the stock in the long run.

- ✔ **Does the report include information on the company's competitors and related matters?** You should know who the company's competitors are because they have a direct effect on the company's success. If customers are choosing the competitor over your firm, the slumping sales and earnings will ultimately hurt the stock's price.

Financial statements

Look over the various financial statements and find the relevant numbers. Every annual report should have (at the very least) a balance sheet and an income statement. Catching the important numbers on a financial statement isn't that difficult to do. However, it certainly helps when you pick up some basic accounting knowledge. Chapter 11 can give you more details on evaluating financial statements.

First, review the income statement (also known as the profit and loss statement, or simply P&L). It gives you the company's sales, expenses, and the result (net income or net loss).

Next, look at the balance sheet. It provides a snapshot of a point in time (annual reports usually provide a year-end balance sheet) that tells you what the company owns (*assets*), what it owes (*liabilities*), and the end result (*net worth*). For a healthy company, assets should always be greater than liabilities.

Carefully read the footnotes to the financial statements. Sometimes big changes are communicated in small print. In current times, especially be wary of small print pointing out other debt or derivatives. *Derivatives* are complicated and (lately) very risky vehicles. Problems with derivatives were one of the major causes of the market turmoil that destroyed financial firms on Wall Street during late 2008. AIG, for example, is a major insurer that had to be bailed out by the Federal Reserve before it went bankrupt (shareholders suffered huge losses).

Derivatives are a huge land mine, and large money center banks still carry them. According to the Bank for International Settlements (www.bis.org), major money center banks are carrying more than 500 trillion dollars' worth of derivatives. (Whew! Now I see why they give away so many toasters.) Derivatives are especially worth being aware of if you're considering bank or other financial stocks for your portfolio.

Summary of past financial figures

The summary of past financial figures gives you a snapshot of the company's overall long-term progress. How many years does the annual report summarize? Some reports summarize three years, but most go back two years.

Management issues

The annual report's management issues section includes a reporting of current trends and issues, such as new developments happening in the industry that affect the company. See whether you agree with management's assessment of economic and market conditions that affect the firm's prospects. What significant developments in society does management perceive as affecting the company's operations? Does the report include information on current or pending lawsuits?

CPA opinion letter

Annual reports typically include comments from the company's independent accounting firm. It may be an opinion letter or a simple paragraph with the accounting firm's views regarding the financial statements.

The CPA opinion letter offers an opinion about the accuracy of the financial data presented and information on how the statements were prepared. Check to see whether the letter includes any footnotes regarding changes in certain numbers or how they were reported. For example, a company that wants to report higher earnings may use a conservative method of measuring depreciation rather than a more aggressive approach. In any case, you should verify the numbers by looking at the company's 10K document filed with the Securities and Exchange Commission (SEC; I describe this document in more detail later in this chapter).

Company identity data

The company identity data section informs you about the company's subsidiaries (or lesser businesses that it owns), brands, and addresses. It also contains standard data such as the headquarters location and names of directors and officers. Many reports also include data on the directors' and officers' positions in stock ownership at year's end.

Stock data

The stock data section may include a history of the stock price, along with information such as what exchange the stock is listed on, the stock symbol, the company's dividend reinvestment plan (if any), and so on. It also includes information on stockholder services and who to contact for further information.

Going through the proxy materials

As a shareholder (or stockholder — same thing), you're entitled to vote at the annual shareholders meeting. If you ever get the opportunity to attend one, do so. You get to meet other shareholders and ask questions of management and other company representatives. Usually, the shareholder services department provides you with complete details. At the meetings, shareholders vote on company matters, such as approving a new accounting firm or deciding whether a proposed merger with another company will go forward.

If you can't attend (which is usually true for the majority of shareholders), you can vote by proxy. *Voting by proxy* essentially means that you vote by mail. You indicate your votes on the proxy statement (or card) and authorize a representative to vote at the meeting on your behalf. The proxy statement is usually sent to all shareholders, along with the annual report, just before the meeting.

Dig Deeper: Getting a Second Opinion

A wealth of valuable information is available for your investing pursuits. The resources in this section are just a representative few — a good representation, though. To get a more balanced view of the company and its prospects (instead of relying only on the annual report that I describe in the preceding section), take a look at several different sources of information for the stocks you're researching.

The information and research they provide can be expensive if you buy or subscribe on your own, but fortunately, most of the resources mentioned are usually available in the business reference section of a well-stocked public library.

Company documents filed with the SEC

The serious investor doesn't overlook the wealth of information that he can cull from documents filed with the SEC. Take the time and effort to review the documents in the following sections, because they offer great insight regarding the company's activities.

Here's how to obtain the main documents that investors should be aware of:

- ✔ **Drop by the company itself.** Stockholder service departments keep these publicly available documents on hand and usually give them out at no cost to interested parties.

- ✔ **Visit the SEC, either in person or online.** These documents are available for public viewing at the SEC offices. You can find out more by contacting the Securities and Exchange Commission, Publications Unit, 450 Fifth St. NW, Washington, DC 20549.

  At the SEC's website (www.sec.gov), you can check out EDGAR (Electronic Data Gathering, Analysis, and Retrieval system) to search public documents filed. It's a tremendous source of documents that date back to 1994. You can search, print, or download documents very easily. Documents can be located either by document number or keyword search.

Form 10K

Gee, how intimidating. Just the report name alone makes you scratch your head. To some people, 10K refers to running a race of 10 kilometers. But if you're reading (not running) a 10K, you may wish you were running one instead.

Form 10K is a report that companies must file with the SEC annually. It works like the annual report that you get from the company, except that it provides more detailed financial information. It can be a little intimidating because the text can be dry and cumbersome. It's not exactly Shakespeare (although 10K reports would've also driven Lady Macbeth insane); then again, the data isn't laden with as much spin as the annual report the company sends to shareholders. Without going crazy, go through each section of the 10K. Take some extra time to scrutinize the section on financial data. Ask the same questions that you do when you're looking at the annual report.

The following websites can help you make sense of 10K reports:

- ✔ FreeEDGAR (www.freeedgar.com)
- ✔ Morningstar Document Research (www.10Kwizard.com)
- ✔ Edgar Online, Inc. (www.edgr.com)

Form 10Q

Form 10Q is a quarterly report that gives you the same basic information as the 10K, but it details only three months' worth of activity. Because a long time can pass between 10Ks (after all, it is a year), don't wait 12 months to see how your company is progressing. Make a habit of seeing how the company is doing by comparing its recent 10Q with one that covers the same quarter last year. Is the profit higher or lower? How about sales? Debt?

Keep in mind that not every company has the same fiscal year. A company with a calendar year fiscal year (ending December 31) files a 10Q for each of the first three quarters and files a 10K for the final quarter. The company reports its fourth quarter data in the 10K, along with the statistics for the full year.

Insider reports

Two types of insiders exist: those who work within a company and those outside the company who have a significant (10 percent or more) ownership of company stock. Tracking insider activity is very profitable for investors who want to follow in the footsteps of the people in the know. See Chapter 20 for information about monitoring and benefiting from insider activity.

Every time an insider (such as the CEO or controller) buys or sells stock, the transaction has to be reported to the SEC. The insider actually reports the trade prior to transacting it. These reports are publicly available documents that allow you to see what the insiders are actually doing. Hearing what they say in public is one thing, but seeing what they're actually doing with their stock transactions is more important.

Value Line

The Value Line Investment Survey, one of many information products provided by Value Line Publishing, Inc., is considered a longtime favorite by many stock investing professionals. You can look it over at any library that has a good business reference department. In the survey, Value Line covers the largest public companies and ranks them according to financial strength and several other key business factors. To get more information about Value Line, either head to the library or visit www.valueline.com.

Standard & Poor's

Another ubiquitous and venerable publisher is Standard & Poor's (S&P). Although it has a number of quality information products and services for both individual and institutional investors, the three you should take a look at are the following:

✔ **S&P Stock Reports:** Available at many libraries, this guide comes out periodically and reports on stocks on the New York Stock Exchange and the largest firms listed on Nasdaq. It gives a succinct, two-page summary of each stock, offering a snapshot of the company's current finances, along with a brief history and commentary on the company's activities. This guide also rates companies based on their financial strength.

✔ **The S&P Industry Survey:** S&P gives detailed reports on the top industries, cramming a lot of information about a given industry in four to seven pages. This annual publication provides a nice summary of what's happened in each industry in the past 12 months, what the industry looks like today, and what the prospects are for the coming year. It also provides the important numbers (earnings, sales, and industry ranking) for the top 50 to 100 firms in each industry.

✔ **S&P Bond Reports:** Yes, I know this book is about stocks. But a company's bond rating is invaluable for stock investors. S&P analyzes the strength of the bond issuer and ranks the bond for creditworthiness. If S&P gives a company a high rating, you have added assurance that the company is financially strong. You want the company to have a bond rating of AAA, AA, or A, because these ratings tell you that the company is "investment-grade."

Check out S&P's website at www.standardandpoors.com for more information about its publications.

Moody's Investment Service

Another stalwart publisher, Moody's offers vital research on stocks and bonds. *Moody's Handbook of Common Stocks* is usually available in the reference section of a well-stocked library. It offers stock and bond guides similar to S&P and also provides an independent bond-rating service. Check out www.moodys.com for more information.

A stock rated highly by both Moody's and S&P is a great choice for investors hunting for value investments.

Brokerage reports: The good, the bad, and the ugly

Clint Eastwood, where are you? Traditionally, brokerage reports have been a good source of information for investors seeking informed opinions about stocks. And they still are, but in recent years some brokers have been penalized for biased reports. Brokers should never be your sole source of information. (Otherwise, Clint may ask them whether they're lucky punks.) The following sections describe the good, the bad, and the ugly of brokerage reports.

The good

Research departments at brokerage firms provide stock reports and make them available for their clients and investment publications. The firms' analysts and market strategists generally prepare these reports. Good research is critical, and brokerage reports can be very valuable. What better source of guidance than full-time experts backed up by million-dollar research departments? Brokerage reports have some strong points:

- ✔ The analysts are professionals who should understand the value of a company and its stock. They analyze and compare company data every day.

- ✔ Analysts have at their disposal tremendous information and historical data that they can sift through to make informed decisions.

- ✔ If you have an account with the firm, you can usually access the information at no cost.

The bad

Well, brokerage reports may not be bad in every case, but at their worst, they're quite bad. Brokers make their money from commissions and investment banking fees (nothing bad here). However, they can find themselves in the awkward position of issuing brokerage reports on companies that are (or could be) customers of the brokerage firm that employs them (hmmm — could be bad). Frequently, this relationship results in a brokerage report that paints an overly positive picture of a company that can be a bad investment (yup, that's bad).

The ugly

During 1998–2000, an overwhelming number of brokerage reports issued glowing praise of companies that were either mediocre or dubious. Investors bought up stocks such as tech stocks and Internet stocks. The sheer demand pushed up stock prices, which gave the appearance of genius to analysts' forecasts, yet the stock prices rose essentially as a self-fulfilling prophecy. The stocks were way overvalued and were cruisin' for a bruisin'. Analysts and investors were feeling lucky.

Investors, however, lost a ton of money (ooh, ugly). Money that people painstakingly accumulated over many years of work vanished in a matter of months as the bear market of 2000 hit (ooh, ugly). Of course, the bear market that hit in 2008–2009 was equally brutal. Retirees who had trusted the analysts saw nest eggs lose 40 to 70 percent in value (yikes, very ugly). Investors lost trillions during these major downturns, much of it needlessly. I'm sure that lots of those folks thought that they should have put that money in things that had enduring value instead . . . such as cookies and cases of merlot.

During that bear market of 2000-2002, a record number of lawsuits and complaints were filed against brokerage firms. Wall Street and Main Street learned some tough lessons. Regarding research reports from brokerage firms, the following points can help you avoid getting a bad case of the uglies:

- ✔ Always ask yourself, "Is the provider of the report a biased source?" In other words, is the broker getting business in any way from the company he's recommending?

- ✔ Never, never, *never* rely on just one source of information, especially if it's the same source that's selling you the stock or other investment.

- ✔ Do your research first before you rely on a brokerage report. Check out annual reports and the other documents I recommend earlier in this chapter.

- ✔ Do your due diligence before you buy stocks anyway. Look at Parts I and II to understand your need for diversification, risk tolerance, and so on.

- ✔ Verify the information provided to you with a trip to the library or websites (see Appendix A).

Although I generally don't rely on Wall Street brokerage analysts, I do track some independent investment analysts. I mention some of my favorites in Appendix A.

Do It Yourself: Compiling Your Own Research Department

You don't need to spend an excessive amount of time or money, but you should maintain your own library of resources. You may only need one shelf (or a small amount of memory on your computer's hard drive), but why not have a few investment facts and resources at your fingertips? I maintain my own library loaded with books, magazines, newsletters, and tons of great stuff downloaded on my computer for easy search and reference. When you start your own collection, follow these tips:

✔ **Keep some select newspapers.** *Barron's, The Wall Street Journal,* and *Investor's Business Daily* regularly have some editions that are worth keeping. For example, *The Wall Street Journal* and *Investor's Business Daily* usually publish a year-in-review issue the first business week in January. *Barron's* has special issues reviewing brokers and financial websites.

✔ **Subscribe to financial magazines.** Publications such as *Forbes* and *SmartMoney* offer great research and regularly review stocks, brokers, and resources for investors.

✔ **Keep annual reports.** Regarding the stocks that are the core holdings in your portfolio, keep all the annual reports (at the very least, the most recent three).

✔ **Go to the library's business reference section periodically to stay updated.** Hey, you pay the taxes that maintain the public library — you may as well use it to stay informed.

✔ **Use the Internet for research.** The web offers plenty of great sites to peruse; I list some of the best in Appendix A.

Financial reports are very important and easier to read than most people think. An investor can easily avoid a bad investment by simply noticing the data in what seems like a jumble of numbers. Figure out how to read them. For a great book to help you with reading financial reports (without needless technicality), check out *How to Read a Financial Report: Wringing Vital Signs Out of the Numbers,* 7th edition, by John A. Tracy or the latest edition of *Reading Financial Reports For Dummies* by Lita Epstein (both published by Wiley).

Chapter 13

Emerging Sector and Industry Opportunities

Suppose that you have to bet your entire nest egg on a one-mile race. All you need to do is select a winning group. Your choices are the following:

Group A: Thoroughbred race horses

Group B: Overweight Elvis impersonators

Group C: Lethargic snails

This isn't a trick question, and you have one minute to answer. Notice that I didn't ask you to pick a single winner out of a giant mush of horses, Elvii, and snails; I only asked you to pick the winning group in the race. The obvious answer is the thoroughbred race horses (and no, they weren't ridden by the overweight Elvis impersonators because that would take away from the eloquent point being made). In this example, even the slowest member of Group A easily outdistances the fastest member of either Group B or C.

Industries, like groups A, B, and C in my example, aren't equal, and life isn't fair. After all, if life were fair, Elvis would be alive, and the impersonators wouldn't exist. Fortunately, picking stocks doesn't have to be as difficult as picking a winning racehorse. The basic point is that it's easier to pick a successful stock from a group of winners (a growing, vibrant industry). Understanding industries only enhances your stock-picking strategy.

A successful, long-term investor looks at the industry (or the basic sector) just as carefully as he looks at the individual stock. Luckily, choosing a winning industry to invest in is easier than choosing individual stocks, as you find out in this chapter. I know some investors who can pick a winning stock in a losing industry, and I also know investors who've chosen a losing stock in a winning industry (the former is far outnumbered by the latter). Just think how well you do when you choose a great stock in a great industry! Of course, if you repeatedly choose bad stocks in bad industries, you may as well get out of the stock market altogether (maybe your calling is to be a celebrity impersonator instead!).

Note: Chapter 14 goes into megatrends, which are a different animal from sectors and industries. *Megatrends* are major developments that have a monumental effect on various parts of our economy. Those "parts" are the various sectors that are the benefactors (or victims) of these effects.

Telling the Difference between a Sector and an Industry

Very often, investors confuse an industry with a sector. Even though it may not be a consequential confusion, some clarity is needed here.

A *sector* is simply a group of interrelated industries. An *industry* is typically a category of business that performs a more precise activity; you can call an industry a subsector. Investing in a sector and investing in an industry can mean different things for the investor. The result of your investment performance can also be very different.

Healthcare is a good example of a sector that has different industries. Within the sector of healthcare, there are a variety of industries: pharmaceuticals, drug retailers, health insurance, hospitals, medical equipment manufacturers, and so on.

Healthcare is actually a good (great!) example of why you should know the distinction between a sector and an industry. Within a given sector (like healthcare), you have industries that behave differently during the same economic conditions. Some of the industries are cyclical (like medical equipment manufacturers), whereas some are defensive (like drug retailers). In a bad economy, cyclicals tend to go down while defensive stocks generally hold their value. In a good or booming economy, cyclicals do very well while defensive stocks tend to lag behind. (I talk more about cyclical and defensive industries later in this chapter.)

Given that fact, an exchange-traded fund (ETF) that reflected the general healthcare sector would be generally flat because some of the industries that went up would be offset by those that went down. Flip to Chapter 5 for more about ETFs.

Interrogating the Sectors and Industries

Your common sense is an important tool in choosing sectors and industries with winning stocks. This section explores some of the most important questions to ask yourself when you're choosing a sector or industry.

Which category does the industry fall into?

Most industries can neatly be placed in one of two categories: cyclical and defensive. In a rough way, these categories generally translate into what society wants and what it needs. Society buys what it *wants* when times are good and holds off when times are bad. It buys what it *needs* in both good and bad times. A want is a "like to have," whereas a need is a "must have." Kapish?

Cyclical industries

Cyclical industries are industries whose fortunes rise and fall with the economy's rise and fall. In other words, if the economy and the stock market are doing well, consumers and investors are confident and tend to spend and invest more money than usual, so cyclical industries tend to do well. Real estate and automobiles are great examples of cyclical industries.

Your own situation offers you some common-sense insight into the concept of cyclical industries. Think about your behavior as a consumer, and you get a revealing clue into the thinking of millions of consumers. When you (and millions of others) feel good about your career, your finances, and your future, you have a greater tendency to buy more (and/or more expensive) stuff. When people feel financially strong, they're more apt to buy a new house or car or make some other large financial commitment. Also, people take on more debt because they feel confident that they can pay it back. In light of this behavior, what industries do you think would do well?

The same point holds for business spending. When businesses think that economic times are good and foresee continuing good times, they tend to spend more money on large purchases such as new equipment or technology. They think that when they're doing well and are flush with financial success, it's a good idea to reinvest that money in the business to increase future success.

Defensive industries

Defensive industries are industries that produce goods and services that are needed no matter what's happening in the economy. Your common sense kicks in here, too. What do you buy even when times are tough? Think about what millions of people buy no matter how bad the economy gets. A good example is food — people still need to eat regardless of good or bad times. Other examples of defensive industries are utilities and healthcare.

In bad economic times, defensive stocks tend to do better than cyclical stocks. However, when times are good, cyclical stocks tend to do better than defensive stocks. Defensive stocks don't do as well in good times because people don't necessarily eat twice as much or use up more electricity.

So how do defensive stocks grow? Their growth generally relies on two factors:

- **Population growth:** As more and more consumers are born, more people become available to buy.

- **New markets:** A company can grow by seeking out new groups of consumers to buy its products and services. Coca-Cola, for example, found new markets in Asia during the 1990s. As communist regimes fell from power and more societies embraced a free market and consumer goods, the company sold more beverages, and its stock soared.

One way to invest in a particular industry is to take advantage of exchange-traded funds (ETFs), which have become very popular in recent years. ETFs are structured much like mutual funds but are fixed portfolios that trade like a stock. If you find a winning industry but you can't find a winning stock (or don't want to bother with the necessary research), then ETFs are a great consideration. You can find out more about ETFs at websites such as www.etfdb.com or by turning to Chapter 5.

Is the sector growing?

The question may seem obvious, but you still need to ask it before you purchase stock. The saying "the trend is your friend" applies when choosing a sector in which to invest, as long as the trend is an upward one. If you look at three different stocks that are equal in every significant way but you find that one stock is in a sector growing 15 percent per year while the other two stocks are in sectors that have either little growth or are shrinking, which stock would you choose?

Sometimes the stock of a financially unsound or poorly run company goes up dramatically because the sector it's in is very exciting to the public. The most obvious example is Internet stocks from 1998–2000. Stocks such as Pets.com shot up to incredible heights because investors thought the Internet was the place to be. Sooner or later, however, the measure of a successful company is its ability to be profitable (Pets.com went bankrupt in 2000). Serious investors look at the company's fundamentals (see Chapter 11 to find out how to do this) and the prospects for the industry's growth before settling on a particular stock.

To judge how well a sector or industry is doing, various information sources monitor all the sectors and industries and measure their progress. Some reliable sources include the following:

- MarketWatch (www.marketwatch.com)
- Standard & Poor's (www.standardandpoors.com)
- Hoover's (www.hoovers.com)
- Yahoo! Finance (finance.yahoo.com)
- *The Wall Street Journal* (www.wsj.com)

The preceding sources generally give you in-depth information about the major sectors and industries. Visit their websites to read their current research and articles along with links to relevant sites for more details. For example, *The Wall Street Journal* (published by Dow Jones & Co.), whose website is updated daily (or more frequently), publishes indexes for all the major sectors and industries so that you can get a useful snapshot of how well each one is doing.

Standard and Poor's (S&P) Industry Survey is an excellent source of information on U.S. industries. Besides ranking and comparing industries and informing you about their current prospects, the survey also lists the top companies by size, sales, earnings, and other key information. What I like is that each industry is covered in a few pages, so you get the critical information you need without reading a novel. The survey and other S&P publications are available on the S&P website or in the business reference section of most libraries (your best bet is to head for the library because the survey is rather expensive).

Are the sector's products or services in demand?

Look at the products and services that are provided by a sector or an industry. Do they look like things that society will continue to want? Are there products and services on the horizon that could replace them? What does the foreseeable future look like for the sector?

When evaluating future demand, look for a *sunrise industry* — one that's new or emerging or has promising appeal for the future. Good examples of sunrise industries in recent years are biotech and Internet companies. In contrast, a *sunset industry* is one that's either declining or has little potential for growth. For example, you probably shouldn't invest in the DVD manufacturing industry because demand is shifting toward digital delivery instead. Owning stock in a strong, profitable company in a sunrise industry is obviously the most desirable choice.

Current research unveils the following megatrends (see Chapter 14 for more information):

- ✔ **The aging of the U.S.:** More senior citizens than ever before are living in the U.S. Because of this fact, financial and healthcare services that touch on eldercare or financial concerns of the elderly will prosper.

- ✔ **Advances in high technology:** Internet, telecom, medical, and biotechnology innovations will continue.

- ✔ **Security concerns:** Terrorism, international tensions, and security issues on a personal level mean more attention for national defense, homeland security, and related matters.

- ✔ **Energy challenges:** Traditional and nontraditional sources of energy (such as solar, fuel cells, and so on) will demand society's attention as it faces Peak Oil (shrinking supplies of the world's available sweet crude oil).

What does the industry's growth rely on?

An industry doesn't exist in a vacuum. External factors weigh heavily on its ability to survive and thrive. Does the industry rely on an established megatrend? Then it will probably be strong for a while. Does it rely on factors that are losing relevance? Then it may begin to decline soon. Technological and demographic changes are other factors that may contribute to an industry's growth or fall.

Keep in mind that a sector will either continue to grow, shrink, or be level, but individual industries can grow, shrink, or even be on a track to disappear. If a sector is expanding, you may see new industries emerge. For example, the graying of the U.S. is an established megatrend. As millions of Americans climb into their later years, profitable opportunities await companies that are prepared to cater to them. Perhaps an industry (subsector) offers great new medical products for senior citizens. What are the prospects for growth?

Is the industry dependent on another industry?

This twist on the prior question is a reminder that industries frequently are intertwined and can become codependent. When one industry suffers, you may find it helpful to understand which industries will subsequently suffer. The reverse can also be true — when one industry is doing well, other industries may reap the benefits.

In either case, if the stock you choose is in an industry that's highly dependent on other industries, you should know about it. If you're considering stocks of resort companies and you see the headlines blaring, "Airlines losing money as public stops flying," what do you do? This type of question forces you to think logically and consider cause and effect. Logic and common sense are powerful tools that frequently trump all the number-crunching activity performed by analysts.

Who are the leading companies in the industry?

After you've chosen the industry, what types of companies do you want to invest in? You can choose from two basic types:

- **Established leaders:** These companies are considered industry leaders or have a large share of the market. Investing in these companies is the safer way to go; what better choice for novice investors than companies that have already proven themselves?

- **Innovators:** If the industry is hot and you want to be more aggressive in your approach, investigate companies that offer new products, patents, or technologies. These companies are probably smaller but have a greater potential for growth in a proven industry.

Is the industry a target of government action?

You need to know if the government is targeting an industry, because intervention by politicians and bureaucrats (rightly or wrongly) can have an impact on an industry's economic situation. Find out about any political issues that face a company, industry, or sector (see Chapter 15 for political considerations).

Investors need to take heed when political "noise" starts coming out about a particular industry. An industry can be hurt either by direct government intervention or by the threat of it. Intervention can take the form of lawsuits, investigations, taxes, regulations, or sometimes an outright ban. In any case, being on the wrong end of government intervention is the greatest external threat to a company's survival.

Sometimes, government action helps an industry. Generally, beneficial action takes two forms:

- **Deregulation and/or tax decreases:** Government sometimes reduces burdens on an industry. During the late 1990s, for example, government deregulation led the way to more innovation in the telecommunications industry. This trend, in turn, laid the groundwork for more innovation and growth in the Internet and expansion of cellphone service.

✔ **Direct funding:** Government has the power to steer taxpayer money toward business as well. In recent years, federal and state governments have provided tax credits and other incentives for alternative energy such as solar power.

Outlining Key Sectors and Industries

In this section, I highlight some sectors and industries that investors should take note of. Consider investing some of your stock portfolio in those that look promising (and, of course, avoid those that look problematic).

Many investors can benefit from a practice referred to as *sector rotation* (not quite like crop rotation, but close enough). The idea is that you shift money from one sector to another based on current or expectant economic conditions. There are a number of variations of this concept, but in most cases, they follow some essential ideas. If the economy is doing poorly or if the outlook appears bearish, you shift to defensive sectors such as consumer staples and utilities. If the economy is doing well, you shift money to cyclicals such as technology and base materials. Given today's problematic economic conditions, sector rotation makes sense and is worth a look by long-term investors. Find out more using the resources I mention in the earlier section "Is the sector growing?" and in Appendix A.

Moving in: Real estate

I include real estate as a key sector because it's a cyclical *bellwether industry* — one that has a great effect on many other industries that may be dependent on it. Real estate is looked at as a key component of economic health because so many other industries — including building materials, mortgages, household appliances, and contract labor services — are tied to it. A booming real estate industry bodes well for much of the economy.

Housing starts are one way to measure real estate activity. This data is an important leading indicator of health in the industry. Housing starts indicate new construction, which means more business for related industries.

Keep an eye on the real estate industry for negative news that could be bearish for the economy and the stock market. Because real estate is purchased with mortgage money, investors and analysts watch the mortgage market for trouble signs such as rising delinquencies and foreclosures. These statistics serve as a warning for general economic weakness.

In recent years, the real estate mania hit its zenith during 2005–2006. A *mania* is typically the final (and craziest) part of a mature bull market. In a mania, the prices of the assets experiencing the bull market (such as stock or real estate) skyrocket to extreme levels, which excites more and more investors to jump in, causing prices to rise even further. It gets to the point where seemingly everyone thinks that it's easy to get rich by buying this particular asset, and almost no one notices that the market has become unsustainable. After prices are exhausted and start to level off, investor excitement dies down, and then investors try to exit by selling their holdings to realize some profit. As more and more sell off their holdings, demand decreases while supply increases. The mania dissipates, and the bear market appears. This is definitely what happened to real estate in 2007–2008, when the industry fell on hard times as the housing bubble popped.

The real estate industry first soared during 2000–2006 and then cratered during 2007–2012. As I write this, the real estate industry is stabilizing after several very difficult years. As you read this, the industry may very well start its path to normalization. Whether you're a real estate investor or a stock investor looking at real estate–related companies and industries, it's probably an appropriate time to see a slow return to normalization for the real estate world.

For real estate investors, start looking for companies that are showing consistent profits and taking advantage in a rebounding sector. Although the sector may not be out of the woods yet, the opportunities do outnumber the pitfalls. Stay tuned and do your homework (research) here.

Driving it home: Automotive

Cars are big-ticket items and are another barometer of people's economic well-being — people buy new cars when they're doing well financially (or at least perceive that they're well-off). A rise in car sales is usually considered to be a positive indicator for the economy.

The automotive sector is still feeling its way. Although the government has used taxpayer funds to rescue some individual companies (such as General Motors), the automotive industry is still not on a healthy track (as I write this in late 2012). The growth opportunities are not yet clear for stock investors.

Talking tech: Computers and related electronics

In recent years, technology stocks have become very popular with investors. Indeed, technology is a great sector, and its impact on the economy's present and future success can't be underestimated. The share price of technology companies can rise substantially because investors buy shares based on expectations — today's untested, unproven companies may become the Googles and Apples of tomorrow.

With the success of Apple as it forges a path in the world of personal electronics (such as the iPhone and related technology), this area will continue to show growth as worldwide consumer demand continues to show strength. Don't lose sight of the fundamentals as this industry continues to mature.

In spite of the sector's potential, companies can still fail if customers don't embrace their products. Even in technology stocks, you still must apply the rules and guidelines about financially successful companies that I discuss throughout this book. Pick the best in a growing industry, and you'll succeed over the long haul.

Banking on it: Financials

Banking and financial services are intrinsic parts of any economy. Debt is the most important sign of this industry for investors. If a company's debt is growing faster than the economy, you need to watch how that debt impacts stocks and mutual funds. If debt gets out of control, it can be disastrous for the economy.

As one of my favorite credit specialists, Doug Noland, points out (you can find his column at www.prudentbear.com), the amount of debt and debt-related securities recently reached historic and troublesome levels. This trend means that many financial stocks are at risk if a recession hits anytime soon.

As this book goes to press, financial stocks have emerged from a tough period of troubles in subprime debt and related difficulties. Because this is an area susceptible to debt troubles, problems will persist during 2013–2014. Investors should be very selective in this industry and should only embrace those lenders that are conservative in their balance sheet and are generally avoiding overexposure in areas such as international finance and derivatives.

Chapter 14

Investing with Megatrends

I'm thrilled to include this chapter again in this 4th edition of *Stock Investing For Dummies*. Had you read this chapter in the previous edition and acted accordingly, you could have made a fortune (I kid you not). So I think that it earns an encore. A lot of this book is about making your own decisions and doing your own research, but what the heck — if I can save you some time and effort, why not? You can thank me later. (I don't just want you to read some stuff on "what is a stock" and so on; I want you to succeed!) Anyway, it's time to make you privy to what my research tells me are unfolding megatrends that offer the greatest potential rewards (or risks) for stock investors. This chapter provides some background on megatrends and talks about both bullish (up) and bearish (down) opportunities.

Setting the Stage for Megatrends

Only a handful of changes in your portfolio over the past four decades would have made you tremendously rich. Had you put your money into natural resources (such as gold, silver, and oil) at the beginning of the 1970s and let them stay put until the end of the decade, you would have made a fortune. Then, had you cashed in and switched to Japanese stocks in 1980 and held them for the rest of the decade, you would have made another fortune. Then, had you switched in 1990 to U.S. stocks for the entire decade, you would have made yet another fortune. What if you had cashed in your stocks in 2000? Well, for starters, you would have avoided huge losses in the down bear market.

What is a megatrend? A *megatrend* is a larger-than-life trend, a development that affects millions socially and economically, either now or in the near future. This change may be demographic, political, or technological (or some combination thereof), which, in turn, has a major economic impact. Stock investors take note because some companies can end up being big winners (or losers) as these megatrends unfold.

How about being bullish? During 2000–2006, real estate was in hyperactive bullish mode until the housing bubble popped and the devastation hit during 2007–2009. Precious metals and most commodities were the enduring bull market for 2000–2010. But that's all history now . . . what looks like a strong bull market for the second decade of the 21st century?

By and large, this decade will be a time of both great opportunity and great peril. As I write this, the U.S. economy is still in deep trouble with high unemployment, poor growth, and tremendous debt. Investors will have to be more cautious than ever, but opportunities for gains will be there. In the rest of this chapter, I get the chance to highlight the major areas to address. Here are some challenges for investors:

- Stubbornly high unemployment
- Rising inflation (as the dollar and other currencies are increased in supply)
- International conflict (ranging from the middle east to surprises across the globe)
- A sluggish or recessionary domestic economy
- Rising prices for natural resources (grains, metals, energy, lumber, and so on)

However, this decade has more to consider, including the following:

- **Debt, debt, and more debt** ($55 trillion as of September 2012 — more than three and a half times the U.S. gross domestic product [GDP] total of $14 trillion). The national debt for the federal government alone has exceeded $16 trillion as of October 2012! The U.S. is now the world's largest debtor nation.
- **The U.S. as a major importer** (versus being an exporter in the '70s)
- **China, Russia, Brazil, and India as major economic competitors** (and consumers of resources)
- **Domestic instability** due to the financial difficulties (and bankruptcies) of many municipalities and even some states (such as California)

> ✔ **More than 700 trillion dollars' worth of derivatives** (25 times larger than the world's total GDP)! Many of these derivatives, which are complicated investment vehicles, are arcane and ultra-risky.

> ✔ **Total Social Security and Medicare liabilities** (along with state and local pension liabilities) that are now projected to exceed $100 trillion. (Rising costs started in 2008 as the oldest baby boomers started to retire at age 62, and escalated in 2011 and beyond as more and more folks turned 65.)

This list isn't comprehensive due to space limitations. (Yikes! What's next? Finding out that your blind date has flesh-eating bacteria?!) Anyway, those preceding points are enough to make you understand that this investing environment has changed dramatically, and you need to refocus your overall game plan to keep your money growing. It also makes you want to race off to Gilligan's island!

You'll see two types of opportunities in the rest of this chapter: bullish and bearish. I recommend that you read Chapter 13 on sectors and industries as well. If I can't help you find the winning stocks, then by golly, I can at least show you what potential problem areas to stay away from.

Benefitting from Bullish Opportunities

Being bullish (or going "long") is the natural inclination for most investors. It's an easy concept — buy low, sell high. No rocket science there. The following sections don't identify every bullish opportunity, but they do cover the most obvious ones (at least to me).

In the examples in the following sections, I reference time frames of several years. Why? You'll see these stocks dip by 10 or 20 percent or more over a given short time frame, such as a few weeks or a few months. But investing wisely means that time ultimately will get the stock price to higher ground, especially if you ride the megatrends.

Honing in on human need

In 2011, the world population passed another milestone — 7 billion! Whew . . . think of all the mouths to feed . . . think food, water, clothing, shelter, and so on. Logical investing strategies based on demographics such as population tend to be solid winners.

An increasing total world population is only part of the picture. Think of the underlying sub-demographics. The growth of the middle class in some countries will have a major impact on demand for those things I refer to as "human need" investments. When you think of human need, you can think of commodities, energy, food, and water.

As long as most (or even all) of your portfolio is geared toward those goods and services that the public will need no matter how good or bad the economy is, you should do well in the long run. Remember, not *want*, but *need* — it's a safer bet in the coming years.

Commodities

Two countries that figure to have a mega-impact on the world in the near future are China and India. In the past ten years, these countries have put their economies on the fast track. Consider the following:

- ✔ They've generally turned away from socialism and a command economy and have turned to a free market or more capitalistic system.

- ✔ Industrialization, privatization, and profit incentives have ignited tremendous booms in these countries.

- ✔ Both nations' populations have continued to grow, with more than 3 billion people combined.

What do these facts mean for stock investors? Somebody has to sell them what they need. China, for example, has a voracious appetite for natural resources like building materials, copper, grain, and so on. Companies that have provided these needed goods and services do very well.

Of course, China and India are only a part of the world's emerging markets, but they're certainly the most important to Americans in terms of economic impact. They are indeed megatrends that will either help or hurt your portfolio. In the coming years, demand will likely continue to be strong, and investors will see the obvious positive implications for solid companies that meet this demand.

To find out more, check out the resources in Appendix A, such as Jim Rogers's book titled *Hot Commodities* (Random House). You can also conduct research at sites such as www.resourceinvestor.com and the commodities sections of www.marketwatch.com and www.bloomberg.com.

Energy

As I write this, North Dakota is experiencing a booming economy with an unemployment rate that's hovering around 3 percent (nice!). This status is particularly eye-opening because most of the other states are struggling with sluggish economies, high unemployment (ranging from 8 to 12 percent), and very difficult government budgets. A big part of North Dakota's success is that it has greatly expanded the ability to find and develop domestic energy.

For modern economies, energy — relatively cheap and plentiful energy — is like sweets and amusement parks . . . inseparable! Energy has been a minefield for our economy in recent years. Whether we're talking triple-digit crude oil, conflicts in the Middle East, or issues about off-shore drilling, we've had a love-hate relationship with fossil fuels. But we can't live without them . . . yet.

Fortunately for investors, the energy sector has more opportunities than problems. The energy sector actually has something for many different types of investors:

- ✔ **For environmentally conscious investors,** opportunities in "green energy" are certainly there, but patience will be necessary as the transition is slow. Our economy is huge and diverse, and transitioning to solar, wind, and similar sources of energy will take time. Many companies have not yet established consistent profits, growth, and product development, but that will come in due course. Cautious investors are better off looking for mutual funds and/or exchange-traded funds (ETFs; see Chapter 5) in this industry until leading companies and profitable technologies emerge.

- ✔ **For growth-oriented investors,** domestic energy production and new technologies in areas such as natural gas and shale oil are gaining traction and offer some good opportunities for growth. (Check out Chapter 8 for more about investing for growth.)

- ✔ **For income-oriented investors,** plenty of opportunities are available to mine (pardon the pun!). Many energy firms offer solid dividends, so do your research. Check out Chapter 9 on income investing (you know the drill! . . . sorry, I couldn't resist).

- ✔ **For conservative investors,** the large cap oil and gas companies are still good energy plays, and most of them are adapting well in the new and diverse energy environment. (Large cap companies are valued at $10 billion to $50 billion; see Chapter 1 for details.)

In the previous edition of this book, I brought up my concerns over peak oil, and those are still there. The world production of sweet crude oil (the primary staple of modern economies) has indeed hit its peak — supply is getting more and more difficult to find. As of October 2012, oil is still north of $80 a barrel. That will continue to be a drag on economic growth until alternate energy production kicks in in some meaningful way.

Overall, the energy sector for the foreseeable future offers strong opportunities for most stock investors. A good example is how energy has performed since the 2008 financial crisis. The price of oil fell to less than $40 a barrel in late 2008 but has risen 125 percent since. In the same time frame, leading oil and gas companies like Exxon Mobil (XOM), for example, went from around $61 per share to $90 in October 2012. That's a rise of about 47 percent (not including dividends). Not spectacular, but still a decent rise.

As you read this chapter, you may not be sure about what particular company you should invest in. If that's the case, why not consider a convenient way to invest in an entire industry or sector? A good consideration is an exchange-traded fund (ETF); see Chapter 5 for more details. An example is an ETF with the symbol XLE. XLE has a cross section of the largest public oil and gas companies, such as Exxon Mobil, Chevron, and others. In 2003, I bought XLE for $18 per share. By October 2012, it was at $75 (not including dividends along the way). Because of the new opportunities in the energy sector, more stock and ETF opportunities are surely on the way. You can do more research on this important megatrend with the resources listed in Appendix A.

Food and water

When the economy is tough and uncertain, it's a good idea to stick to profitable companies that sell stuff that people will buy no matter how good or bad the economy is. Food and water — you can't get more basic than that! This is a reference to "human need" that couldn't get more intimate. (I'm waiting for some good choices in oxygen because that's the only thing closer to real human need.) By sheer dint of demographics — more people! — food and water have good built-in demand.

Think about this example: Say you bought into the S&P 500 on January 1, 2008, and you also bought stocks in food and beverage companies. An easy way to reflect both investments is to use ETF proxys for each. Say that for the S&P 500, you bought the ETF "SPY," and you got the food and beverage ETF "PBJ." How did they fare from the beginning of 2008 to today (October 2012)?

ETF	January 1, 2008	October 31, 2012	Gain/Loss
S&P 500 (SPY)	$132.15	$141.35 *	Up 6.9%
Food/Bev. (PBJ)	$15.76	$19.75 *	Up 25.3 %

*Price is adjusted for dividends and stock splits.

The table clearly shows that human-need investing (represented by the food & beverage ETF "PBJ") outdid the generic S&P 500 (represented by the ETF "SPY") with a gain of 25.3 percent versus SPY's 6.9 percent gain. Investing in human need has fared well in recent years, and considering how the economy is unfolding during 2013–2014, it should have a prominent place in today's stock portfolio.

Going for gold and other precious metals

Over the ages, gold (and silver) has come to be synonymous with wealth. In modern times, gold has become known as an inflation hedge and investment insurance, especially during times of inflation and geopolitical uncertainty. After being in a 20-year bear market (from its high of $850 in 1980 to its low of $252 in 2000), gold has been in a long-term bull market since 2001. As the conditions for precious metals look compelling for the next few years, aggressive investors should be investigating gold stocks and ETFs. Why now?

Most of the countries of the world are currently in the process of expanding the supply of their currencies to (hopefully) mitigate the effects of a hobbled economy and of massive debt and pension burdens. More money supply growth means more inflation. More inflation means that precious metals become a bullish play.

Because gold does well in an inflationary environment, understanding inflation itself is important. Inflation isn't the price of things going up; it's the value of the currency going down. The reason it goes down in value is primarily because the government can print money at will, thereby increasing the money supply. When you significantly increase the money supply, you create a bullish environment for hard assets such as gold. (For more about inflation, see Chapter 15.)

Gold analysts such as Bill Murphy, Doug Casey, Jay Taylor, James Sinclair, and many others accurately forecasted that the price of gold would hit four figures (it did in March 2008) and that the current environment (circa 2012–2013) may see gold zigzagging to new highs in the coming years. If that's the case, gold-mining stocks and ETFs will perform very well (not unlike their heyday in the late 1970s). For conservative investors, consider large cap mining firms and ETFs. For the more daring, consider junior mining stocks. Do your research using the websites mentioned in Appendix A.

As an additional note, the general precious metals market is strong and is a good consideration for solid gains because of the current inflationary environment. I think that silver and even uranium (for energy) offer investors good opportunities. To find out more, check out my book *Precious Metals Investing For Dummies* (published by Wiley).

Looking at healthcare

I'm sure you've heard much about the "graying of America." This phrase obviously represents a firm megatrend in place. For stock investors, this megatrend is a purely demographic play, and the numbers are with them.

The number of people over the age of 50, and especially those considered senior citizens, represents the fastest growing segment of American society. The same megatrend is in place across the globe (especially in Europe). As more and more people move into this category, the idea that companies that serve this segment will also prosper becomes a no-brainer. Well-managed companies that run nursing homes and eldercare services will see their stocks rise.

Be careful about which healthcare firms you select because this sector includes stocks that are cyclical and also some that are defensive.

- ✔ **Cyclical:** Companies that sell expensive equipment (such as CAT scans or MRI technology) may not do that well in an economic downturn because hospitals and other healthcare facilities may not want to upgrade or replace their equipment. Therefore, healthcare companies that sell big-ticket items can be considered cyclical.

- ✔ **Defensive:** On the other hand, businesses that sell necessary items like medicine and bandages (such as pharmaceuticals and drug retailers) can be considered defensive. People who need medicine (such as aspirin or antacids) will buy it no matter how bad the economy is. In fact, people will probably buy even more aspirin and antacids in bad economic times.

Also be wary of political trends and government initiatives as they affect healthcare. In 2012, the Supreme Court substantially upheld the landmark healthcare legislation officially known as the Patient Protection and Affordable Care Act, and this means major changes for healthcare in 2013 and beyond. Whether this legislation remains intact still remains to be seen; a growing number of politicians are seeking to either discontinue it or (more likely) get it modified.

Whatever occurs, it's safe to say that healthcare will continue to be a major source of both concern and opportunity for investors. This is where your logic comes into play. Healthcare is a diverse sector; it will contain both winners and losers in the coming years. The U.S. may be slowly lurching toward socialized medicine. If this possibility develops, turn your bullish expectations into bearish ones. History (and my experience) tells me that a government takeover of an industry like healthcare spells danger for investors (and patients, too).

To find out more about healthcare opportunities, check out the industry and main stocks by using the resources in Appendix A.

Taking note of personal and national security

The horrific events of September 11, 2001, ushered in an era where Americans became mindful of the idea that the U.S. is an enduring target where extremists and militants bring harm directly onto its shores. You can't calculate the seriousness of this on most levels, but it has become a reality Americans deal with. This era brought entities Americans had never dealt with before, such as the Transportation Security Administration (TSA) and a greater presence of video cameras almost everywhere.

In addition, recent economic difficulties have engendered a situation where crime and fraud have clearly upticked and the populace is more mindful of personal safety. Recent data shows that gun purchases have hit record highs. In addition, many municipalities have experienced very bad financial times. Unfortunately, much of this was self-inflicted as these local governments spent more than the tax revenues they received. Consequently, many of them have had painful shortfalls in their budgets, and the result is cutbacks in their workforce (such as police and firemen).

The bottom line with all of these factors is that the public has seen fit to find more ways to increase its security. For stock investors, the objective is clear. Find those companies that are profitably filling this demand with security-related products and services.

The U.S. will continue to retool its military and seek ways to monitor, track, and attack terrorists. Defense companies that sell certain products and services will benefit. For publications that do a great job informing investors and speculators regarding the war economy, check out the U.S. & World Early Warning Report at www.chaostan.com.

Taking a Bearish Outlook

Stocks are versatile in that you can even make money when they go down in value. Techniques range from using put options to going short, or doing a short sale of stock (see Chapter 17). For traditional investors, the more appropriate strategy is first and foremost to avoid or minimize losses. Making money betting that a stock will fall is closer to speculating than actual investing, so all I want is for investors to see the pitfalls and act accordingly. The following sections offer cautionary alerts to keep you away from troubled areas in the economy (or to help you find speculative opportunities to short stocks).

The Dow Jones Industrial Average (DJIA) hit a high of 11,722 in January 2000 and, after seven roller-coaster years, hit an all-time high of 14,164.53 on October 9, 2007. (As of October 2012, the DJIA is about 13,100.) As you can see, the general market gain since January 2000 has been mediocre (although the roller-coaster ride has been unnerving for many). Although some stock groups have grown quite well, stocks in general have struggled, and some sectors have done rather poorly. Choosing the right sector is critical for your stock investing success (for more on sectors, check out Chapter 13).

Avoiding consumer discretionary sectors

When the economy is struggling or contracting and people are concerned about their financial situation, some sectors will undoubtedly suffer. If you have money tied up in stocks attached to companies in these sectors, you may suffer as well. In today's economic environment, I would generally avoid sectors such as "consumer discretionary," which refers to companies that sell products or services that people may want but usually don't need. In other words, when consumers (both individuals and organizations) have to make hard choices on tighter budgets, the first areas of spending that will logically shrink are those goods and services that simply aren't that necessary in people's daily lives.

Here's an example: In trying times, those who typically eat at fancy, expensive restaurants will cut back. Maybe they'll eat at fast food places or simply opt for good ol' home cooking. Multiply this choice by millions of consumers, and you see that high-end restaurants (and their stocks, if they're public companies) will see their fortunes sink. Your logic and common sense are very useful here.

Waiting for real estate to return

Real estate is a major sector, of course, but it has really been licking its wounds in recent years. Real estate may take a few years to truly recover before stock investors can see some obvious opportunities. I think that cautious investors should wait until the industry shows some consistent traction in terms of housing starts and a strong shrinkage in the national inventory of unsold property.

Are there opportunities for "contrarians" and speculators? Sure! Of course, the risks are still high, so if you're talking investing, then having some patience is a better bet for now.

To find out more about what's going on with this sector, check out www.realtor.com and www.realestatetopsites.com.

The great credit monster

Too much debt means that someone will get hurt. The unprecedented explosion in debt may have given the economy a huge boost in the late 1990s, but debt now poses great dangers for the rest of this decade. This massive debt problem is obviously tied to real estate. However, it goes much further. Individuals, companies, and government agencies are carrying too much debt for comfort. It's not just mortgage debt; it's also consumer, business, government, and margin debt. The latest addition to this horror show is college debt, which recently surpassed $1 trillion (as of September 2012).

With total debt now in the vicinity of more than $50 trillion, saying that a lot of this debt won't be repaid is probably a safe bet. Individual and institutional defaults will rock the economy and the financial markets. Bankruptcy is (and will continue to be) a huge issue.

Debt will (and does) weigh heavily on stocks, either directly or indirectly. Because every type of debt is now at record levels, no one is truly immune. Say you have a retail stock of a company that has no debt whatsoever. Are you immune? Not really, because consumer debt (credit cards, personal loans, and so on) is at an all-time high. If consumer spending declines, the retailer's sales go down, its profits shrink, and ultimately, its stock goes down.

Exposure to debt is quite pervasive. Check your 401(k) plan, your bond funds, and your insurance company's annuity. Why? Banks and mortgage companies issued trillions of dollars' worth of mortgages in recent years, but after the mortgages were issued, they were sold to other financial institutions. A huge number of mortgages were sold to the most obvious buyers, the Federal National Mortgage Association (FNM) and the Federal Mortgage Assurance Corporation (FRE). These giant, government-sponsored entities are usually referred to as "Fannie Mae" and "Freddie Mac." They were taken over in 2008 by the federal government because of gross mismanagement and overindebtedness (in the trillions!). Hmm . . . there goes that alarmist robot with the flailing arms again.

What's a stock investor to do?

- ✔ Well, remember that first commandment to avoid or minimize losses? Make sure that you review your portfolio and sell stocks that may get pulverized by the credit monster. That includes many banks and brokerage firms.

- ✔ Make sure that the companies themselves have no debt, low debt, or at least manageable debt. (Check their financial reports; see Chapter 12 for more details.)

- ✔ For the venturesome, seek shorting opportunities in those companies most exposed to the dangers of debt. (For more information on shorting, go to Chapter 17.)

Cyclical stocks

Another type of stock that I think you should be cautious about is cyclical stocks. Heavy equipment, automobiles, and technology tend to be cyclical and are very susceptible to downturns in the general economy. Conversely, cyclical stocks do very well when the economy is growing or on an upswing (hence the label).

As individuals and corporations get squeezed with more debt and less disposable income, hard choices need to be made. Ultimately, the result is that people buy fewer big-ticket items. That means that a company selling those items ends up selling less and earning less profit. This loss of profit, in turn, makes that company's stock go down.

In a struggling, recessionary economy, investing in cyclical stocks is like sunbathing on an anthill and using jam instead of sunblock — not a pretty picture.

Important Considerations for Bulls and Bears

I don't presume that stocks go straight up or that they zigzag upward indefinitely. Your due diligence is necessary for your success. Make sure that you're investing appropriately for your situation. If you're 35, heading into your peak earnings years, want to ride a home-run stock, and you understand the risks, then go ahead and speculate with that small cap gold mining stock or the solar power technology junior stock.

But if you're more risk averse or your situation is screaming out loud for you to be conservative, then don't speculate. Go instead with a more diversified portfolio of large cap stocks or get the ETF for that particular sector. And don't forget the trailing stop-loss strategy (see Chapter 17). 'Nuff said.

For those people who want to make money by going short in those sectors that look bearish, again take a deep breath and remember what's appropriate. Conservative investors simply avoid the risky areas. Aggressive investors or speculators may want to deploy profitable bearish strategies (with a portion of their investable funds). Here are some highlights for all of you.

Conservative and bullish

Being conservative and bullish is proper when you're in (or near) retirement, have a family to support, or live in a very large shoe with so many kids that you don't know what to do. After you choose a promising sector, just select large cap companies that are financially strong, are earning a profit, have low debt, and are market leaders. This entire book shows you how to do just that.

However, you may not like the idea of buying stocks directly. In that case, consider either sector mutual funds or ETFs (see Chapter 5). That way, you can choose the industry and effectively buy a basket of the top stocks in that area. ETFs have been a hot item lately, and I think that they're a great choice for most investors because they offer some advantages over mutual funds. For example, you can put stop-loss orders on them (see Chapter 17) or borrow against them in your stock portfolio. Check with your financial advisor to see whether ETFs are appropriate for you.

Aggressive and bullish

If you're aggressive and bullish, you want to buy stocks directly. For real growth potential, look at mid caps or small caps. Keep in mind that you're speculating, so you understand the downside risk but are willing to tolerate it because the upside potential can reward you so handsomely. Few things in the investment world give you a better gain than a supercharged stock in a hot sector.

Conservative and bearish

For many (if not most) investors, making money on a falling market isn't generally a good idea. Doing so takes a lot of expertise and risk tolerance. Really, for conservative investors, the key word is safety. Analyze your portfolio with an advisor you trust and sell the potentially troubled stocks. If you're not sure what to do on a particular stock, then (at the very least) put in stop-loss orders and make them GTC (good-til-canceled). (See Chapter 17 for details.) As odd as it sounds, sometimes losing less than others makes you come out ahead if you play it right.

For example, look at the bear market that hit the U.S. in the mid-1970s. In 1974–1975, the stock market fell 45 percent. Stocks didn't recover until 1982. If you had a stock that was at $100, it would have fallen to $55 and not returned to $100 until seven or eight years later. Whew! Sometimes just burying your money in the backyard sounds like genius. What if you had a stop loss at $90? You would have gotten out with a minimal loss and could have reinvested the money elsewhere (such as in bonds or CDs) and looked much brighter than your neighbor feverishly digging for money in his backyard.

Aggressive and bearish

Being aggressive in a bearish market isn't for the faint of heart. However, this is where the quickest fortunes have been made by some of history's greatest investors. Going short can make you great money when the market is bearish, but it can sink you if you're wrong. I usually don't tell my clients and students to short a stock because it can backfire. Yes, ways to go short with less risk are out there, but I prefer to buy put options.

Put options are a way to make money with limited risk when you essentially make a bet that an investment (such as stocks) will go down. Obviously, options go beyond the scope of this book, but at least let me give you some direction, because there's an appropriate options strategy for most stock port-folios. You can find great (free) tutorials on using options at websites such as the Chicago Board Options Exchange (www.cboe.com) and the Options Industry Council (www.888options.com).

Chapter 15

The Big Economic and Political Picture

In This Chapter

▶ Looking at the effects of politics and government on stocks

▶ Checking out a few handy political resources

*P*olitics can be infuriating, disruptive, meddlesome, corrupting, and harmful. Don't let that fool you — it has its bad side, too! Even if politics doesn't amuse or interest you, you can't ignore it. If you aren't careful, it can wreak great havoc on your portfolio. Politics wields great influence on the economic and social environments, which in turn affects how companies succeed or fail. This success or failure in turn either helps or hurts your stock's price. Politics (manifested in taxes, regulations, price controls, capital controls, and other government actions) can make or break a company, industry, or sector quicker than any other external force.

What people must understand (especially government policymakers) is that a new tax, law, regulation, or government action has a *macro* effect on a stock, an industry, a sector, or even an entire economic system, whereas a company has a *micro* effect on an economy. The following gives you a simple snapshot of these effects:

Politics → policy → economy → sector → industry → company → stock → stock investor

Now, this chapter doesn't moralize about politics or advocate a political point of view; after all, this book is about stock investing. In general, policies can be good or bad regardless of their effect on the economy — some policies are enacted to achieve greater purposes even if they kick you in the wallet. However, in the context of this chapter, politics is covered from a cause-and-effect perspective: How does politics affect prosperity in general and stock investing in particular?

A proficient stock investor can't — must not — look at stocks as though they exist in a vacuum. My favorite example of this rule is the idea of fish in a lake. You can have a great fish (your stock) among a whole school of fish (the stock market) in a wonderful lake (the economy). But what if the lake gets polluted (bad policy)? What happens to the fish? Politics controls the lake and can make it hospitable — or dangerous — for the participants. You get the point. The example may sound too simple, yet it isn't. So many people — political committees, corporate managers, bureaucrats, and politicians — still get this picture so wrong time and time again, to the detriment of the economy and stock investors. Heck, I don't mind if they get it wrong with *their* money, but their actions make it tough for *your* money.

Although the two inexorably get intertwined, I do what I can to treat politics and economics as separate issues.

Tying Together Politics and Stocks

The campaigns heat up. Democrats, Republicans, and smaller parties vie for your attention and subsequent votes. Conservatives, liberals, socialists, moderates, and libertarians joust in the battlefield of ideas. But after all is said and done, voters make their decisions. Election Day brings a new slate of politicians into office, and they in turn joust and debate on new rules and programs in the legislative halls of power. Before and after election time, investors must keep a watchful eye on the proceedings. In the following sections, I explain some basic political concepts that relate to stock investing.

Seeing the general effects of politics on stock investing

For stock investors, politics manifests itself as a major factor in investment-making decisions in the ways shown in Table 15-1.

Table 15-1	Politics and Investing
Possible Legislation	*Effect on Investing*
Taxes	Will a new tax affect a particular stock (industry, sector, or economy)? Generally, more or higher taxes ultimately have a negative impact on stock investing. Income taxes and capital gains taxes are good examples.
Laws	Will Congress (or, in some instances, state legislatures) pass a law that will have a negative impact on a stock, the industry, the sector, or the economy? Price controls — laws that set the price of a product, service, or commodity — are examples of negative laws. I discuss price controls in more detail later in this chapter.
Regulations	Will a new (or existing) regulation have a negative (or positive) effect on the stock of your choice? Generally, more or tougher regulations have a negative impact on stocks.
Government spending and debt	If government agencies spend too much or misallocate resources, they may create greater burdens on society, which in turn will be bearish for the economy and the stock market.
Money supply	The U.S. money supply — the dollars you use — is controlled by the Federal Reserve. It's basically a governmental agency that serves as America's central bank. How can it affect stocks? Increasing or decreasing the money supply results in either an inflationary or a deflationary environment, which can help or hurt the economy, specific sectors and industries, and your stock picks.
Interest rates	The Federal Reserve has crucial influence here. It can raise or lower key interest rates that in turn can have an effect on the entire economy and the stock market. When interest rates go up, it makes credit more expensive for companies. When interest rates go down, companies can get cheaper credit, which can be better for profits.
Government bailouts	A bailout is when the government intervenes directly in the marketplace and uses either tax money or borrowed money to bail out a troubled enterprise. This is generally a negative because funds are diverted by force from the healthier private economy to an ailing enterprise.

Politics, stocks, and "taxmageddon"

As I write this edition, the United States is in the throes of the 2012 presidential election campaign (ugh . . . it's time for an adult beverage). Stock investors (both individuals and portfolio managers) will make decisions based on the outcomes . . . especially who ends up in the White House. By the time you read this in 2013, either the stock market was happy with the decision or it wasn't. However, I will take a leap of faith and say that if the winner doesn't reverse the pending effects of what is referred to as "taxmaggedon" (a major and worrisome batch of tax increases scheduled to go into effect as of January 2013), then the effect on the economy (hence the stock market) will be very negative. Whether this reversal will actually happen or not remains to be seen as this book goes to press, but it's safe to write that increased taxes (especially if they're too onerous) will have a negative impact on stocks (regardless of which political party dominates the presidency and/or congress). We must remember (and we must remind politicians . . . constantly) that increasing taxes means taking money out of the private sector (where goods and services are produced) and shifting these funds to venues (good or bad) that are not productive for the growth of the economy.

When many of the factors in Table 15-1 work in tandem, they can have a magnified effect that can have tremendous consequences for your stock portfolio. Alert investors keep a constant vigil when the legislature is open for business, and they adjust their portfolios accordingly.

Ascertaining the political climate

The bottom line is that you ignore political realities at your own (economic) risk. To be and stay aware, ask yourself the following questions about the stock of each company in which you invest:

- ✔ What laws will directly affect my stock investment adversely?

- ✔ Will any laws affect the company's industry and/or sector?

- ✔ Will any current or prospective laws affect the company's sources of revenue?

- ✔ Will any current or prospective laws affect the company's expenses or supplies?

- ✔ Am I staying informed about political and economic issues that may possibly have a negative impact on my investment?

- ✔ Will such things as excessive regulations, price controls, or new taxes have a negative impact on my stock's industry?

Here's an example: Oil and gas service and exploration companies benefited from the need of the U.S. for more energy supplies. But investment opportunities didn't stop there. As overseas oil (the type we use most, which is sweet crude oil) became more problematic to access (due to shrinking supplies and growing geopolitical tensions), alternative and domestic sources of energy became more desirable. New sources of energy, such as shale oil, and new ways to extract traditional energy, such as natural gas, ignited an energy boom in the Midwest. Consequentially, the stock of those public energy-related companies did well. The interplay between economics and politics was interesting to view at the state level.

In the midst of a slumping national economy, North Dakota has a booming state economy (fueled by an energy exploration boom operated by the private sector). The state's unemployment rate has fallen below 4 percent compared to a national rate of more than 8 percent. Meanwhile, in states like California, the contrast has been stark. In spite of having a large natural supply of energy (such as oil), the state government in California has banned or greatly restricted any companies from exploring this abundant supply. Consequently, many of the firms have left the state to head to friendlier jurisdictions, and the state has dealt with an unemployment rate much higher than the national average.

Regardless of the merits (or demerits) of the situation, investors must view it through the lens of economic causes and effects, which in turn leads to their decisions on which companies (and their stocks) are impacted positively or negatively.

Distinguishing between nonsystemic and systemic effects

Politics can affect your investments in two basic ways: nonsystemic and systemic.

- ✔ *Nonsystemic* means that the system isn't affected but a particular participant is affected.
- ✔ *Systemic* means that all the players in the system are affected. Laws typically affect more than just one company or group of companies; rather, they affect an entire industry, sector, or the entire economy — more "players" in the economic system.

In this case, the largest system is the economy at large: To a lesser extent, an entire industry or sector can be the system that's affected. Politics imposes itself (through taxes, laws, regulations, and so on) and can have an undue influence on all (or most) of the members of that system.

Playing monopoly

Government action against large companies for real (or alleged) abuses has happened many times. Longtime investors remember how companies such as IBM (in the 1970s) and Microsoft (during 1999 and 2000) faced monopolistic allegations. And in 2004, the New York attorney general targeted insurer American International Group, Inc. (AIG) for fraud, bid-rigging, and other alleged improprieties. In a few months, AIG's stock fell from $74 to a low of $50 in April 2005. How irony moves in strange ways! In 2008, the federal government bailed out AIG with an $80 billion loan as the company was pulled away from the brink of collapse. As for AIG's stock? It went DOA.

The federal government is a massive entity, and it has trillions at its disposal (whether from taxpayer funds or unlimited borrowing). When it targets a company, regardless of the merits of the case, avoid investing in that company until the trouble has passed. Investors should be wary when the government starts making noise about any company and potential legal actions against it.

Nonsystemic effects

Say that you decide to buy stock in a company called Golf Carts Unlimited, Inc. (GCU). You believe that the market for golf carts has great potential and that GCU stands to grow substantially. How can politics affect GCU?

What if politicians believe that GCU is too big and that it controls too much of the golf cart industry? Maybe they view GCU as a monopolistic entity and want the federal government to step in to shrink GCU's reach and influence for the sake of competition and for the ultimate benefit of consumers. Maybe the government believes that GCU engages in unfair or predatory business practices and that it's in violation of antitrust (or antimonopoly) laws. If the government acts against GCU, the action is a nonsystemic issue: The action is directed toward the participant (in this case, GCU) and not the golf cart industry in general. (See the nearby sidebar for more about monopolies.)

What happens if you're an investor in GCU? Does your stock investment suffer as a result of government action directed against the company? Let's just say that the stock price will "hook left" and could end up "in the sand trap."

Systemic effects

Say that politicians want to target the golf industry for intervention because they maintain that golf should be free or close to free for all to participate in and that a law must be passed to make it accessible to all, especially those people who can't afford to play. So to remedy the situation, the following law is enacted: "Law #67590305598002 declares that from this day forward, all golf courses must charge only one dollar for any golfer who chooses to participate."

That law sounds great to any golfer. But what are the unintended effects when such a law becomes reality? Many people may agree with the sentiment of the law, but what about the actual cause-and-effect aspects of it? Obviously, all things being equal, golf courses will be forced to close. Staying in business is uneconomical if their costs are higher than their income. If they can't charge any more than a dollar, how can they possibly stay open? Ultimately (and ironically), no one can play golf. The law would be a "triple bogey" for sure!

What happens to investors of Golf Carts Unlimited, Inc.? If the world of golf shrinks, demand for golf carts shrinks as well. The value of GCU's stock will certainly be stuck in a sand trap.

Examples of politics creating systemic problems are endless, but you get the point. Companies are ultimately part of a system, and those that control or maintain the rules overseeing that system can have far-reaching effects. All investors are advised to be vigilant about systemic effects on their stocks.

Understanding price controls

Stock investors should be very wary of price controls, which are a great example of regulation. A *price control* is a fixed price on a particular product, commodity, or service mandated by the government.

Price controls have been tried continuously throughout history, and they've continuously been removed because they ultimately do more harm than good. It's easy to see why (unless, of course, you're an overzealous politician or bureaucrat eager to apply them). Imagine that you run a business that sells chairs, and a law is passed that states, "From this point onward, chairs can only be sold for $10." If all your costs stay constant at $9 or less, the regulation wouldn't be harmful at that point. However, price controls put two dynamics in motion:

✔ First, the artificially lower price encourages consumption — more people buy chairs.

✔ Second, production is discouraged. What company wants to make chairs if it can't sell them for a decent profit (or at the very least cover its costs)?

What happens to the company with a fixed sales price (in this example, $10) coupled with rising costs? Profits shrink, and depending on how long the price controls are in effect, the company eventually experiences losses. The chair producer is eventually driven out of business. The chair-building industry shrinks, and the result is a chair shortage. Profits (and jobs) soon vanish. So what happens if you own stock in a company that builds chairs? I'll just say that if I tell you how badly the stock price is pummeled, you'd better be sitting down (if, of course, you have a chair).

Central banks

Central banks are the governmental entities that are charged with the responsibility of managing the supply of currency that's used in the economy. The problem with this is the tendency of central banks to overproduce the supply of currency. This overproduction leads to the condition of having too much currency, which leads to the problematic condition of inflation. If too many units of currency (such as dollars or yen, for example) are chasing a limited supply of goods and services, consumers end up paying more money for goods and services (ugh!), but this is the reality that occurs when central banks (in the case of the U.S., the Federal Reserve) create too much of the currency.

Poking into Political Resources

Ignoring what's going on in the world of politics is like sleepwalking near the Grand Canyon — a bad idea! You have to be aware of what's going on. Governmental data, reports, and political rumblings are important clues to the kind of environment that's unfolding for the economy and financial markets. Do your research with the following resources so you can stay a step ahead in your stock-picking strategies.

Government reports to watch out for

The best analysts look at economic reports from both private and government sources. The following sections list some reports/statistics issued by the government to watch out for. For private reports and commentaries on the economy, investors can turn to sources such as the American Institute for Economic Research (www.aier.org), the Mises Institute (www.mises.org), and Moody's (www.economy.com). Usually general sources, such as MarketWatch (www.marketwatch.com) and Bloomberg (www.bloomberg.com), are good as well.

Alas, government reports aren't totally reliable because errors and/or purposeful fudging happen and usually have a political component to them. Take the gross domestic product (GDP), for instance. In the second quarter of 2008, the GDP was reported at a surprisingly robust 3.3 percent — a very healthy number given the fact that the economy was struggling at the time. A closer examination revealed that the GDP was calculated using a very low inflation rate of just 1.2 percent, a ten-year low. Yet in a separate report for the same quarter, the same agency (the Bureau of Labor Statistics, or BLS) reported that inflation was at 5.6 percent, a 17-year high! Had the BLS used this more believable inflation rate, the GDP would have actually been at –1.1 percent. I doubt that the fact that 2008 was an election year is a coincidence because games like this have been played by administrations of all stripes dating back to Franklin Roosevelt's day. A good way to round out your economic analysis is to compare government data from other sources that scrutinize the same data. One that I like is Shadow Government Statistics (www.shadowstats.com).

GDP

Gross domestic product (GDP), which measures a nation's total output of goods and services for the quarter, is considered the broadest measure of economic activity. Although the U.S. GDP is measured in dollars (as of 2012, annual GDP is in the ballpark of $14 trillion), it's usually quoted as a percentage. You typically hear a news report that says something like, "The economy grew by 2.5 percent last quarter." Because the GDP is an important overall barometer of the economy, the number should be a positive one. The report on the GDP is released quarterly by the U.S. Department of Commerce (www.commerce.gov).

You should regularly monitor the GDP along with economic data that relates directly to your stock portfolio. The following list gives some general guidelines for evaluating the GDP:

- ✔ **More than 3 percent:** This number indicates strong growth and bodes well for stocks. At 5 percent or higher, the economy is sizzling!

- ✔ **1 to 3 percent:** This figure indicates moderate growth and can occur either as the economy is rebounding from a recession or as it's slowing down from a previously strong period.

- ✔ **0 percent or negative (as low as –3 percent):** This number isn't good and indicates that the economy either isn't growing or is actually shrinking a bit. A negative GDP is considered *recessionary* (meaning that the economy's growth is receding).

- ✔ **Less than –3 percent:** A GDP this low indicates a very difficult period for the economy. A GDP less than –3 percent, especially for two or more quarters, indicates a serious recession or possibly a depression.

Looking at a single quarter isn't that useful. Track the GDP over many consecutive quarters to see which way the general economy is trending. When you look at the GDP for a particular quarter of a year, ask yourself whether it's better (or worse) than the quarter before. If it's better (or worse), then ask yourself to what extent it has changed. Is it dramatically better (or worse) than the quarter before? Is the economy showing steady growth, or is it slowing? If several quarters show solid growth, the overall economy is generally bullish.

Higher economic growth typically translates into better sales and profits for companies, which in turn bodes well for their stocks (and, of course, the investors that hold these stocks).

Traditionally, if two or more consecutive quarters show negative growth (an indication that economic output is shrinking), the economy is considered to be in a recession. A recession can be a painful necessity; it usually occurs when the economy can't absorb the total amount of goods being produced because of too much excess production. A bear market in stocks usually accompanies a recession.

The GDP is just a rough estimate at best. It can't possibly calculate all the factors that go into economic growth. For example, crime has a negative effect on economic growth, but it's not reflected in the GDP. Still, most economists agree that the GDP provides an adequate ballpark snapshot of the overall economy's progress.

Unemployment

The National Unemployment Report is provided by the Bureau of Labor Statistics (www.bls.gov). It gives investors a snapshot of the health and productivity of the economy.

The Consumer Price Index

The Consumer Price Index (CPI) is a statistic that tracks the prices of a representative basket of goods and services monthly. This statistic, which is also computed by the Bureau of Labor Statistics, is meant to track price inflation. *Inflation* is the expansion of the money supply. This is referred to as *monetary inflation,* and it usually leads to *price inflation,* which means that the price of goods and services rises. Inflation, therefore, is not the price of goods and services going up; it's actually the price or value of money going down. Investors should pay attention to the CPI because a low-inflation environment is generally good for stocks (and bonds, too), whereas high inflation is generally more favorable for sectors such as commodities and precious metals.

Websites to surf

To find out about new laws being passed or proposed, check out Congress and what's going on at its primary websites: the U.S. House of Representatives (www.house.gov) and the U.S. Senate (www.senate.gov). For presidential information and proposals, check the White House's website at www.whitehouse.gov.

You also may want to check out THOMAS, the service provided by the Library of Congress, at http://thomas.loc.gov. THOMAS is a search engine that helps you find any piece of legislation, either by bill number or keyword. This search engine is an excellent way to find out whether an industry is being targeted for increased regulation or deregulation. In the late 1980s, real estate was hit hard when the government passed new regulations and tax rules (related stocks went down). When the telecom industry was deregulated in the mid-1990s, the industry grew dramatically (related stocks went up).

Turn to the following sources for economic data:

- Conference Board, www.conferenceboard.org
- U.S. Department of Commerce, www.doc.gov
- The Federal Reserve, www.federalreserve.gov
- Free Lunch, www.freelunch.com
- Grandfather Economic report, www.grandfathereconomicreport.com

You can find more resources in Appendix A. The more knowledge you pick up about how politics and government actions can help (or harm) an investment, the better you'll be at growing (and protecting) your wealth.

Part IV
Investment Strategies and Tactics

The 5th Wave   By Rich Tennant

EARLY INVESTORS TRACKING A STOCK

©RICHTENNANT

In this part . . .

Successful stock investing entails more than choosing
a particular stock — how you go about doing it matters, too. Successful investors go beyond merely picking
good stocks and watching the financial news. They implement techniques and strategies that help them either minimize losses or maximize gains (hopefully both). The
chapters in this part introduce some of the most effective
investing techniques (including brokerage orders and
trade triggers) and describe some smart ways to hold
onto more of your profits when tax time rolls around.

Chapter 16

Choosing among Investing, Trading, and Speculating

*Y*ou may have heard of stock trading and wondered how it compares to stock investing. While I'm at it, I may as well toss another verbal hand grenade — stock speculating. Rest assured that trading and investing are two different animals (speculating is a hybrid, and it can have a foot in both trading and investing).

Trading is advantageous when you're looking to profit from short-term swings in the market due to volatility. However, trading can be dangerous because the market's short-term movements can be quite unpredictable. The only reason I'm including trading in this book is because you, dear reader, should get some do's and don'ts in this short-term venture. If you're going to trade stocks, you should have some guidelines to keep the downside to a minimum. I explain what you need to know about trading and speculating in this chapter.

Distinguishing among Investing, Trading, and Speculating

Stock investing, stock trading, and stock speculating may sound similar, but they're actually pretty different:

- ✔ **Stock investing:** Investing looks primarily at fundamentals (earnings, sales, industry outlook, and so on), which tend to be long-term drivers of stock prices. The long-term investor waits out the zigzags as long as the bullish outlook and the general uptrend are intact. The good part is that investing involves fewer transaction costs (you aren't constantly buying and selling stock) and usually lower taxes (long-term capital gains typically are taxed at a lower rate than short-term gains). The bad part is that sometimes the stock can correct (go down temporarily) or have periods of flat performance, which the long-term investor has to patiently tolerate.

- ✔ **Stock trading:** In trading, much more activity takes place during a range of a few days, weeks, or months. Traders may dump losers immediately and cash out winners to lock in some profit before the next dip in price. Trading can mean more costs due to frequent commissions and short-term taxable gains. For trading, the fundamentals are either not a factor or at best a secondary or minor factor because short-term movements in a stock price are more geared to momentum and sentiment, which are reflected in the data found in charts along with price and volume statistics.

- ✔ **Stock speculating:** Speculating is a form of "financial gambling," which may sound too harsh, but at least helps you understand that you're not investing but making an educated guess about which way the price will go on a particular investment. Speculating is typically associated with a short-term time frame (like trading), but it can also be long-term.

   I think it's safe to say that much of trading is short-term speculating and that speculating is a much smaller dimension of investing. In other words, speculating simply overlaps both worlds (trading and investing), but the much greater overlap is in the world of trading.

The following sections give you the full scoop on the differences among investing, trading, and speculating.

The time factor

When I first started investing in stocks, it was easy to delineate what was *short term, intermediate term,* and *long term:*

- ✔ **Short term** was less than one year (some would say less than two years).
- ✔ **Intermediate term** was usually one to three years or one to five years, depending on your personal outlook.
- ✔ **Long term** was beyond that time frame (longer than five years).

In recent years, however, investors have become very impatient. For some investors, short term is now measured in days, intermediate term in weeks, and long term in months. In the old days (here's where I date myself), investors were akin to cooks using the crockpot; today, they use the microwave. But these people are actually traders, not investors. If an investment does well, they sell it immediately and move on to another (hopefully) profitable investment. If the investment is down, they sell it immediately to minimize losses and move on to (hopefully) greener pastures elsewhere.

There's no such thing as a three-month investment when it comes to stocks. Stocks require time for the marketplace to discover them. Sometimes great stocks see their prices move very little because the market (again, millions of individual and institutional investors) hasn't noticed them yet. In trading, on the other hand, you jump in and out relatively quickly. Typical trades occur over the span of a few days or a few weeks. Of course, if a position you take on grows more profitable and your expectations are positive, you can stay in longer. But many experienced traders won't tempt fate and stay in too long because a reversal of fortune can always occur, so they're not shy about cashing out and taking a profit.

What's the time factor for speculating? Usually it's short term (less than a year), but it can be much longer. Speculating with options is short term by definition because options have a finite shelf life (even long-term options are typically two years or less). However, an investor who's speculating using stocks (such as small cap stocks) can do so for a longer term because no finite time period is involved. It's up to the individual to ultimately decide, but keep in mind that the research you do will be the major deciding factor.

The psychology factor

In investing, you can be very analytical. You can look at a stock and its fundamentals and then at the prospects for the stock's industry and the general economy, and you can make a good choice knowing that you're not worried about the price going up or down a few percentage points in the next few days or weeks. If you've done your homework, your stock will probably go up and do well over the long haul.

In stock investing, the focus is on the underlying company, which is very real and measurable. I look at the underlying value of a company and decide whether the stock price is fair to pay. If I believe that the stock is worth $50 per share based on factors such as net worth, sales, profits, and so on and I can buy it at $40, then that's a good deal.

Now if that stock goes to $38 in the short term, I won't sweat it because from the start, the fundamentals have indicated to me that it's worth $50 per share. The psychology here is simple: I got a good deal, and if I've chosen well, sooner or later the market will discover my gem, and market action (more buyers than sellers) will push the stock higher to its true intrinsic value.

Trading is different. Trading involves looking at stocks that have the ability to move quickly, regardless of the direction; you look very little, if at all, at the company's underlying fundamentals. The reason for this lack of scrutiny is that seasoned traders want to make money quickly and capitalize on crowd psychology and market movements. It matters little whether investors are bidding up or down; the trader is primarily looking for a stock with momentum.

Stock trading is indeed short-term speculating because the trader is making an educated guess about something that's not readily measured: figuring out which way the market (again, a group of buyers and sellers) will move.

Some people say that stock traders do have ways of measuring activity for a reliable forecast of a stock's movement (using technical analysis, which is covered later in this chapter and in Chapter 10). However, technical analysis isn't always reliable as a predictive tool because there's no statistical means to accurately and consistently gauge the unpredictable impulses and acts of human beings. In other words, if you can't figure out what your spouse or kid is doing and why he or she is doing it, no worries! Stock traders can't figure out your kid or your spouse . . . or the sudden (short-term) impulses of a group of mercurial folks known as buyers and sellers.

I'm not saying that trading is a hopeless pursuit; I'm saying that the prudent trader doesn't make large bets on a single outcome (such as a stock rising or falling in a given day or week) because no one is 100 percent sure. A successful trader makes a number of "bets" on a number of different outcomes (bullish or bearish) to increase the chances of success.

Checking out an example

The stock investor takes the long view and stays patient and focused. As I try to stress throughout this book, investing should be measured in years, and the stock's *fundamentals* (a company's profits, sales, industry, and so on) are the foundation. A patient and successful investor holds on as the stock zigzags upward. When the inevitable correction occurs, a successful investor either just waits it out or takes that moment as a buying opportunity and adds shares to her holdings. In a bullish (up) outlook, the investor expects the stock to generally trend upward. If the investor expects a stock to have a downward path, then obviously she simply avoids it.

The stock trader sees things differently. The trader may indeed be just as bullish on a particular stock but may also bet on the occasional pullback or correction that's typical of most stocks. The trader may buy 100 shares of a stock and keep it as a core holding, but he may also make different bets on its price movement.

For an example, take a look at the chart in Figure 16-1. This is a chart of Zig Zag Corporation (ZZC), and it's helpful in showing you how investing and trading behave differently during the same time frame.

Figure 16-1:
A chart tracking the movements of ZZC stock.

What an investor would do

An investor would have bought ZZC stock in 2011 and held on. As long as the fundamentals don't change, the investor just "buys right and sits tight." Although some traders may smirk at such a simple strategy, it's a time-tested approach. Look at billionaire Warren Buffet for a great example of this. He has been known to hold stocks for decades. Many investors (and traders, too) envy his extraordinary success, but relatively few try to emulate it. Patience and discipline aren't always popular or fashionable in investing, but a patient, disciplined approach has proven to be superior to many trading systems that tell you to jump in and jump out.

What a trader would do

Looking at Figure 16-1, how would successful traders have performed with ZZC? The trader may have started off as an investor and made that initial investment in the stock. As time passed, the trader would have watched technical indicators to time an entry or exit point. A *technical indicator* is a result of a mathematical calculation based on prices and the volume of trading, typically displayed as a chart. (See the later section "On the charts: Technical analysis.")

Stock traders typically use options (such as calls and puts) because they're cheap and can provide a magnified move with the underlying stock. In other words, options are a form of leverage, meaning that the price swing can be greater (up or down) than the move in the underlying stock. If a stock moves up 10 percent, then an option (in this case a call option) could go up 20 percent or more. Of course, if the stock goes down 10 percent, then that same option could easily go down 20 percent or more.

What are call and put options?

- **A call option** is a bet that a particular stock (or exchange-traded fund) will go up during the life of the option.

- **A put option** is a bet that a particular stock (or exchange-traded fund) will go down during the life of the option.

Think of the following (very rough) rules of thumb:

- If the stock goes up 10 percent, a call option on that stock could go up 20 percent. Of course, a put option on that same stock would lose 20 percent (or more).

- If the stock goes down 10 percent, a call option could go down 20 percent. Of course, a put option on that same stock would gain 20 percent (or more).

- If the stock stays flat or neutral, both the call and put options would start to lose value because options have a finite life and can potentially be worthless by the time they expire.

Referring back to Figure 16-1, the trader may have seen his stock rise from about $55 per share in October 2011 to $70 in December. Technical indicators may have flashed that the stock was overbought. Some traders would have cashed in and sat with the cash, waiting for the next opportunity. Other traders would have kept the stock but cashed in any call options that were purchased before that time frame for a nice profit. The money from cashing out the sale of the call options would sit waiting for the next entry point. Perhaps the trader would then use the money to purchase put options, betting that a correction was soon due. Then you see the huge move up by ZZC starting at about $70 in December 2011 and hitting $115 in October 2012 before correcting in a zigzag fashion down to about $73 in February 2013.

Had the trader employed both calls and puts, he would have had plenty of opportunities for profit. During the summer of 2012, the call options would have been profitable and could have been cashed out. In that scenario, a call option could easily reward the astute trader with triple-percentage gains. Of course, the puts in the same time frame would have greatly lost value. Heading into the November 2012–February 2013 period, the bearish strategies would have paid off because put options would rise in value as the underlying asset (in this case the stock of ZZC) declined.

As you can see, the successful trader must diligently monitor his positions and frequently enter more than one position on the same stock to try to capitalize on the stock's movements. Whenever you take opposing positions on the same security, you're doing a form of hedging. Hedging takes into consideration the idea that the market can easily go against you, which is an especially likely scenario if the market is volatile. In that case, why not profit from the move?

Keep in mind that any profits are offset by any losses from options that lose value (or expire worthless) and by transaction costs.

Scores of books have been written about options, so I won't go into great detail here, but you should get familiar with options, especially if short-term speculating or trading greatly interests you. You can start with *Trading Options For Dummies* by George A. Fontanills, published by Wiley.

Utilizing the Tools of the Trade(r)

As you can judge from the example I provide earlier in this chapter, successful trading requires lots of diligent attention. Because stocks can go all over the place, the trader uses various tools to determine entry and exit points. I cover some of those tools and strategies in the following sections.

On the charts: Technical analysis

The most common tool of short-term speculators and traders is technical analysis. *Technical analysis* looks at the recent price movements and volume of trading for particular securities and commodities. The price movements are depicted on charts, so "charting a security" is a common practice among those who use technical analysis.

The technical analyst uses some useful short-term indicators, including

- ✔ **Moving averages** to gauge the general trend for a particular stock. Typical moving averages are the 10-day, 20-day, 50-day, and 200-day averages. Stocks that stay above these averages tend to be bullish, whereas stocks that keep falling below these averages tend to be bearish.

- ✔ **Relative Strength Indicators (RSI)** to see whether a stock is considered oversold or overbought. A technical analyst sees an oversold stock as a buying opportunity and an overbought stock as a selling opportunity.

Technical analysis is a complex topic, and although I cover it in Chapter 10, I just can't do it justice. I don't mean to shortchange it, because it's worthy of study for serious traders. I mention it here because traders should be aware of it, regardless of how extensively they use it. I strongly recommend that serious traders do some extensive research on the topic. Consider starting your research with the latest edition of *Technical Analysis For Dummies* by Barbara Rockefeller (Wiley).

As most longtime readers probably know by now, I'm not an ardent fan of technical analysis. Don't get me wrong; I respect it as a short-term trading tool. It can be remarkably useful over a period of a few weeks or months. However, it's not that useful for long-term investing. Yes, you can use it to maximize or time an entry or exit point, but over the long haul, a company's fundamentals are the primary drivers of the stock's price. When you look at the pantheon of consistently successful investors in history, it's no accident that most of them use fundamental analysis and are into some form of value investing.

Fast moves: Brokerage orders

Because trading in the market's short-term gyrations can be a fast-moving activity, it pays to get proficient with brokerage orders and trading triggers to help you manage your trading portfolio and take advantage of the market's swift moves.

The moment after a diligent trader buys a stock or an option, she'll enter her next order very quickly — often even before the stock has made a major move. For example, if she buys a stock for $50 at 10 a.m. on a weekday morning, she may enter a stop-loss order at, say, $45 at 11 a.m. and simultaneously put in a sell order at $60. That way she can limit the loss to $5 per share and maybe catch a $10 profit on the upside. These moves are possible now due to the sophisticated technology that most brokers have on their websites.

That's just an example of what you can do with brokerage orders. Find out more about brokerage orders and trade triggers in Chapters 17 and 18.

Help is here: Advisory services

You don't have to go it alone with your trading strategies because the world is filled with advisory services, newsletters, and websites that cater to the art and science of short-term trading. Some notable ones that I respect include Elliott Wave International (www.elliottwave.com) and Roger Wiegand's Trader Tracks (www.tradertracks.com). A monthly publication that covers the realm of trading is *Futures Magazine* (www.futuresmag.com). Of course, you can do your own diligent research at the library and on the Internet (check Appendix A for resources).

Following the Basic Rules of Trading

If you're going to trade, adhere to some golden rules to help you maximize your success (or at least minimize potential losses):

- ✔ **Don't commit all your cash at once:** In a fast-moving market, opportunities come up all the time. Try to keep some cash on hand to take advantage of those opportunities.

- ✔ **Have a plan:** Try to have predetermined points at which you cut losses or take profits.

- ✔ **Understand that taking profits is not a sin:** Sometimes, a bird in the hand is worth two in the bush. Markets can reverse fairly quickly. If you have a stock position sitting there with a fat profit, it can't hurt to take the profit. This action gives you cash for the next opportunity.

- ✔ **Discover hedging techniques:** Just because you're bullish doesn't mean that you can't also put on a bearish position. Hedging techniques protect you when the market moves against you.

- ✔ **Find out which events move markets:** Research the market and discover what types of events tend to move it (either up or down). Serious short-term traders keep one eye on their positions and the other on what's going on in the world. Keep informed by regularly reading financial publications and websites (see Appendix A for resources).

- ✔ **Check the stock's trading history:** Charts and related data tell you how a particular stock has moved in recent weeks, months, and years. Do you see any seasonality or reliable patterns that may help you judge future movements?

✔ **Use stop-loss and limit orders:** Using trade orders is an integral part of the trader's overall strategy. Find out more in Chapter 17.

✔ **Use discipline and patience versus emotion and panic:** Part of the human equation in the world of financial markets is that fear and greed can become irrational, short-term drivers of prices. Instead of joining the crowd, watch them to give you an advantage in assessing a stock's price movements. Stick with your plan and use discipline and patience.

✔ **Minimize transaction costs:** Keep in mind that because trading is typically active and short-term, transaction costs are significant. Active trading can mean lots of brokerage commissions, even in this age of Internet-based brokerage firms. Therefore, traders who trade frequently should shop around for brokerage firms that charge low commissions (check out brokerage firms in Appendix A). In addition, short-term trading leads to short-term capital gains, which are taxed at a higher rate than long-term transactions (see Chapter 21 for more details).

✔ **Understand the beta of a stock:** The volatility of a stock is an important consideration for traders. The more volatile a stock is, the greater its ups and downs are. Therefore, traders should regularly check the stock's beta. *Beta* is a statistical measure of how volatile a particular stock is relative to a market standard (such as the S&P 500 index).

How is it measured? The S&P 500 (for example) is given a beta of 1. A stock with a beta of 2 is considered twice as volatile as the index. In other words, if the index falls by 10 percent, the stock in question has the potential of falling by 20 percent. A stock with a beta of 0.5 is considered to be half as volatile as the index. In other words, if the index falls by 10 percent, that low-beta stock would only be expected to fall 5 percent.

Traders looking for fast (and hopefully profitable) movement look for high-beta opportunities. A stock's beta can be found on various financial websites (see the resources in Appendix A).

✔ **Read and learn from top traders:** Last (but not least), learn from the great ones out there, such as the legendary Jesse Livermore. You can read all about his trading exploits in the book *Reminiscences of a Stock Operator* by Edwin Lefèvre and Jon D. Markman (Wiley).

Because trading can be very risky, you need to know as much as you can. Don't use your rent money or retirement money, and for crying out loud, don't break open your kid's piggy bank. Trading should only be done with *risk capital* (money that, if lost, doesn't hurt your lifestyle). And don't forget the advice from the immortal Will Rogers: "Don't gamble. Take all your savings and buy some good stock and hold it till it goes up; then sell it. If it don't go up, don't buy it."

A Final Note on Speculating

In my estimation, the biggest point of speculating is that you're putting your money where you think the rest of the market will be putting their money — before it happens. This is where the "financial gambling" part comes in. The following sections discuss two types of speculation: that stocks will go up and that stocks will go down.

Beginners should consider investing and should wait before they do any trading or speculating because the latter require more experience — along with expendable capital (money that you can afford to lose if you're wrong).

Speculating on the upside

If you're expecting the market to go long on a particular stock (or commodity or other investment vehicle), then you're speculating as to where the buyers will be heading. Don't forget that the main reason that a stock or other investment goes up is because there are more buyers of it than there are sellers. More buyers means that the investment will see its price be bid up.

Therefore, speculators attempt to be forward thinkers and "early birds," hoping to buy early and then cash out when the stampede of buyers show up. Of course, the speculator can be wrong. The investment may not go up, and if sellers outnumber buyers, the investment can lose money.

Given that painful possibility, successful speculators spend a lot of time researching to make sure that their facts and "cause-and-effects" logic are as sound as possible. Speculators can do their research with the resources in Appendix A.

Speculating on the downside

Speculating isn't just about anticipating (and hopefully profiting from) upside moves before the market jumps in. It can also be about making money speculating that some investment will go down. Many speculators look for what they believe will be the "next stock to crash," and they establish a short position in that stock (such as going short, which I discuss in Chapter 17, or buying put options, which I discuss earlier in this chapter). Some made a killing when stocks like Enron and GM plummeted. Although speculating from down-side market moves is usually short term in nature (under a year), it can be long term too in some cases.

The final point is that speculating on stocks soaring or falling can indeed be very profitable (much like buying a winning lottery ticket), but because you're doing it before the crowd, the danger is that you can lose big (much like buying a lot of losing lottery tickets). Still intent on speculating? Go ahead — just do lots of research to enhance your chance of succeeding (you can start with Appendix A). Because a speculator is being more aggressive and riskier, more research should be done. This means not only looking at the resources in Appendix A but also drilling down into publications that are read by executives in that particular industry or sector.

If, for example, I was speculating that gold would skyrocket and I was looking for big gains on a small cap mining stock, I'd read as many mining newsletters and works by mining experts as possible and even call and interview executives at mining companies.

Chapter 17

Understanding Brokerage Orders and Trading Techniques

· ·

In This Chapter

▶ Looking at different types of brokerage orders

▶ Trading on margin to maximize profits

▶ Making sense of going short

· ·

*I*nvestment success isn't just about *which* stocks to choose; it's also about *how* you choose those stocks. Frequently, investors think that good stock-picking means doing your homework and then making that buy (or sell). However, you can take it a step further to maximize profits (or minimize losses).

In 2008, millions of investors were slammed mercilessly by a tumultuous market; many could have used some simple techniques and orders that could have saved them some grief. Investors who used stop-loss orders avoided some of the trillion-dollar carnage that hit the stock market during that scary time. As a stock investor, you can take advantage of this technique and others available through your standard brokerage account (see Chapter 7 for details). This chapter presents some of the best ways you can use these powerful techniques, which are useful whether you're buying or selling stock.

Checking Out Brokerage Orders

Orders you place with your stockbroker fit neatly into three categories:

✔ Time-related orders

✔ Condition-related orders

✔ Advanced orders (such as "trade triggers"; more about these in Chapter 18)

At the very least, get familiar with the first two types of orders because they're easy to implement, and they're invaluable tools for wealth-building and (more importantly) wealth-saving! Advanced orders usually are combinations of the first two types.

Using a combination of orders helps you fine-tune your strategy so that you can maintain greater control over your investments. Speak with your broker about the different types of orders you can use to maximize the gains (or minimize the losses) from your stock-investing activities. You also can read the broker's policies on stock orders at the brokerage website.

On the clock: Time-related orders

A time-related order is just that — the order has a time limit. Typically, investors use these orders in conjunction with condition-related orders, which I describe later in this chapter. The two most common time-related orders are day orders and good-til-canceled (GTC) orders.

Day orders

A *day order* is an order to buy or sell a stock that expires at the end of that particular trading day. If you tell your broker, "Buy BYOB, Inc., at $37.50 and make it a day order," you mean that you want to purchase the stock at $37.50. But if the stock doesn't hit that price, your order expires, unfilled, at the end of the trading day. Why would you place such an order? Maybe BYOB is trading at $39, but you don't want to buy it at that price because you don't believe the stock is worth it. Consequently, you have no problem not getting the stock that day.

When would you use day orders? It depends on your preferences and personal circumstances. I rarely use day orders because few events cause me to say, "Gee, I'll just try to buy or sell between now and the end of today's trading action." However, you may feel that you don't want a specified order to linger beyond today's market action. Perhaps you want to test a price. ("I want to get rid of stock A at $39 to make a quick profit, but it's currently trading at $37.50. However, I may change my mind tomorrow.") A day order is the perfect strategy to use in this case.

If you make a trade and don't specify a time limit with the order, most (if not all) brokers will automatically treat it as a day order.

Good-til-canceled orders

A good-til-canceled (GTC) order is the most commonly requested order by investors, and it's one that I use and recommend often. The GTC order means just what it says: The order stays in effect until it's transacted or until the investor cancels it. Although GTC orders are time-related, they're always tied to a condition, such as the stock achieving a certain price.

Although the order implies that it can run indefinitely, most brokers have a limit of 30 or 60 days (or more). I've seen the limit as high as 120 days. By that time, either the broker cancels the order or contacts you (usually by e-mail) to see whether you want to extend it. Ask the broker about his particular policy.

GTC orders are always coupled with condition-related orders (see the next section for the lowdown on conditional orders). For example, say that you think ASAP Corp. stock would make a good addition to your portfolio, but you don't want to buy it at the current price of $48 per share. You've done your homework on the stock, including looking at the stock's price-to-earnings ratio, price-to-book ratio, and so on (see Appendix B for more on ratios), and you say, "Hey, this stock isn't worth $48 a share. I'd only buy it at $36 per share." (It's overpriced or overvalued according to your analysis.) How should you proceed? Your best bet is to ask your broker to do a GTC order at $36. This request means that your broker will buy the shares if and when they hit the $36 mark (unless you cancel the order). Just make sure that your account has the funds available to complete the transaction.

GTC orders are very useful, so you should become familiar with your broker's policy on them. While you're at it, ask whether any fees apply. Many brokers don't charge for GTC orders because if they happen to result in a buy (or sell) order, they generate a normal commission just as any stock transaction does. Other brokers may charge a small fee (but that's rare).

To be successful with GTC orders, you need to know the following:

- **When you want to buy:** In recent years, people have had a tendency to rush into buying a stock without giving some thought to what they could do to get more for their money. Some investors don't realize that the stock market can be a place for bargain-hunting consumers. If you're ready to buy a quality pair of socks for $16 in a department store but the sales clerk says that those same socks are going on sale tomorrow for only $8, what do you do — assuming that you're a cost-conscious consumer? Unless you're barefoot, you probably decide to wait. The same point holds true with stocks.

  Say that you want to buy SOX, Inc., at $26, but it's currently trading at $30. You think that $30 is too expensive, but you'd be happy to buy the stock at $26 or lower. However, you have no idea whether the stock will move to your desired price today, tomorrow, next week, or even next month (or maybe never). In this case, a GTC order is appropriate.

- **When you want to sell:** What if you buy some socks at a department store and you discover that they have holes (darn it!)? Wouldn't you want to get rid of them? Of course you would. If a stock's price starts to unravel, you want to be able to get rid of it as well.

Perhaps you already own SOX at $25 but are concerned that market conditions may drive the price lower. You're not certain which way the stock will move in the coming days and weeks. In this case, a GTC order to sell the stock at a specified price is a suitable strategy. Because the stock price is $25, you may want to place a GTC order to sell it if it falls to $22.50, to prevent further losses. Again, in this example, GTC is the time frame, and it accompanies a condition (sell when the stock hits $22.50).

At your command: Condition-related orders

A *condition-related order* (also known as a *conditional order*) is an order that's executed only when a certain condition is met. Conditional orders enhance your ability to buy stocks at a lower price, to sell at a better price, or to minimize potential losses. When stock markets become bearish or uncertain, conditional orders are highly recommended.

A good example of a conditional order is a *limit order*. A limit order may say, "Buy Mojeski Corp. at $45." But if Mojeski Corp. isn't at $45 (this price is the condition), then the order isn't executed. I discuss limit orders, as well as market orders and stop-loss orders, in the following sections.

Market orders

When you buy stock, the simplest type of order is a *market order* — an order to buy or sell a stock at the market's current best available price. Orders don't get any more basic than that. Here's an example: Kowalski, Inc., is available at the market price of $10. When you call your broker and instruct her to buy 100 shares "at the market," the broker implements the order for your account, and you pay $1,000 plus commission.

I say "current best available price" because the stock's price is constantly moving, and catching the best price can be a function of the broker's ability to process the stock purchase. For very active stocks, the price change can happen within seconds. It's not unheard of to have three brokers simultaneously place orders for the same stock and get three different prices because of differences in the brokers' capabilities. The difference may be pennies, but it's a difference nonetheless. (Some computers are faster than others.)

The advantage of a market order is that the transaction is processed immediately, and you get your stock without worrying about whether it hits a particular price. For example, if you buy Kowalski, Inc., with a market order, you know that by the end of that phone call (or website visit), you're assured of getting the stock. The disadvantage of a market order is that you can't control the price at which you purchase the stock. Whether you're buying or selling your shares, you may not realize the exact price you expect (especially if you're dealing with a volatile stock).

Market orders get finalized in the chronological order in which they're placed. Your price may change because the orders ahead of you in line cause the stock price to rise or fall based on the latest news.

Stop-loss orders

A _stop-loss order_ (also called a _stop order_) is a condition-related order that instructs the broker to sell a particular stock in your portfolio only when the stock reaches a particular price. It acts like a trigger, and the stop order converts to a market order to sell the stock immediately.

The stop-loss order isn't designed to take advantage of small, short-term moves in the stock's price. It's meant to help you protect the bulk of your money when the market turns against your stock investment in a sudden manner.

Say that your Kowalski, Inc., stock rises to $20 per share and you seek to protect your investment against a possible future market decline. A stop-loss order at $18 triggers your broker to sell the stock immediately if it falls to the $18 mark. In this example, if the stock suddenly drops to $17, it still triggers the stop-loss order, but the finalized sale price is $17. In a volatile market, you may not be able to sell at your precise stop-loss price. However, because the order automatically gets converted into a market order, the sale will be done, and you'll be spared further declines in the stock.

The main benefit of a stop-loss order is that it prevents a major loss in a stock that you own. It's a form of discipline that's important in investing in order to minimize potential losses. Investors can find it agonizing to sell a stock that has fallen. If they don't sell, however, the stock often continues to plummet as investors continue to hold on while hoping for a rebound in the price.

Most investors set a stop-loss amount at about 10 percent below the market value of the stock. This percentage gives the stock some room to fluctuate, which most stocks tend to do from day to day. If you're extra nervous, consider a tighter stop-loss, such as 5 percent or less.

Please keep in mind that this order is a trigger and a particular price is not guaranteed to be captured because the actual buy or sell occurs immediately after the trigger is activated. If the market at the time of the actual transaction is particularly volatile, then the price realized may be significantly different.

In the following sections, I describe a certain type of stop-loss order (called a trailing stop), and I talk about the use of beta measurement with stop-loss orders.

Trailing stops

Trailing stops are an important technique in wealth preservation for seasoned stock investors and can be one of your key strategies in using stop-loss orders. A *trailing stop* is a stop-loss order that an investor actively manages by moving it up along with the stock's market price. The stop-loss order "trails" the stock price upward. As the stop-loss goes upward, it protects more and more of the stock's value from declining.

Imagine that you bought stock in Peach Inc. (PI) for $30 a share. A trailing stop is in place at, say, 10 percent, and the order is GTC (presume that this broker places a time limit of 90 days for GTC orders). At $30 per share, the trailing stop is $27. If PI goes to $40, your trailing stop automatically rises to $36. If PI continues to rise to $50, your trailing continues along with it to $45. Now say that PI reverses course (for whatever reason) and starts to plummet. The trailing stop stays put at $45 and triggers a sell order if PI reaches the $45 level.

In the preceding example, I use a trailing stop percentage, but trailing stops are also available in dollar amounts. For example, say that PI is at $30, and I put in a trailing stop of $3. If PI rises to $50, my trailing stop will reach $47. If PI then drops from this peak of $50, the trailing stop stays put at $47 and triggers a sell order if PI actually hits $47. You get the picture. Trailing stops can help you sleep at night . . . especially in these turbulent times.

William O'Neill, founder and publisher of *Investor's Business Daily,* advocates setting a trailing stop of 8 percent below your purchase price. That's his preference. Some investors who invest in very volatile stocks may put in trailing stops of 20 or 25 percent. Is a stop-loss order desirable or advisable in every situation? No. It depends on your level of experience, your investment goals, and the market environment. Still, stop-loss orders (trailing or otherwise) are appropriate in many cases, especially if the market seems uncertain (or you are!).

A trailing stop is a stop-loss order that you actively manage. The stop-loss order is good-til-canceled (GTC), and it constantly trails the stock's price as it moves up. To successfully implement stop-loss orders (including trailing stops), you should

- ✔ **Realize that brokers usually don't place trailing stops for you automatically.** In fact, they won't (or shouldn't) place any type of order without your consent. Deciding on the type of order to place is your responsibility. You can raise, lower, or cancel a trailing stop order at will, but you need to monitor your investment when substantial moves do occur to respond to the movement appropriately.

- ✔ **Change the stop-loss order when the stock price moves significantly.** Hopefully, you won't call your broker every time the stock moves 50 cents. Change the stop-loss order when the stock price moves around

10 percent. For example, if you initially purchase a stock at $90 per share, ask the broker to place the stop-loss order at $81. When the stock moves to $100, cancel the $81 stop-loss order and replace it at $90. When the stock's price moves to $110, change the stop-loss order to $99, and so on.

✔ **Understand your broker's policy on GTC orders.** If your broker usually considers a GTC order expired after 30 or 60 days, you should be aware of it. You don't want to risk a sudden drop in your stock's price without the stop-loss order protection. Make a note of your broker's time limit so that you remember to renew the order for additional time.

✔ **Monitor your stock.** A trailing stop isn't a "set it and forget it" technique. Monitoring your investment is critical. Of course, if the investment falls, the stop-loss order prevents further loss. Should the stock price rise substantially, remember to adjust your trailing stop accordingly. Keep raising the safety net as the stock continues to rise. Part of monitoring the stock is knowing the beta, which you can read more about in the next section.

Using beta measurement

To be a successful investor, you need to understand the volatility of the particular stock you invest in. In stock market parlance, this volatility is also called the beta of a stock. *Beta* is a quantitative measure of the volatility of a given stock (mutual funds and portfolios, too) relative to the overall market, usually the S&P 500 index. (For more information on the S&P 500, see Chapter 5.) Beta specifically measures the performance movement of the stock as the S&P moves 1 percent up or down. A beta measurement above 1 is more volatile than the overall market, whereas a beta below 1 is less volatile. Some stocks are relatively stable in terms of price movements; others jump around.

Because beta measures how volatile or unstable the stock's price is, it tends to be uttered in the same breath as "risk" — more volatility indicates more risk. Similarly, less volatility tends to mean less risk. (Chapter 4 offers more details on the topics of risk and volatility.)

You can find a company's beta at websites that provide a lot of financial information about companies, such as Nasdaq (www.nasdaq.com) or Yahoo! Finance (http://finance.yahoo.com).

The beta is useful to know when it comes to stop-loss orders because it gives you a general idea of the stock's trading range. If a stock is currently priced at $50 and it typically trades in the $48 to $52 range, then a trailing stop at $49 doesn't make sense. Your stock would probably be sold the same day you initiated the stop-loss order. If your stock is a volatile growth stock that may swing up and down by 10 percent, you should more logically set your stop-loss at 15 percent below that day's price.

Practicing discipline with stop-loss orders

I have a stack of several years' worth of investment newsletters in which investment experts made all sorts of calls regarding the prospects of a company, industry, or the economy in general. Some made forecasts that were spectacularly on target, but you should see the ones that were spectacularly wrong — ouch! However, even some of the winners suffered because of a lack of discipline. Those spectacular gains disappeared like balloons at a porcupine convention.

At the height of the housing bubble (circa 2007) many real estate and mortgage companies saw record highs in their stock prices. A good example was Federal National Mortgage Association ("Fannie Mae" with the stock symbol FNMA). FNMA was a public company, but it was technically a government-sponsored entity. Many

thought that because it had the backing (real or imagined) of the federal government, it was a safe investment. In 2007, its stock price was around $75. I was very worried about the housing bubble and felt that any stock tied to this dangerous market was at risk. Yet there were still analysts toting the stock with "strong buy" and/or "buy" orders.

Whenever you own a stock (or an exchange-traded fund, known as an ETF) that you begin to worry about and aren't sure about selling, consider a stop-loss order. A stop-loss order on FNMA, even at a much lower level, such as $50, would have saved investors a fortune. By the end of 2008, FNMA's stock price fell below $1 per share (you read that right . . . under a buck a share!). In less than 12 months, FNMA fell almost 99 percent.

The stock of a large cap company in a mature industry tends to have a low beta — one close to the overall market. Small and mid cap stocks in new or emerging industries tend to have greater volatility in their day-to-day price fluctuations; hence, they tend to have a high beta. (You can find out more about large, small, and mid cap stocks in Chapter 1; Chapter 4 has more about beta.)

Limit orders

A *limit order* is a very precise condition-related order implying that a limit exists either on the buy or the sell side of the transaction. You want to buy (or sell) only at a specified price. Period. Limit orders work well if you're buying the stock, but they may not be good for you if you're selling the stock. Here's how they work in both instances:

   ✔ **When you're buying:** Just because you like a particular company and you want its stock doesn't mean that you're willing to pay the current market price. Maybe you want to buy Kowalski, Inc., but the current market price of $20 per share isn't acceptable to you. You prefer to buy it at $16 because you think that price reflects its true market value. What do you do? You tell your broker, "Buy Kowalski with a limit order at $16" (or you can enter a limit order at the broker's website). You have to specify whether it's a day order or a GTC order, both of which I discuss earlier in this chapter.

What happens if the stock experiences great volatility? What if it drops to $16.01 and then suddenly drops to $15.95 on the next move? Nothing happens, actually, which you may be dismayed to hear. Because your order was limited to $16, it can be transacted only at $16 — no more and no less. The only way for this particular trade to occur is if the stock rises back to $16. However, if the price keeps dropping, then your limit order isn't transacted and may expire or be canceled.

✔ **When you're selling:** Limit orders are activated only when a stock hits a specific price. If you buy Kowalski, Inc., at $20 and you worry about a decline in the share price, you may decide to put in a limit order at $18. If you watch the news and hear that Kowalski's price is dropping, you may sigh and say, "I sure am glad I put in that limit order at $18!" However, in a volatile market, the share price may leapfrog over your specified price. It could go from $18.01 to $17.99 and then continue its descent. Because the stock price never hit $18 on the mark, your stock isn't sold. You may be sitting at home satisfied (mistakenly) that you played it smart, while your stock plummets to $15, $10, or worse! Having a stop-loss order in place is best.

Investors who aren't in a hurry can use a limit order to try to get a better price when they decide to sell. For example, maybe you own a stock whose price is at $50 and you want to sell, but you think that a short-term rally in the stock is imminent. In that case, you can use a limit order such as, "Sell the stock at the sell limit order of $55 and keep the order on for 30 days."

When you're buying (or selling) a stock, most brokers interpret the limit order as "buy (or sell) at this specific price or better." For example, presumably, if your limit order is to buy a stock at $10, you'll be just as happy if your broker buys that stock at $9.95. That way, if you don't get exactly $10 because the stock's price was volatile, you'll still get the stock at a lower price. Talk to your broker to be clear on the meaning of the limit order.

The joys of technology: Advanced orders

Brokers have added sophisticated capabilities to the existing repertoire of orders that are available for stock investors. One example is *advanced orders,* which provide investors with a way to use a combination of orders for more sophisticated trades. An example of an advanced order is something like, "Only sell stock B, and if it sells, use the proceeds to buy stock D." You get the idea. My brokerage firm has the following on its website, and I'm sure that more firms will do the same. Inquire with yours and see the benefit of using advanced orders such as the following:

- ✔ **"One order cancels another order":** In this scenario you enter two orders simultaneously with the condition that if one order is executed, the second order is automatically cancelled.

- ✔ **"One order triggers another order":** Here you submit an order, and if that order is filled, another order is automatically submitted. Many brokers have different names for these types of orders, so ask them if they can provide such an order.

Other types of advanced orders and order strategies are available (and covered in Chapter 18), but you get the picture. Talk to your brokerage firm and find out what's available in your particular account. Investors need to know that today's technology allows them to have more power and control over the implementation of buying and selling transactions. I love it!

Buying on Margin

Buying on margin means buying securities, such as stocks, with funds you borrow from your broker. Buying stock on margin is similar to buying a house with a mortgage. If you buy a house at a purchase price of $100,000 and put 10 percent down, your equity (the part you own) is $10,000, and you borrow the remaining $90,000 with a mortgage. If the value of the house rises to $120,000 and you sell (for the sake of simplicity, I don't include closing costs in this example), you make a profit of 200 percent. How is that? The $20,000 gain on the property represents a gain of 20 percent on the purchase price of $100,000, but because your real investment is $10,000 (the down payment), your gain works out to 200 percent (a gain of $20,000 on your initial investment of $10,000).

Buying on margin is an example of using leverage to maximize your gain when prices rise. *Leverage* is simply using borrowed money when you make an asset purchase in order to increase your potential profit. This type of leverage is great in a favorable (bull) market, but it works against you in an unfavorable (bear) market. Say that a $100,000 house you purchase with a $90,000 mortgage falls in value to $80,000 (and property values can decrease during economic hard times). Your outstanding debt of $90,000 exceeds the value of the property. Because you owe more than you own, you're left with a negative net worth.

Leverage is a double-edged sword. Don't forget that you need approval from your brokerage firm before you can buy on margin. To buy on margin, you typically fill out the form provided by that brokerage firm to be approved. Check with the broker because each firm has different requirements.

In the following sections, I describe the potential outcomes of buying on margin, I explain how to maintain a balance, and I provide some pointers for successfully buying on margin.

Examining marginal outcomes

Suppose you think that the stock for the company Mergatroid, Inc., currently at $40 per share, will go up in value. You want to buy 100 shares, but you have only $2,000. What can you do? If you're intent on buying 100 shares (versus simply buying the 50 shares that you have cash for), you can borrow the additional $2,000 from your broker on margin. If you do that, what are the potential outcomes?

If the stock price goes up

This outcome is the best for you. If Mergatroid goes to $50 per share, your investment is worth $5,000, and your outstanding margin loan is $2,000. If you sell, the total proceeds will pay off the loan and leave you with $3,000. Because your initial investment was $2,000, your profit is a solid 50 percent because your $2,000 principal amount generated a $1,000 profit. (For the sake of this example, I leave out any charges, such as commissions and interest paid on the margin loan.) However, if you pay the entire $4,000 upfront without the margin loan, your $4,000 investment generates a profit of $1,000, or 25 percent. Using margin, you double the return on your money.

Leverage, when used properly, is very profitable. However, it's still debt, so understand that you must pay it off eventually, regardless of the stock's performance.

If the stock price fails to rise

If the stock goes nowhere, you still have to pay interest on that margin loan. If the stock pays dividends, this money can defray some of the margin loan's cost. In other words, dividends can help you pay off what you borrow from the broker. (Flip to Chapter 3 for an introduction to dividends.)

Having the stock neither rise nor fall may seem like a neutral situation, but you pay interest on your margin loan with each passing day. For this reason, margin trading can be a good consideration for conservative investors if the stock pays a high dividend. Many times, a high dividend from 4,000 dollars' worth of stock can exceed the margin interest you have to pay from the $2,000 (50 percent) you borrow from the broker to buy that stock.

If the stock price goes down, buying on margin can work against you. What if Mergatroid goes to $38 per share? The market value of 100 shares is then $3,800, but your equity shrinks to only $1,800 because you have to pay your $2,000 margin loan. You're not exactly looking at a disaster at this point, but you'd better be careful, because the margin loan exceeds 50 percent of your stock investment. If it goes any lower, you may get the dreaded *margin call,* when the broker actually contacts you to ask you to restore the ratio between the margin loan and the value of the securities. See the following section for information about appropriate debt to equity ratios.

Maintaining your balance

When you purchase stock on margin, you must maintain a balanced ratio of margin debt to equity of at least 50 percent. If the debt portion exceeds this limit, you're required to restore that ratio by depositing either more stock or more cash into your brokerage account. The additional stock you deposit can be stock that's transferred from another account.

To continue the example from the previous section: If Mergatroid goes to $28 per share, the margin loan portion exceeds 50 percent of the equity value in that stock — in this case, because the market value of your stock is $2,800 but the margin loan is still at $2,000, the margin loan is a worrisome 71 percent of the market value ($2,000 divided by $2,800 = 71 percent). Expect to get a call from your broker to put more securities or cash into the account to restore the 50 percent balance.

If you can't come up with more stock, other securities, or cash, the next step is to sell stock from the account and use the proceeds to pay off the margin loan. For you, that means realizing a capital loss — you lose money on your investment.

The Federal Reserve Board governs margin requirements for brokers with Regulation T. Discuss this rule with your broker to understand fully your (and the broker's) risks and obligations. Regulation T dictates margin requirements set by brokers for their customers. For most listed stocks, it's 50 percent.

Striving for success on margin

Margin, as you can see from the previous sections, can escalate your profits on the up side but magnify your losses on the down side. If your stock plummets drastically, you can end up with a margin loan that exceeds the market value of the stock you used the loan to purchase. In the emerging bear market of 2000–2002, stock losses hurt many people, and a large number of those losses were made worse because people didn't manage the responsibilities involved with margin trading. In 2008, margin debt again hit very high levels, and that subsequently resulted in tumbling stock prices.

If you buy stock on margin, use a disciplined approach. Be extra careful when using leverage, such as a margin loan, because it can backfire. Keep the following points in mind:

- ✔ **Have ample reserves of cash or marginable securities in your account.** Try to keep the margin ratio at 40 percent or less to minimize the chance of a margin call.

- ✔ **If you're a beginner, consider using margin to buy stocks in large companies that have relatively stable prices and pay good dividends.** Some people buy income stocks that have dividend yields that exceed the margin interest rate, meaning that the stock ends up paying for its own margin loan. Just remember those stop-loss orders, which I discuss earlier in this chapter.

- ✔ **Constantly monitor your stocks.** If the market turns against you, the result will be especially painful if you use margin.

- ✔ **Have a payback plan for your margin debt.** Taking margin loans against your investments means that you're paying interest. Your ultimate goal is to make money, and paying interest eats into your profits.

Going Short and Coming Out Ahead

The vast majority of stock investors are familiar with buying stock, holding onto it for a while, and hoping its value goes up. This kind of thinking is called *going long,* and investors who go long are considered to be *long on stocks.* Going long essentially means that you're bullish and seeking your profits from rising prices. However, astute investors also profit in the market when stock prices fall. *Going short* (also called *shorting a stock, selling short,* or *doing a short sale*) on a stock is a common technique for profiting from a stock price decline. Investors have made big profits during bear markets by going short. A short sale is a bet that a particular stock is going down.

Most people easily understand making money by going long. It boils down to "buy low and sell high." Piece of cake. Going short means making money by selling high and then buying low. Huh? Thinking in reverse isn't a piece of cake. Although thinking of this stock adage in reverse may be challenging, the mechanics of going short are really simple. Consider an example that uses a fictitious company called DOA, Inc. As a stock, DOA ($50 per share) is looking pretty sickly. It has lots of debt and plummeting sales and earnings, and the news is out that DOA's industry will face hard times for the foreseeable future. This situation describes a stock that's an ideal candidate for shorting. The future may be bleak for DOA, but it's promising for savvy investors. The following sections provide the full scoop on going short.

To go short, you have to be deemed (by your broker) creditworthy — your account needs to be approved for short selling. When you're approved for margin trading, you're probably set to sell short, too. Talk to your broker (or check on the broker's website for information) about limitations in your account regarding going short.

You must understand brokerage rules before you conduct short selling. The broker must approve you for it (see Chapter 7 for information on working with brokers), and you must meet the minimum collateral requirement, which is typically $2,000 or 50 percent (whichever is higher) of the shorted stock's market value. If the stock generates dividends, those dividends are paid to the stock's owner, not to the person who borrows to go short. Check with your broker for complete details, and review the resources in Appendix A.

Because going short on stocks has greater risks than going long, I strongly advise beginning investors to avoid shorting stocks until they become more seasoned.

Setting up a short sale

This section explains how to go short. Say that you believe DOA is the right stock to short — you're pretty sure its price is going to fall. With DOA at $50, you instruct your broker to "go short 100 shares on DOA." (It doesn't have to be 100 shares; I'm just using that as an example.) Here's what happens next:

1. **Your broker borrows 100 shares of DOA stock, either from his own inventory or from another client or broker.**

   That's right. The stock can be borrowed from a client, no permission necessary. The broker guarantees the transaction, and the client/stock owner never has to be informed about it because he never loses legal and beneficial right to the stock. You borrow 100 shares, and you'll return 100 shares when it's time to complete the transaction.

2. **Your broker then sells the stock and puts the money in your account.**

   Your account is credited with $5,000 (100 shares × $50) in cash — the money gained from selling the borrowed stock. This cash acts like a loan on which you're going to have to pay interest.

3. **You buy the stock back and return it to its rightful owner.**

   When it's time to close the transaction (because either you want to close it or the owner of the shares wants to sell them, so you have to give them back), you must return the number of shares you borrowed (in this case, 100 shares). If you buy back the 100 shares at $40 per share (remember that you shorted this particular stock because you were sure its price was going to fall) and those 100 shares are returned to their owner, you make a $1,000 profit. (To keep the example tidy, I don't include brokerage commissions.)

Oops! Going short when prices grow taller

I bet you guessed that the wonderful profitability of selling short has a flip side. Say that you were wrong about DOA and that the stock price rises from the ashes as it goes from $50 to $87. Now what? You still have to return the 100 shares you borrowed. With the stock's price at $87, that means you have to buy the stock for $8,700 (100 shares at the new, higher price of $87). Ouch! How do you pay for it? Well, you have that original $5,000 in your account from when you initially went short on the stock. But where do you get the other $3,700 ($8,700 less the original $5,000)? You guessed it — your pocket! You have to cough up the difference. If the stock continues to rise, that's a lot of coughing.

How much money do you lose if the stock goes to $100 or more? A heck of a lot. As a matter of fact, there's no limit to how much you can lose. That's why going short can be riskier than going long. When going long, the most you can lose is 100 percent of your money. When you go short, however, you can lose more than 100 percent of the money you invest. Yikes!

Because the potential for loss is unlimited when you short a stock, I suggest that you use a stop order (also called a *buy-stop order*) to minimize the damage. Better yet, make it a good-til-canceled (GTC) order, which I discuss earlier in this chapter. You can set the stop order at a given price, and if the stock hits that price, you buy the stock back so that you can return it to its owner before the price rises even higher. You still lose money, but you limit your losses. Like a stop-loss order, a buy-stop order effectively works to limit your loss.

The uptick rule

For many years, the stock market had something called "the uptick rule." This rule stated that you could enter into a short sale only when the stock had just completed an uptick. "Tick" in this case means the actual incremental price movement of the stock you're shorting. For a $10 stock that was just $9.95 a moment ago, the 5-cent difference represents an uptick. If the $10 stock was just $10.10 a moment before, the 10-cent difference is a downtick. The amount of the tick doesn't matter. So, if you short a stock at the price of $40, the immediate prior price must have been $39.99 or lower. The reason for this rule (a Federal Reserve regulation) is that short selling can aggravate declining stock prices in a rapidly falling market. In practice, going short on a stock whose price is already declining can make the stock price fall even farther. Excessive short selling can make the stock more volatile than it would be otherwise.

In 2007, however, the uptick rule was removed. This action contributed to the increased volatility that investors saw during 2007–2008. Investors had to adapt accordingly. It meant getting used to wider swings in stock price movements on days of heavy activity.

Feeling the squeeze

If you go short on a stock, you have to buy that stock back sooner or later so that you can return it to its owner. What happens when a lot of people are short on a particular stock and its price starts to rise? All those short sellers are scrambling to buy the stock back so that they can close their transactions before they lose too much money. This mass buying quickens the pace of the stock's ascent and puts a squeeze (called a *short squeeze*) on the investors who've been shorting the stock.

In the earlier section "Setting up a short sale," I explain that your broker can borrow stock from another client so that you can go short on it. What happens when that client wants to sell the stock in her account — the stock that you borrowed and which is therefore no longer in her account? When that happens, your broker asks you to return the borrowed stock. That's when you feel the squeeze — you have to buy the stock back at the current price.

Going short can be a great maneuver in a declining (bear) market, but it can be brutal if the stock price goes up. If you're a beginner, stay away from short selling until you have enough experience (and money) to risk it.

Chapter 18

Using Trade Triggers and Advanced Conditional Orders

*I*n the age of knowledge, grasshopper, we must be one with the technology. Especially, locust, when technology can help you make more profit. In that spirit, uh . . . cricket, I take the topic of brokerage orders from Chapter 17 to another level.

Brokerage orders that you can automate on a website are (in my humble opinion) one of the greatest uses of technology. Chapter 17 is about placing single transaction orders, such as a stop-loss order or a trailing stop. In this chapter, I introduce you to more advanced brokerage orders, whereby it's possible to enter a combination order containing two or more orders that may be triggered by market events (this stuff is cool . . .).

No one says that you need to use a trade trigger or an advanced conditional order. For most folks (even yours truly), the basic orders that I describe in Chapter 17 suffice most of the time. However, it's good to know that if you encounter a challenging situation due to market conditions and/or your changing preferences and circumstances, you can structure an order or a set of orders to satisfy your investing/trading/speculating needs.

Trying Trade Triggers

A trade trigger is any event that sets a trade in motion (stock or otherwise). The trade trigger can be a singular event (such as the movement of an individual stock) or a market-wide event (such as a major index reaching a certain level). Trade triggers are used to make something automatically occur, such as the selling or buying of stock shares when a particular price level is reached. Essentially, trade triggers carry out the function of "if this happens, then do that." If a trigger is, well, triggered, the trade is deployed, and the stock trader receives an e-mail notice as soon as the transaction is done.

Those who trade (versus invest in) stocks use trade triggers regularly to keep from constantly monitoring the daily swings in market movements. Most brokerage firms offer this technology for frequent traders. (See Chapter 16 for the differences between investing and trading.)

In the following sections, I explain the different types of trade triggers and provide pointers on how to set one up.

Surveying different types of trade triggers

I think that trade triggers can be extremely useful to stock investors (and those who do options and/or track indexes). The following sections cover the three different types of trade triggers.

Using a stock

Chapter 17 gives you the scoop on basic triggers such as limit orders. A buy limit order, for example, says that "if and when XYZ stock hits the price of $50, then buy 100 shares." And usually a time is attached, such as "this order is good for the day" or "this order is good-til-canceled."

However, a more sophisticated trade trigger can be set in motion by a separate event that's not directly associated with the movement of a particular stock. The trade trigger may be the movement of an entirely different stock. It may be one you own, or one you don't.

With trade triggers, the activity or attributes of any stock can trigger an order for another stock. If you feel there's a correlation between the prices of two different stocks, you can set up a trade trigger similar to the one in the following example.

Say that you want to buy 100 shares of Apple (APPL) stock, but only when Google's (GOOG) stock price falls to $400 per share within the next 30 days. The trade trigger would be set to "buy 100 shares of APPL when GOOG is equal to (or less than) $400, and this order will be GTC (good-til-canceled) but will expire 30 days from when the order is entered."

As you can see, your creativity can take you to new levels of investing nirvana (whatever that may be!). Use triggers such as these when you come across opportunities in your favorite stocks. Do your research on stocks that you would like to buy; start with Chapter 6 and also use the resources in Appendix A.

Using an index

The investor can make a buy or sell trade using a major market index (rather than a stock) as the trigger. If you feel that certain movements of indexes may influence or correlate to the movement of individual stocks (or options), you can set up a trigger to place an order if the conditions you specify are met. (Indexes include the Dow Jones Industrial Average and the S&P 500; see Chapter 5 for details.)

You can do a sell order on a particular stock, for example, which is triggered when the Dow rises to a certain level. Or if, say, the S&P 500 index is reflecting a strong rally and you think it will be overbought when it reaches, say, 1650, you can set your order to sell a stock when this index reaches that level.

Very frequently, major market movements set up buying or selling opportunities in the stocks that you're following. The idea that you can automate the process with trade triggers is very appealing. The timing is entirely up to you, but Chapter 16 (on investing, speculating, and trading) and Chapter 17 (on brokerage orders) can come in handy for setting up your scenarios and related trade triggers.

Using an option

Call and put options can also be part of your trade trigger strategy. Options are speculative vehicles that have an expiration date, where you're betting on the direction of an underlying asset; you buy a call option if you're "betting" that the underlying asset will go up, and you buy a put option if you're "betting" that the underlying option will go down. (For more information on options and how to use them, go to the educational sections of websites such as www.cboe.com and www.888options.com.)

For instance, say you're bullish on XYZ stock (the world's most famous noncompany!); you'd like to buy a call option but only on a day when XYZ is down so that you get a favorable price for the call option. Say that XYZ is at $70, and you'd like to buy a call option when the price dips to $65.

Perhaps the particular call option you're eyeing (say it's "XYZ call option $67.50") is priced at a premium of $175. (This would be quoted as a premium of $1.75 because a single option is based on 100 shares; therefore, a multiplier of 100 is in the price.) But you want to buy it for $150 (quoted as $1.50) or better. You would set your trigger as follows: When XYZ stock goes to $65 or better (meaning that the stock price hits the price of $65 or lower — that $65 price acts as the "trigger"), buy "XYZ call option $67.50" at the specific price of $1.50 or better (meaning that you would be glad to purchase at a price lower than $1.50).

If XYZ stock does indeed fall to $65, your broker would enter an order at $1.50 (this would specifically be called a "buy limit order"). When (and if) the particular call option falls to the price of $1.50, a purchase would be made, and you would end up buying that call option for $150 (plus commissions).

Entering trade triggers

So you're excited to use a trade trigger, but how, exactly, do you enter one? Every brokerage firm has the glossary and tutorials necessary to guide you through the process of placing an order. The main components of the trade trigger order are

- ✔ **The order action:** Is it a buy or sell order?

- ✔ **The order type:** Is it a market order, a stop-loss order, or a limit order? See Chapter 17 for more information.

- ✔ **The quantity to be bought or sold:** 100 shares? More? Less?

- ✔ **The symbol of the security to be bought or sold:** This one's self-explanatory.

- ✔ **The limit price and/or activation price for the order:** This may or may not be applicable based on the type of order selected.

- ✔ **The expiration for the order:** Is it a day order or good-til-canceled? See Chapter 17 for details.

Keep in mind that not every broker performs these transactions the same way or labels these orders as I do. Speak to your broker and discuss this list with him.

Here are a few more handy hints for establishing a trade trigger:

- ✔ A trigger alert can be "activated" by a variety of sources. For example, you can have a trigger alert occur when a major market index, such as the DJIA, hits a certain level. Or, these alerts can be based on a particular stock that's on the New York Stock Exchange (which includes the old American Stock Exchange), Nasdaq, the Over the Counter Bulletin Board (OTCBB), or even "The Pink Sheets" (where you find small cap and micro cap stocks).

- ✔ Some brokers can get very sophisticated with trade triggers, while other brokers may not do them at all (yet). Talk with your brokerage firm's customer service department to see what triggers are available for traders and investors to use.

✔ Triggers on stocks and options are normally activated during regular market hours (9:30 a.m. to 4:00 p.m. ET).

✔ Talk with your broker about how long the triggers will stay on (until the triggers are activated or until they expire). Some brokers may have different time frames from the usual good-til-canceled time frame. The broker will usually send you an e-mail if the trigger is activated or if it expires.

✔ If the trigger involves the purchase of a security, make sure that you either have enough cash for the order amount or enough margin to cover the purchase (see Chapter 17 for details on buying on margin). Do a tally of the total amount you need — a combination of triggers or conditional orders may involve more than one purchase.

Considering Advanced Conditional Orders

Advanced conditional orders let you combine two or three orders that, if filled, will either cancel or trigger additional orders. Conditional orders are available for both stocks and call or put option orders (make sure that you're approved for options trading by your brokerage firm). In the following sections, I list different kinds of advanced conditional orders and explain how to place them.

Checking out different types of advanced conditional orders

Imagine saying to yourself, "Gee, I'm committed to my current stock, Stock A, and I hope it continues to go up. I'd love to get Stock B, but the only way I'd buy Stock B is if Stock A were crashing and I sold it because I lost hope in its future."

It's kinda like being at the supermarket and saying, "I'll buy the veal only if the beef isn't on sale, but if the beef is on sale, I'll get that (unless it's Tuesday, which is chicken day, of course). Well, you get the point. Sometimes the situation (whether in the stock market or just real-life) is a combination "what-if/then-that" scenario.

The following are three of the most common advanced conditional orders that you'll encounter:

✔ **One cancels another (OCA) order:** In this case, you actually submit two simultaneous orders. If one is filled, the other is automatically canceled. Say you want to buy one of two stocks but not both. With the OCA order, you can do that because filling the order to buy Stock A will automatically cancel the order to buy Stock B.

✔ **One triggers another (OTA) order:** If this order is filled, another order is automatically and subsequently submitted. Say you have a stock (Stock A) and would like to buy another stock (Stock B) but only if you can use the purchase money from the proceeds from the sale of Stock A. The OTA order says that if Stock A hits a certain price, sell Stock A and then subsequently buy Stock B.

✔ **One triggers two (OTT) order:** If this order is filled, it automatically submits two subsequent orders. Say you own a stock (Stock A) at $50 a share, and you're worried that it may fall below $48. You would like to buy Stock B at $45 and then enter a stop-loss order for Stock B at $40. The OTT order would sell Stock A when it hits $48 and then enter two subsequent orders: buy Stock B at $45 and put on a stop-loss order for Stock B at $40.

As you get more knowledgeable and confident in your investing pursuits, you may want to try the following advanced conditional orders, which build on those in the preceding list.

✔ **OT/OCA:** One order triggers an OCA order. When you submit an order and it's filled, two orders are simultaneously submitted. If one of the second set of orders is filled, the other one is canceled.

✔ **OT/OTA:** One order triggers an OTA order. When you submit an order and it's filled, another order is subsequently submitted, and if that second order is filled, a third order is subsequently submitted.

✔ **OT/OTT:** If one order is filled, it automatically submits two subsequent orders simultaneously. Oh yeah . . . you can get crazy with this stuff. (Keep in mind that every broker treats these orders a bit differently, so check with your broker to get the specifics.)

I guess the only order left is the OT/DOA (don't ask — just kidding).

Placing advanced conditional orders

Although advanced conditional orders may seem complicated, like anything else, they become easy as you break down the process.

Before I get to the actual process, remember that you need to set clearly in your mind what you actually want to occur and what possibilities you want to take into account long before you talk to your broker or head to your broker's website to create the orders. You may want to write down your thoughts as clearly as possible.

Some of these steps will vary because every brokerage firm runs things a little differently, but the essential steps should be the same.

1. **Choose the security.**

   In this order, are you trading a stock, exchange-traded fund (ETF), or option?

2. **Search out the symbol.**

   What is the symbol of the stock or ETF (or option)?

3. **Choose the quantity.**

   How many shares of the stock or ETF do you want? Or how many option contracts?

4. **Figure out the basic order type.**

   Is it a market order, limit order, or other type of order? (See Chapter 17 for details.)

5. **Check the condition.**

   Indicate that this order is conditional.

6. **Check the "What if" operator in your order.**

   Did you mean "greater than or equal to" or "less than or equal to"? Check with your broker to be sure your order does exactly what you intend for it to do.

7. **Choose the second security.**

   Repeat Steps 2–6 for this security.

8. **Choose the third security.**

   Repeat Steps 2–6 for this security.

9. **Set the cancellation condition.**

   Under what circumstance should the order be canceled? Say you want to buy XYZ stock when it hits $50 but not above that price. In that case, you set the cancellation condition at $50.

10. **Set the time factor.**

    Specify that the order(s) is good for a day or provide an expiration date.

11. **Review and confirm your order.**

    Lastly, review that the order is structured to your specifications. Not sure? Cancel and try again!

Your success with trade triggers doesn't mean you need to master all the different types that I mention in this chapter. However, it's good to master at least one or two to make your trading and investing more successful.

Chapter 19

Getting a Handle on DPPs, DRPs, and DCA . . . PDQ

*W*ho says you must buy 100 shares of a stock to invest? And who says that you must buy your stock only from a broker? (There goes that little voice in my head. . . .) Can you buy direct instead? What if you only want to put your toe in the water and buy just one share for starters? Can you do that without paying through the nose for transaction costs, such as commissions?

The answer to these questions is that you can buy stocks directly (without a broker) and save money in the process. That's what this chapter is about. In this chapter, I show you how direct purchase programs (DPPs) and dividend reinvestment plans (DRPs) make a lot of sense for long-term stock investors, and I show how you can do them on your own — no broker necessary. I also show you how to use the method of dollar cost averaging (DCA) to acquire stock, a technique that works especially well with DRPs. All these programs are well-suited for people who like to invest small sums of money and plan on doing so consistently in the same stock (or stocks) over a long period of time.

Don't invest in a company just because it has a DPP or DRP. DPPs and DRPs are simply a means for getting into a particular stock with very little money. They shouldn't be a substitute for doing diligent research and analysis on a particular stock.

Going Straight to Direct Purchase Programs

If you're going to buy a stock anyway, why not buy it directly from the company and bypass the broker (and commissions) altogether? Several hundred companies now offer *direct purchase programs* (DPPs), also called *direct investment programs* (DIPS), which give investors an opportunity to buy stock directly from these companies. In the following sections, I explain the steps required for investing in a DPP, describe alternatives to DPPs, and warn you of a few minor DPP drawbacks.

DPPs give investors the opportunity to buy stock with little upfront money (usually enough to cover the purchase of one share) and usually no commissions. Why do companies give investors this opportunity? For their sake, they want to encourage more attention and participation from investors. For your purposes, however, a DPP gives you what you may need most: a low-cost entry into that particular company's dividend reinvestment plan, or DRP (which you can read more about in the section "Delving In to Dividend Reinvestment Plans," later in this chapter).

Investing in a DPP

If you have your sights set on a particular company and have only a few bucks to start out, a DPP is probably the best way to make your initial investment. The following steps guide you toward your first stock purchase using a DPP:

1. **Decide what stock you want to invest in (I explain how to do so in Parts II and III) and find the company's contact information.**

   Say that you do your homework and decide to invest in Yumpin Yimminy Corp. (YYC). You can get YYC's contact information through the stock exchange YYC trades on. For example, if YYC trades on the New York Stock Exchange, you can call the NYSE and ask for YYC's contact information, or you can visit the NYSE's website (www.nyse.com). So, you can contact the NYSE to reach YYC for its DPP ASAP. OK?

2. **Find out whether YYC has a DPP (before it's DOA!).**

   Call YYC's shareholder services department and ask whether it has a DPP. If it does, great; if it doesn't, ask whether it plans to start one. At the very least, it may have a DRP. If you prefer, you can check out the company's website, because most corporate websites have plenty of information on their stock purchase programs.

3. **Look into enrolling.**

    The company will send you an application along with a prospectus — the program document that serves as a brochure and, hopefully, answers your basic questions. Usually, the enrollment forms are downloadable from the company's website.

    The processing is typically handled by an organization that the company designates (known as the *plan administrator*). From this point forward, you're in the dividend reinvestment plan. The DPP acts as the entry point to the dividend reinvestment plan so that you make future purchases through the dividend reinvestment plan.

Finding DPP alternatives

Although several hundred companies offer DPPs, the majority of companies don't. What if you want to invest in a company directly and it doesn't have a DPP? The following sections present some alternatives.

Buying your first share through a broker to qualify for a DRP

Yes, buying your first share through a broker costs you a commission; however, after you make the purchase, you can contact that company's shareholder services department and ask about its DRP. After you're an existing stockholder, qualifying for the DRP is a piece of cake.

To qualify for the DRP, you must be on the book of record with the transfer agent. A *book of record* is simply the database the company uses to track every single outstanding share of stock and the stock's owner. The *transfer agent* is the person or organization responsible for maintaining the database. Whenever stock is bought or sold, the transfer agent must implement the change and update the records. In many cases, you must have the broker issue a stock certificate in your name after you own the stock. Getting a stock certificate is the most common way to get your name on the book of record, hence qualifying you for the DRP.

Sometimes, simply buying the stock isn't enough to get your name on the book of record. Although you technically and legally own the stock, brokers, for ease of transaction, often keep the stock in your account under what's referred to as a *street name*. (For instance, your name may be Jane Smith, but the street name can be the broker's firm name, such as Jones & Co., simply for administrative purposes.) Having the stock in a street name really doesn't mean much to you until you want to qualify for the company's DRP. Be sure to address this point with your broker. (Flip to Chapter 7 for more details on brokers.)

Getting started in a DRP directly through a broker

These days, more brokers offer the features of the DRP (like compounding interest) right in the brokerage account itself, which is more convenient than going to the trouble of setting up a DRP with the company directly. This service is most likely a response to the growing number of long-term investors who have fled traditional brokerage accounts for the benefits of direct investing that DPPs and DRPs offer.

The main drawback of a broker-run DRP is that it doesn't usually allow you to make stock purchases through optional cash payments without commission charges (a big negative!). See the section "Building wealth with optional cash payments," later in this chapter, for more on this topic.

Purchasing shares via alternate buying services

Organizations have set up services to help small investors buy stock in small quantities. The primary drawback to these middlemen is that you'll probably pay more in transaction costs than you would if you approached the companies directly. Check out the most prominent services, which include the following:

- ✔ DRIP Central at www.dripcentral.com
- ✔ First Share at www.firstshare.com
- ✔ National Association of Investors Corporation at www.better investing.org
- ✔ ShareBuilder at www.sharebuilder.com

Recognizing the drawbacks

As beneficial as DPPs are, they do have some minor drawbacks (doesn't everything?). Keep the following points in mind when considering DPPs as part of your stock portfolio:

- ✔ Although more and more companies are starting to offer DPPs, relatively few (approximately 500) companies have them.

- ✔ Some DPPs require a high initial amount to invest (as much as $250 or more) or a commitment of monthly investments. In any case, ask the plan administrator about the investing requirements.

- ✔ A growing number of DPPs have some type of service charge. This charge is usually very modest and lower than typical brokerage commissions. Ask about all the incidents — such as getting into the plan, getting out, and so on — that may trigger a service charge.

Delving In to Dividend Reinvestment Plans

Sometimes, *dividend reinvestment plans* (DRPs) are called "DRIPs," which makes me scratch my head. "Reinvestment" is one word, not two, so where does that "I" come from? But I digress. Whether you call them DRIPs or DRPs, they're great for small investors and people who are truly long-term investors in a particular stock. A company may offer a DRP to allow investors to accumulate more shares of its stock without paying commissions.

A DRP has two primary advantages:

- ✔ **Compounding:** The dividends (cash payments to shareholders) get reinvested and give you the opportunity to buy more stock.

- ✔ **Optional cash payments (OCPs):** Most DRPs give participants the ability to make investments through the plan for the purpose of purchasing more stock, usually with no commissions. The OCP minimum for some DRPs is as little as $25 (or even nothing).

Here are the requirements to be in a DRP:

- ✔ You must already be a stockholder of that particular stock.
- ✔ The stock must be paying dividends (you had to guess this one!).

In the following sections, I go into more detail on compounding and OCPs, explain the cost advantages of using DRPs, and warn you of a few drawbacks.

As technology (the Internet and so on) changes and improves, it becomes easier to participate in programs like DRPs because most brokerage firms now make it easier to participate right inside your brokerage account.

Getting a clue about compounding

Dividends are reinvested, offering a form of compounding for the small investor. Dividends buy more shares, in turn generating more dividends. Usually, the dividends don't buy entire shares but fractional ones.

For example, say that you own 20 shares of Fraction Corp. at $10 per share for a total value of $200. Fraction Corp.'s annual dividend is $1, meaning that a quarterly dividend of 25 cents is issued every three months. What happens if this stock is in the DRP? The 20 shares generate a $5 dividend payout in the first quarter (20 shares × 25 cents), and this amount is applied to the stock purchase as soon as it's credited to the DRP account (buying you half of a share). If you presume for this example that the stock price doesn't change, the DRP has 20.5 total shares valued at $205 (20.5 shares × $10 per share). The dividend payout isn't enough to buy an entire share, so it buys a fractional share and credits that to the account.

Now say that three months pass and that no other shares have been acquired since your prior dividend payout. Fraction Corp. issues another quarterly dividend for 25 cents per share. Now what?

- ✔ The original 20 shares generate a $5 dividend payout.
- ✔ The 0.5, or half share, in the account generates a 12.5-cent dividend (half the dividend of a full share because it's only half a share).
- ✔ The total dividend payout is $5.125 (rounded to $5.13), and the new total of shares in the account is 21.01 (the former 20.5 shares plus 0.513 share purchased by the dividend payout and rounded off; the 0.513 fraction was gained by the cash from the dividends). Full shares generate full dividends, and fractional shares generate fractional dividends.

To illustrate my point easily, the preceding example uses a price that doesn't fluctuate. In reality, stock in a DRP acts like any other stock — the share price changes constantly. Every time the DRP makes a stock purchase, whether it's monthly or quarterly, the purchase price will likely be different.

Building wealth with optional cash payments

Most DRPs (unless they're run by a broker) give the participant the opportunity to make *optional cash payments* (OCPs), which are payments you send in to purchase more stock in the DRP. DRPs usually establish a minimum and a maximum payment. The minimum is typically very modest, such as $25 or $50. A few plans even have no minimum. This feature makes it very affordable to regularly invest modest amounts and build up a sizable portfolio of stock in a short period of time, unencumbered by commissions.

DRPs also have a maximum investment limitation, such as specifying that DRP participants can't invest more than $10,000 per year. For most investors, the maximum isn't a problem because few would typically invest that much anyway. However, consult with the plan's administrator, because all plans are a little different.

OCPs are probably the most advantageous aspect of a DRP. If you can invest $25 to $50 per month consistently, year after year, at no (or little) cost, you may find that doing so is a superb way to build wealth.

OCPs work well with dollar cost averaging (DCA). Find out more in the upcoming section "The One-Two Punch: Dollar Cost Averaging and DRPs."

Checking out the cost advantages

In spite of the fact that more and more DRPs are charging service fees, DRPs are still an economical way to invest, especially for small investors. The big savings come from not paying commissions. Although many DPPs and DRPs do have charges, they tend to be relatively small (but keep track of them, because the costs can add up).

Some DRPs actually offer a discount of between 2 and 5 percent (a few are higher) when buying stock through the plan. Others offer special programs and discounts on the company's products and services. Some companies offer the service of debiting your checking account or paycheck to invest in the DRP. One company offered its shareholders significant discounts to its restaurant subsidiary. In any case, ask the plan administrator because any plus is . . . well . . . a plus.

Weighing the pros with the cons

When you're in a DRP, you reap all the benefits of stock investing. You get an annual report, and you qualify for stock splits, dividend increases, and so on. But you must be aware of the risks and responsibilities.

So before you start to salivate over all the goodies that come with DRPs, be clear-eyed about some of their negative aspects as well. Those negative aspects include the following:

- ✔ **You need to get that first share.** You have to buy that initial share in order to get the DRP started (but you knew that).

- ✔ **Even small fees cut into your profits.** More and more DRP administrators have added small fees to cover administrative costs. Find out how much they are and how they're transacted to minimize your DRP costs. The more costs you incur, of course, the more your net profit will be diminished over time.

- ✔ **Many DRPs may not have added services that you may need.** For example, you may want to have your DRP in a vehicle such as an Individual Retirement Account (IRA). (Chapter 21 offers more information on IRAs.) Many investors understand that a DRP is a long-term commitment, so having it in an IRA is an appropriate strategy. Some administrators have the ability to set up your DRP as an IRA, but some don't, so you need to inquire about this.

✔ **DRPs are designed for long-term investing.** Although getting in and out of the plan are easy, the transactions may take weeks to process because stock purchases and sales are typically done all at once on a certain day of the month (or quarter).

✔ **You need to read the prospectus.** You may not consider this a negative point, but for some people, reading a prospectus is not unlike giving blood by using leeches. Even if that's your opinion, you need to read the prospectus to avoid any surprises, such as hidden fees or unreasonable terms.

✔ **You must understand the tax issues.** There, ya see? I knew I'd ruin it for you. Just know that dividends, whether or not they occur in a DRP, are usually taxable (unless the DRP is in an IRA, which is a different matter). I cover tax issues in detail in Chapter 21.

✔ **You need to keep good records.** Keep all your statements together and use a good spreadsheet program or accounting program if you plan on doing a lot of DRP investing. These records are especially important at tax time, when you have to report any subsequent gains or losses from stock sales. Because capital gains taxes can be complicated as you sort out short-term versus long-term capital gains on your investments, DRP calculations can be a nightmare without good record-keeping.

Moving money out of DRPs to pay off debt

DRPs are a great way to accumulate a large stock holding over an extended period of time. Moreover, think about what you can do with this stock. Say that you accumulate 110 shares of stock, valued at $50 per share, in your DRP. You can, for example, take out $5,000 worth of stock (100 shares at $50 per share) and place those 100 shares in your brokerage account. The remaining 10 shares can stay in your account to keep the DRP and continue with dividend reinvestment to keep your wealth growing. Why remove those shares?

All things being equal, you're better off keeping the stock in the DRP, but what if you have $2,500 in credit card debt and don't have extra cash to pay off that debt? Brokerage accounts still have plenty of advantages, such as, in this example, the use of margin (a topic I discuss in detail in Chapter 17). If your situation merits it, you can borrow up to 50 percent of the $5,000, or $2,500, as a margin loan and use it to pay off that credit card debt. Because you're replacing unsecured debt (credit card debt that may be charging 15 percent, 18 percent, or more) with secured debt, you can save a lot of money (borrowing against stock in a brokerage account is usually cheaper than credit card debt). Another benefit is that the margin loan with your broker doesn't require monthly payments, as do the credit card balances. Additionally, ask your tax consultant about potential tax benefits — investment interest expense is deductible, but consumer credit card debt is not.

The One-Two Punch: Dollar Cost Averaging and DRPs

Dollar cost averaging (DCA) is a splendid technique for buying stock and lowering your cost for doing so. The example in Table 19-1 shows that it's not uncommon for investors to see a total cost that reflects a discount to the market value. DCA works especially well with DRPs.

DCA is a simple method for acquiring stock. It rests on the idea that you invest a fixed amount of money at regular intervals (monthly, usually) over a long period of time in a particular stock. Because a fixed amount (say, $50 per month) is going into a fluctuating investment, you end up buying less of that stock when it goes up in price and more of it when it goes down in price. Your average cost per share is usually lower than if you were to buy all the shares at once.

DCA is best presented with an example. Say you decide to get into the DRP of the company Acme Elevator, Inc. (AE). On your first day in the DRP, AE's stock is at $25, and the plan allows you to invest a minimum of $25 through its optional cash purchase (OCP) program. You decide to invest $25 per month and assess how well (hopefully) you're doing six months from now. Table 19-1 shows how this technique works.

Table 19-1		Dollar Cost Averaging (AE)		
Months	*Investment Amount*	*Purchase Price*	*Shares Bought*	*Accumulated Shares*
1	25	25	1	1
2	25	20	1.25	2.25
3	25	17.5	1.43	3.68
4	25	15	1.67	5.35
5	25	17.5	1.43	6.78
6	25	20	1.25	8.03
Totals	150	N/A	8.03	8.03

To assess the wisdom of your decision to invest in the DRP, ask yourself some questions:

- ✔ **How much did you invest over the entire six months?** Your total investment is $150. So far, so good.

- ✔ **What's the first share price for AE, and what's the last share price?** The first share price is $25, but the last share price is $20.

- ✔ **What's the market value of your investment at the end of six months?** You can easily calculate the value of your investment. Just multiply the number of shares you now own (8.03 shares) by the most recent share price ($20). The total value of your investment is $160.60.

- ✔ **What's the average share price you bought at?** The average share price is also easy to calculate. Take the total amount of your purchases ($150) and divide it by the number of shares you acquired (8.03 shares). Your average cost per share is $18.68.

Be sure to take note of the following:

- ✔ Even though the last share price ($20) is lower than the original share price ($25), your total investment's market value is still higher than your purchase amount ($160.60 compared to $150)! How can that be? You can thank dollar cost averaging. Your disciplined approach (using DCA) overcame the fluctuations in the stock price to help you gain more shares at the lower prices of $17.50 and $15.

- ✔ Your average cost per share is only $18.68. The DCA method helped you buy more shares at a lower cost, which ultimately helped you make money when the stock price made a modest rebound.

DCA not only helps you invest with small sums, but also helps you smooth out the volatility in stock prices. These benefits help you make more money in your wealth-building program over the long haul. The bottom line for long-term stock investors is that DCA is a solid investing technique, and DRPs are a great stock investment vehicle for building wealth. Can you visualize that retirement hammock yet?

Dollar cost averaging is a fantastic technique in a bull market and an okay technique in a flat or sideways market, but it's really not a good consideration during bear markets because the stock you're buying is going down in price and the market value can very easily be lower than your total investment. If you plan on holding on to the stock long-term, then simply cease your dollar cost averaging approach until times improve for the stock (and its industry, and the economy). Find out more about sectors and industries in Chapter 13 and megatrends in Chapter 14.

Chapter 20

Corporate and Government Skullduggery: Looking at Insider Activity

*I*magine that you're boarding a cruise ship, ready to enjoy a hard-earned vacation. As you merrily walk up the plank, you notice that the ship's captain and crew are charging out of the vessel, flailing their arms, and screaming at the top of their lungs. Some are even jumping into the water below. Pop quiz: Would you get on that ship? You get double credit if you can also explain why (or why not).

What does this scenario have to do with stock investing? Plenty. The behavior of the people running the boat gives you important clues about the near-term prospects for the boat. Similarly, the actions of company insiders can provide important clues into the near-term prospects for their company.

Company *insiders* are key managers or investors in the company. Insiders include the president of the company, the treasurer, or another managing officer. An insider can also be someone who owns a large stake in the company or someone on the board of directors. In any case, insiders usually have a bird's-eye view of what's going on with the company and a good idea of how well (or how poorly) the company is doing.

In this chapter, I describe different kinds of insider activities, such as insider buying, insider selling, corporate stock buybacks, and stock splits. I also show you how to keep track of these activities with the help of a few resources.

Keep tabs on what insiders are doing, because their buy/sell transactions do have a strong correlation to the near-term movement of their company's stock. However, don't buy or sell stock only because you heard that some insider did. Use the information on insider trading to confirm your own good sense in buying or selling stock. Insider trading sometimes can be a great precursor to a significant move that you can profit from if you know what to look for. Many shrewd investors have made their profits (or avoided losses) by tracking the activity of insiders.

Tracking Insider Trading

Fortunately, we live in an age of disclosure and the Internet. Insiders who buy or sell stock must file reports that document their trading activity with the Securities and Exchange Commission (SEC), which makes the documents available to the public. You can view these documents at either a regional SEC office (see www.sec.gov/contact/addresses.htm) or on the SEC's website, which maintains the EDGAR (Electronic Data Gathering, Analysis, and Retrieval) database (www.sec.gov/edgar.shtml). Just click on "Search for Company Filings." Some of the most useful documents you can view there include the following:

- **Form 3:** This form is the initial statement that insiders provide. They must file Form 3 within ten days of obtaining insider status. An insider files this report even if he hasn't made a purchase yet; the report establishes the insider's status.

- **Form 4:** This document shows the insider's activity, such as a change in the insider's position as a stockholder, how many shares the person bought and sold, or other relevant changes. Any activity in a particular month must be reported on Form 4 by the 10th of the following month.

- **Form 5:** This annual report covers transactions that are small and not required on Form 4, such as minor, internal transfers of stock.

- **Form 144:** This form serves as the public declaration by an insider of the intention to sell *restricted stock* — stock that the insider was awarded, or received from the company as compensation, or bought as a term of employment. Insiders must hold restricted stock for at least one year before they can sell it. After an insider decides to sell, she files Form 144 and then must sell within 90 days or submit a new Form 144. The insider must file the form on or before the stock's sale date. When the sale is finalized, the insider is then required to file Form 4.

Fighting accounting fraud: The Sarbanes-Oxley Act

Very often, a market that reaches a mania stage sees abuse reach extreme conditions as well. Abuse by insiders is a good example. In the stock market mania of 1997–2000, this abuse wasn't limited to just insider buying and selling of stock; it also covered the related abuse of accounting fraud. (Companies like Enron in 2001 and Fannie Mae in 2008 come to mind.) The top management executives at several prominent companies deceived investors about the companies' financial conditions and subsequently were able to increase the perceived value of the companies' stock. The stock could then be sold at a price that was higher than market value. Congress took notice of these activities and, in 2002, passed the Sarbanes-Oxley Act (SOX). Congress designed this act to protect investors from fraudulent accounting activities by corporations. SOX established a public accounting oversight board and also tightened the rules on corporate financial reporting. To find out more about this act, you can either do a search for it at www.congress.gov or get details from sites such as www.sox-online.com and www.findlaw.com.

For a more comprehensive list of insider forms (among others that are filed by public companies), go to www.sec.gov/info/edgar/forms/edgform.pdf.

Companies are required to make public the documents that track their trading activity. The SEC's website offers limited access to these documents, but for greater access, check out one of the many websites that report insider trading data, such as www.marketwatch.com and www.bloomberg.com.

The SEC has enacted the *short-swing profit rule* to protect the investing public. This rule prevents insiders from quickly buying the stock that they just sold at a profit. The insider must wait at least six months before buying it again. The SEC created this rule to prevent insiders from using their privileged knowledge to make an unfair profit quickly, before the investing public can react. The rule also applies if an insider sells stock — he can't sell it at a higher price within a six-month period.

Looking at Insider Transactions

The classic phrase "Actions speak louder than words" was probably coined for insider trading. Insiders are in the know, and keeping a watchful eye on their transactions — both buying and selling their company's stock — can provide you with very useful investing information. But insider buying and insider selling can be as different as day and night; insider buying is simple, while insider selling can be complicated. In the following sections, I present both sides of insider trading.

Breaking down insider buying

Insider buying is usually an unambiguous signal about how an insider feels about his company. After all, the primary reason that all investors buy stock is that they expect it to do well. If one insider is buying stock, that's generally not a monumental event. But if several or more insiders are buying, those purchases should certainly catch your attention.

Insider buying is generally a positive omen and beneficial for the stock's price. Also, when insiders buy stock, less stock is available to the public. If the investing public meets this decreased supply with increased demand, the stock price rises. Keep these factors in mind when analyzing insider buying:

- **Identify who's buying the stock.** The CEO is buying 5,000 shares. Is that reason enough for you to jump in? Maybe. After all, the CEO certainly knows how well the company is doing. But what if that CEO is just starting her new position? What if before this purchase she had no stock in the company at all? Maybe the stock is part of her employment package.

   The fact that a new company executive is making her first stock purchase isn't as strong a signal urging you to buy as the fact that a long-time CEO is doubling her holdings. Also, if large numbers of insiders are buying, that sends a stronger signal than if a single insider is buying.

- **See how much is being bought.** In the preceding example, the CEO bought 5,000 shares, which is a lot of stock no matter how you count it. But is it enough for you to base an investment decision on? Maybe, but a closer look may reveal more. If she already owned 1 million shares at the time of the purchase, then buying 5,000 additional shares wouldn't be such an exciting indicator of a pending stock rise. In this case, 5,000 shares is a small incremental move that doesn't offer much to get excited about.

   However, what if this particular insider has owned only 5,000 shares for the past three years and is now buying 1 million shares? Now that should arouse your interest! Usually, a massive purchase tells you that particular insider has strong feelings about the company's prospects and that she's making a huge increase in her share of stock ownership. Still, a purchase of 1 million shares by the CEO isn't as strong a signal as ten insiders buying 100,000 shares each. Again, if only one person is buying, that may or may not be a strong indication of an impending rise. However, if lots of people are buying, consider it a fantastic indication.

An insider purchase of any kind is a positive sign, but it's always more significant when a greater number of insiders are making purchases. "The more the merrier!" is a good rule for judging insider buying. All these individuals have their own, unique perspectives on the company and its prospects. Mass buying indicates mass optimism for the company's future. If the treasurer, the president, the vice president of sales, and several other key players are putting their wealth on the line and investing it in a company they know intimately, that's a good sign for your stock investment as well.

✔ **Notice the timing of the purchase.** The timing of insider stock purchases is important as well. If I tell you that five insiders bought stock at various points last year, you may say, "Hmm." But if I tell you that all five people bought substantial chunks of stock at the same time and right before earnings season, that should make you say, "HMMMMM!"

Picking up tips from insider selling

Insider stock buying is rarely negative — it either bodes well for the stock or is a neutral event at worst. But how about insider selling? When an insider sells his stock, the event can be either neutral or negative. Insider selling is usually a little tougher than insider buying to figure out, because insiders may have many different motivations to sell stock that have nothing to do with the company's future prospects. Just because the president of the company is selling 5,000 shares from his personal portfolio doesn't necessarily mean you should sell, too.

Insiders may sell their stock for a couple reasons: They may think that the company won't be doing well in the near future — a negative sign for you — or they may simply need the money for a variety of personal reasons that have nothing to do with the company's potential. Some typical reasons why insiders may sell stock include the following:

✔ **To diversify their holdings:** If an insider's portfolio is heavily weighted with one company's stock, a financial advisor may suggest that she balance her portfolio by selling some of that company's stock and purchasing other securities.

✔ **To finance personal emergencies:** Sometimes an insider needs money for medical, legal, or family reasons.

✔ **To buy a home or make another major purchase:** An insider may need the money to make a down payment, or perhaps to buy something outright without having to take out a loan.

How do you find out about the details regarding insider stock selling? Although insiders must report their pertinent stock sales and purchases to the SEC, the information isn't always revealing. As a general rule, consider the following questions when analyzing insider selling:

- **How many insiders are selling?** If only one insider is selling, that single transaction doesn't give you enough information to act on. However, if many insiders are selling, you should see a red flag. Check out any news or information that's currently available by going to websites such as www.marketwatch.com, www.sec.gov, and http://finance.yahoo.com (along with other sources in Appendix A).

- **Are the sales showing a pattern or unusual activity?** If one insider sold some stock last month, that sale alone isn't that significant an event. However, if ten insiders have each made multiple sales in the past few months, those sales are cause for concern. See whether any new developments at the company are potentially negative. If massive insider selling has recently occurred and you don't know why, consider putting a stop-loss order on your stock immediately. I cover stop-loss orders more fully in Chapter 17.

- **How much stock is being sold?** If a CEO sells 5,000 shares of stock but still retains 100,000 shares, that's not a big deal. But if the CEO sells all or most of his holdings, that's a possible negative. Check to see whether other company executives have also sold stock.

- **Do outside events or analyst reports seem coincidental with the sale of the stock?** Sometimes, an influential analyst may issue a report warning about a company's prospects. If the company's management poohpoohs the report but most of them are bailing out anyway (selling their stock), you may want to do the same. Frequently, when insiders know that damaging information is forthcoming, they sell the stock before it takes a dip.

Similarly, if the company's management issues positive public statements or reports that contradict their own behavior (they're selling their stock holdings), the SEC may investigate to see whether the company is doing anything that may require a penalty (the SEC regularly tracks insider sales).

Considering Corporate Stock Buybacks

When you read the financial pages or watch the financial shows on TV, you sometimes hear that a company is buying its own stock. The announcement may be something like, "SuperBucks Corp. has announced that it will spend $2 billion dollars to buy back its own stock." Why would a company do that, and what does that mean to you if you own the stock or are considering buying it?

When companies buy back their own stock, they're generally indicating that they believe their stock is undervalued and that it has the potential to rise. If a company shows strong fundamentals (for example, good financial condition and increasing sales and earnings; see Chapter 11 for details) and it's buying more of its own stock, it's worth investigating — it may make a great addition to your portfolio.

Just because a company announces a stock buyback doesn't always mean that one will happen. The announcement itself is meant to stir interest in the stock and cause the price to rise. The stock buyback may be only an opportunity for insiders to sell stock, or it may be needed for executive compensation — recruiting and retaining competent management are positive uses of money.

The following sections present some common reasons a company may buy back its shares from investors, as well as some ideas on the negative effects of stock buybacks.

If you see that a company is buying back its stock while most of the insiders are selling their personal shares, that's not a good sign. It may not necessarily be a bad sign, but it's not a positive sign. Play it safe and invest elsewhere.

Understanding why a company buys back shares

You bought this book because you're looking at buying stocks, but individuals aren't alone in the stock-buying universe. No, I don't just mean that mutual funds, pensions, and other entities are buyers; I mean the companies behind the stocks are buyers (and sellers), too. Why would a public company buy stock — especially its own?

Boosting earnings per share

By simply buying back its own shares from stockholders, a company can increase its earnings per share without actually earning extra money (see Chapter 11 and Appendix B for more on earnings per share). Sound like a magician's trick? Well, it is, kind of. A corporate stock buyback is a financial sleight of hand that investors should be aware of. Here's how it works: Noware Earnings, Inc., (NEI) has 10 million shares outstanding, and it's expected to net earnings of $10 million for the fourth quarter. NEI's earnings per share (EPS) would be $1 per share. So far so good. But what happens if NEI buys 2 million of its own shares? Total shares outstanding shrink to

8 million. The new EPS becomes $1.25 — the stock buyback artificially boosts the earnings per share by 25 percent!

The important point to keep in mind about stock buybacks is that actual company earnings don't change — no fundamental changes occur in company management or operations — so the increase in EPS can be misleading. But the marketplace can be obsessive about earnings, and because earnings are the lifeblood of any company, an earnings boost, even if it's cosmetic, can also boost the stock price.

If you watch a company's price-to-earnings ratio (see Chapter 11), you know that increased earnings usually mean an eventual increase in the stock price. Additionally, a stock buyback affects supply and demand. With less available stock in the market, demand necessarily sends the stock price upward.

Whenever a company makes a major purchase, such as buying back its own stock, think about how the company is paying for it and whether it seems like a good use of the company's purchasing power. In general, companies buy their stock for the same reasons any investor buys stock — they believe that the stock is a good investment and will appreciate in time. Companies generally pay for a stock buyback in one of two basic ways: funds from operations or borrowed money. Both methods have a downside. For more details, see the section "Exploring the downside of buybacks," later in this chapter.

Beating back a takeover bid

Suppose you read in the financial pages that Company X is doing a hostile takeover of Company Z. A hostile takeover doesn't mean that Company X sends storm troopers armed with mace to Company Z's headquarters to trounce its management. All a *hostile takeover* means is that X wants to buy enough shares of Z's stock to effectively control Z (and Z is unhappy about being owned or controlled by X). Because buying and selling stock happens in a public market or exchange, companies can buy each other's stock. Sometimes, the target company prefers not to be acquired, in which case it may buy back shares of its own stock to give it a measure of protection against unwanted moves by interested companies.

In some cases, the company attempting the takeover already owns some of the target company's stock. In this case, the targeted company may offer to buy those shares back from the aggressor at a premium to thwart the takeover bid. This type of offer is often referred to as *greenmail*.

Takeover concerns generally prompt interest in the investing public, driving the stock price upward and benefiting current stockholders.

Exploring the downside of buybacks

As beneficial as stock buybacks can be, they have to be paid for, and this expense has consequences. When a company uses funds from operations for the stock buyback, less money is available for other activities, such as upgrading technology, making improvements, or doing research and development. A company faces even greater dangers when it uses debt to finance a stock buyback. If the company uses borrowed funds, not only does it have less borrowing power for other uses, but it also has to pay back the borrowed funds with interest, thus lowering earnings figures.

In general, any misuse of money, such as using debt to buy back stock, affects a company's ability to grow its sales and earnings — two measures that need to maintain upward mobility to keep stock prices rising.

Say that Noware Earnings, Inc. (NEI), typically pays an annual dividend of 25 cents per share of stock and wants to buy back shares, which are currently at $10 each, with borrowed money with a 9 percent interest rate. If NEI buys back 2 million shares, it won't have to pay out $500,000 in dividends (2 million × 25 cents). That's money saved. However, NEI has to pay interest on the $20 million it borrowed ($10 per share × 2 million shares) to buy back the shares. The interest totals $1.8 million (9 percent of $20 million), and the net result from this rudimentary example is that NEI sees an outflow of $1.3 million (the difference between the interest paid out and the dividends savings).

Using debt to finance a stock buyback needs to make economic sense — it needs to strengthen the company's financial position. Perhaps NEI could have used the stock buyback money toward a better purpose, such as modernizing equipment or paying for a new marketing campaign. Because debt interest ultimately decreases earnings, companies must be careful when using debt to buy back their stock.

Stock Splits: Nothing to Go Bananas Over

Frequently, management teams decide to do a stock split. A *stock split* is the exchange of existing shares of stock for new shares from the same company. Stock splits don't increase or decrease the company's capitalization; they just change the number of shares available in the market and the per-share price.

Typically, a company may announce that it's doing a 2-for-1 stock split. For example, a company may have 10 million shares outstanding, with a market price of $40 each. In a 2-for-1 split, the company then has 20 million shares (the share total doubles), but the market price is adjusted to $20 (the share price is halved). Companies do other splits, such as a 3-for-2 or 4-for-1, but 2-for-1 is the most common split.

The following sections present the two basic types of splits: ordinary stock splits and reverse stock splits.

Qualifying for a stock split is similar to qualifying to receive a dividend — you must be listed as a stockholder as of the date of record. Keep good records regarding your stock splits in case you need to calculate capital gains for tax purposes. (For information on the date of record, see Chapter 6. See Chapter 21 for tax information.)

Ordinary stock splits

An *ordinary stock split* — when the number of stock shares increases — is the kind investors usually hear about. If you own 100 shares of Dublin, Inc., stock (at $60 per share) and the company announces a stock split, what happens? If you own the stock in certificate form, you receive in the mail a stock certificate for 100 more shares. Now, before you cheer over how your money just doubled, check the stock's new price. Each share is adjusted to a $30 value.

Not all stock is in certificate form. Stocks held in a brokerage account are recorded in book entry form. Most stock, in fact, is in book entry form. A company only issues stock certificates when necessary or when the investor requests it. If you keep the stock in your brokerage account, check with your broker for the new share total to make sure you're credited with the new number of shares after the stock split.

An ordinary stock split is primarily a neutral event, so why does a company bother to do it? The most common reason is that management believes the stock is too expensive, so it wants to lower the stock price to make the stock more affordable and therefore more attractive to new investors. Studies have shown that stock splits frequently precede a rise in the stock price. Although stock splits are considered a non-event in and of themselves, many stock experts see them as bullish signals because of the interest they generate among the investing public.

Reverse stock splits

A *reverse stock split* usually occurs when a company's management wants to raise the price of its stock. Just as ordinary splits can occur when management believes the price is too expensive, a reverse stock split means the company feels that the stock's price is too cheap. If a stock's price looks too low, that may discourage interest by individual or institutional investors (such as mutual funds). Management wants to drum up more interest in the stock for the benefit of shareholders (some of whom are probably insiders).

The company may also do a reverse split to decrease costs. When you have to send an annual report and other correspondence regularly to all the stockholders, the mailings can get a little pricey, especially if you have lots of investors who own only a few shares each. A reverse split helps consolidate shares and lower overall management costs.

A reverse split can best be explained with an example. TuCheep, Inc. (TCI), is selling at $2 per share on the Nasdaq. At that rock-bottom price, the investing public may ignore it. So TCI announces a 10-for-1 reverse stock split. Now what? If a stockholder had 100 shares at $2 (the old shares), the stockholder now owns 10 shares at $20.

Technically, a reverse split is considered a neutral event. However, just as investors may infer positive expectations from an ordinary stock split, they may have negative expectations from a reverse split because a reverse split tends to occur for negative reasons. One definitive negative reason for a reverse split is if the company's stock is threatened to be delisted. If a stock is on a major exchange and the price falls below $1, the stock will face delisting (basically getting removed from the exchange). A reverse split may be used to ward off such an event.

 If, in the event of a stock split, you end up with an odd number of shares, the company doesn't produce a fractional share. Instead, you get a check for the cash equivalent. For example, if you have 51 shares and the company announces a 2-for-1 reverse split, odds are that you'll get 25 shares and a cash payout for the odd share (or fractional share).

Keeping a Close Eye on Congress

The latest sensation in the world of insider trading has been how congresspeople of both parties have reaped fortunes by doing something that's illegal for you and me — but was legal for them! For those folks who've wondered how someone can spend millions to get a "public service" job and then retire a multimillionaire, now you have a clue: congressional insider trading.

Congressmen and women, as you know, pass laws for a variety of matters. They know which companies stand to lose or benefit as a result. They can then invest in the winners and/or avoid (or go short) the losers. (When you go short on a stock, you make money by selling high and then buying low; to get a good idea about how short selling works, see Chapter 17 for details.) Many were able to easily reap million-dollar gains because of this privileged perch they stood on.

Some folks in Congress made outrageous profits from shorting strategies during the 2008 crash when they learned of pending financial developments behind closed doors before the public (and most investors) found out. It's maddening that these politicians profited (legally!) from activities that you and I would have ended up in jail for doing.

From the furor in late 2011 over this incredible corruption came a new law passed in early 2012: the Stop Trading on Congressional Knowledge (STOCK) Act. Hopefully it will do the trick, but the real lesson for stock investors (and voters) is that we must always be vigilant about what insiders (both corporate and political) are doing. The Act is officially called H.R. 1148, and you can look it up at places such as www.opencongress.org and find other sources through your favorite search engine. Also keep track with some of the resources mentioned in Appendix A.

Chapter 21

Keeping More of Your Money from the Taxman

*A*fter conquering the world of making money with stocks, now you have another hurdle — keeping your money. Some people may tell you that taxes are brutal, complicated, and counterproductive. Others may tell you that they're a form of legalized thievery, and still others may say that they're a necessary evil. And then there are the pessimists. In any case, this chapter shows you how to keep more of the fruits from your hard-earned labor.

Note: Keep in mind that this chapter isn't meant to be comprehensive. For a fuller treatment of personal taxes, you should check with your personal tax advisor and get the publications referenced in this chapter by either visiting the IRS website at www.irs.gov or calling the IRS publications department at 800-829-3676.

However, in this chapter, I cover the most relevant points for stock investors, such as the tax treatment for dividends and capital gains and losses, common tax deductions for investors, some simple tax-reduction strategies, and pointers for retirement investing.

Tax laws can be very hairy and perplexing, and at press time, the rumblings in Washington, D.C., are for more ways to take the fruits of your labor. Higher (and more complicated) taxes generally aren't good for stock investors or the economy at large, so give the legislative folks a piece of your mind. A good way to do this is through taxpayer advocacy groups like the National Taxpayers Union (www.ntu.org). 'Nuff said.

Paying through the Nose: The Tax Treatment of Different Investments

The following sections tell you what you need to know about the tax implications you face when you start investing in stocks. It's good to know in advance the basics on ordinary income, capital gains, and capital losses because they may affect your investing strategy.

Understanding ordinary income and capital gains

Profit you make from your stock investments can be taxed in one of two ways, depending on the type of profit:

✔ **Ordinary income:** Your profit can be taxed at the same rate as wages — at your full, regular tax rate. If your tax bracket is 28 percent, for example, that's the rate at which your ordinary income investment profit is taxed. Two types of investment profits get taxed as ordinary income (Check out IRS Publication 550, "Investment Income and Expenses," for more information):

• **Dividends:** When you receive dividends (either in cash or stock), they're taxed as ordinary income. This is true even if those dividends are in a dividend reinvestment plan (see Chapter 19 to find out more about dividend reinvestment plans, or DRPs.) If, however, the dividends occur in a tax-sheltered plan, such as an IRA or 401(k) plan, then they're exempt from taxes for as long as they're in the plan. (Retirement plans are covered in the section "Taking Advantage of Tax-Advantaged Retirement Investing," later in this chapter.) Keep in mind that qualified dividends are taxed at a lower rate than nonqualified dividends. A *qualified dividend* is a dividend that receives preferential tax treatment versus other types of dividends.

Note: At the time of writing, a provision in the Patient Protection and Affordable Care Act, signed into law in 2010, may push the tax rate on dividends to almost 45 percent (yikes) so stay tuned (it may or may not be repealed or modified by the time you read this). Be sure to check with your accountant on this one.

• **Short-term capital gains:** If you sell stock for a gain and you've owned the stock for one year or less, the gain is considered ordinary income. To calculate the time, you use the *trade date* (or *date of execution*). This is the date on which you executed the order, not the settlement date. (For more on important dates, see Chapter 6.) However, if these gains occur in a tax-sheltered plan, such as a 401(k) or an IRA, no tax is triggered.

✔ **Long-term capital gains:** These are usually much better for you than ordinary income as far as taxes are concerned. The tax laws reward patient investors. After you've held the stock for at least a year and a day (what a difference a day makes!), your tax rate is reduced. Get more information on capital gains in IRS Publication 550.

You can control how you manage the tax burden from your investment profits. Gains are taxable only if a sale actually takes place (in other words, only if the gain is "realized"). If your stock in GazillionBucks, Inc., goes from $5 per share to $87, that $82 appreciation isn't subject to taxation unless you actually sell the stock. Until you sell, that gain is "unrealized." Time your stock sales carefully and hold on to stocks for at least a year to minimize the amount of taxes you have to pay on them.

When you buy stock, record the date of purchase and the *cost basis* (the purchase price of the stock plus any ancillary charges, such as commissions). This information is very important come tax time should you decide to sell your stock. The date of purchase (also known as the date of execution) helps establish the *holding period* (how long you own the stocks) that determines whether your gains are considered short term or long term.

Say you buy 100 shares of GazillionBucks, Inc., at $5 and pay a commission of $8. Your cost basis is $508 (100 shares times $5 plus $8 commission). If you sell the stock at $87 per share and pay a $12 commission, the total sale amount is $8,688 (100 shares times $87 less $12 commission). If this sale occurs less than a year after the purchase, it's a short-term gain. In the 28 percent tax bracket, the short-term gain of $8,180 ($8688 – $508) is also taxed at 28 percent. Read the following section to see the tax implications if your gain is a long-term gain.

Any gain (or loss) from a short sale is considered short term regardless of how long the position is held open. For more information on selling short, check out Chapter 17.

Minimizing the tax on your capital gains

Long-term capital gains are taxed at a more favorable rate than ordinary income. To qualify for long-term capital gains treatment, you must hold the investment for more than one year (in other words, for at least one year and one day).

Debt and taxes: Another angle

If you truly need cash but you don't want to sell your stock because it's doing well and you want to avoid paying capital gains tax, consider borrowing against it. If the stock is listed (on the New York Stock Exchange, for example) and is in a brokerage account with margin privileges, you can borrow up to 50 percent of the value of marginable securities at favorable rates (listed stocks are marginable securities). The money you borrow is considered a margin loan (see Chapter 17 for details), and the interest you pay is low (compared to credit cards or personal loans) because it's considered a secured loan (your stock acts as collateral). On those rare occasions when I use margin, I usually make sure I use stocks that generate a high dividend. That way, the stocks themselves help to pay off the margin loan. In addition, if the proceeds are used for an investment purpose, the margin interest may be tax-deductible. See IRS Publication 550 for more details.

Recall the example in the preceding section with GazillionBucks, Inc. As a short-term transaction at the 28 percent tax rate, the tax is $2,290 ($8,180 × 28 percent). After you revive, you say, "Gasp! What a chunk of dough. I better hold off a while longer." You hold on to the stock for more than a year to achieve the status of long-term capital gains. How does that change the tax? For anyone in the 28-percent tax bracket or higher, the long-term capital gains rate of 15 percent applies. In this case, the tax is $1,227 ($8,180 × 15 percent), resulting in a tax savings to you of $1,063 ($2,290 less $1,227). Okay, it's not a fortune, but it's a substantial difference from the original tax. After all, successful stock investing isn't only about making money . . . it's about keeping it too.

Capital gains taxes *can* be lower than the tax on ordinary income, but they can't be higher. If, for example, you're in the 15 percent tax bracket for ordinary income and you have a long-term capital gain that would normally bump you up to the 28 percent tax bracket, the gain is taxed at your lower rate of 15 percent instead of a higher capital gains rate. Check with your tax advisor on a regular basis, because this rule could change due to new tax laws.

Don't sell a stock just because it qualifies for long-term capital gains treatment, even if the sale eases your tax burden. If the stock is doing well and meets your investing criteria, hold on to it.

Coping with capital losses

Ever think that having the value of your stocks fall could be a good thing? Perhaps the only real positive regarding losses in your portfolio is that they can reduce your taxes. A *capital loss* means that you lost money on your investments. This amount is generally deductible on your tax return, and you can claim a loss on either long-term or short-term stock holdings. This loss can go against your other income and lower your overall tax.

Say you bought Worth Zilch Co. stock for a total purchase price of $3,500 and sold it later at a sale price of $800. Your tax-deductible capital loss is $2,700.

The one string attached to deducting investment losses on your tax return is that the most you can report in a single year is $3,000. On the bright side, though, any excess loss isn't really lost — you can carry it forward to the next year. If you have net investment losses of $4,500 in 2011, you can deduct $3,000 in 2011 and carry the remaining $1,500 loss over to 2012 and deduct it on your 2012 tax return.

Before you can deduct losses, they must first be used to offset any capital gains. If you realize long-term capital gains of $7,000 in Stock A and long-term capital losses of $6,000 in Stock B, then you have a net long-term capital gain of $1,000 ($7,000 gain less the offset of $6,000 loss). Whenever possible, see whether losses in your portfolio can be realized to offset any capital gains to reduce potential tax. IRS Publication 550 includes information for investors on capital gains and losses.

Here's your optimum strategy: Where possible, keep losses on a short-term basis and push your gains into long-term capital gains status. If a transaction can't be tax free, at the very least try to defer the tax to keep your money working for you.

Evaluating gains and losses scenarios

Of course, any investor can come up with hundreds of possible gains and losses scenarios. For example, you may wonder what happens if you sell part of your holdings now as a short-term capital loss and the remainder later as a long-term capital gain. You must look at each sale of stock (or potential sale) methodically to calculate the gain or loss you would realize from it. Figuring out your gain or loss isn't that complicated. Here are some general rules to help you wade through the morass. If you add up all your gains and losses and

- **The net result is a short-term gain:** It's taxed at your highest tax bracket (as ordinary income).

- **The net result is a long-term gain:** It's taxed at 15 percent if you're in the 28 percent tax bracket or higher. If you're in the 15 percent tax bracket or lower, the tax rate on long-term capital gains is 0 percent in 2011.

- ✔ **The net result is a loss of $3,000 or less:** It's fully deductible against other income. If you're married filing separately, your deduction limit is $1,500.

- ✔ **The net result is a loss that exceeds $3,000:** You can only deduct up to $3,000 in that year; the remainder goes forward to future years.

Sharing Your Gains with the IRS

Of course, you don't want to pay more taxes than you have to, but as the old cliché goes, "Don't let the tax tail wag the investment dog." You should buy or sell a stock because it makes economic sense first and consider the tax implications as secondary issues. After all, taxes consume a relatively small portion of your gain. As long as you experience a *net gain* (gain after all transaction costs, including taxes, brokerage fees, and other related fees), consider yourself a successful investor — even if you have to give away some of your gain to taxes.

Try to make tax planning second nature in your day-to-day activities. No, you don't have to consume yourself with a blizzard of paperwork and tax projections. I simply mean that when you make a stock transaction, keep the receipt and maintain good records. When you make a large purchase or sale, pause for a moment and ask yourself whether this transaction will have positive or negative tax consequences. (Refer to the section "Paying through the Nose: The Tax Treatment of Different Investments," earlier in this chapter, to review various tax scenarios.) Speak to a tax consultant beforehand to discuss the ramifications.

In the following sections, I describe the tax forms you need to fill out, as well as some important rules to follow.

Filling out forms

Most investors report their investment-related activities on their individual tax returns (Form 1040). The reports that you'll likely receive from brokers and other investment sources include the following:

- ✔ **Brokerage and bank statements:** Monthly statements that you receive

- ✔ **Trade confirmations:** Documents to confirm that you bought or sold stock

- ✔ **1099-DIV:** Reporting dividends paid to you

- ✔ **1099-INT:** Reporting interest paid to you

- ✔ **1099-B:** Reporting gross proceeds submitted to you from the sale of investments, such as stocks and mutual funds

You may receive other, more obscure forms that aren't listed here. You should retain all documents related to your stock investments.

The IRS schedules and forms that most stock investors need to be aware of and/or attach to their Form 1040 include the following:

- ✔ **Schedule B:** To report interest and dividends

- ✔ **Schedule D:** To report capital gains and losses

- ✔ **Form 4952:** Investment Interest Expense Deduction

- ✔ **Publication 17:** Guide to Form 1040

You can get these publications directly from the IRS at 800-829-3676, or you can download them from the website (www.irs.gov). For more information on what records and documentation investors should hang on to, check out IRS Publication 552, "Recordkeeping for Individuals."

If you plan to do your own taxes, consider using the latest tax software products, which are inexpensive and easy to use. These programs usually have a question-and-answer feature to help you do your taxes step by step, and they include all the necessary forms. Consider getting either TurboTax (www.turbotax.com) or H&R Block At Home (formerly TaxCut) (www.hrblock.com/tax-software) at your local software vendor or the companies' websites. Alternatively, you can get free tax preparation software at www.taxact.com.

Playing by the rules

Some people get the smart idea of, "Hey! Why not sell my losing stock by December 31 to grab the short-term loss and just buy back the stock on January 2 so that I can have my cake and eat it, too?" Not so fast. The IRS puts the kibosh on maneuvers like that with something called the *wash-sale rule*. This rule states that if you sell a stock for a loss and buy it back within 30 days, the loss isn't valid because you didn't make any substantial investment change. The wash-sale rule applies only to losses. The way around the rule is simple: Wait at least 31 days before you buy that identical stock back again.

Some people try to get around the wash-sale rule by doubling up on their stock position with the intention of selling half. Therefore, the IRS makes the 30-day rule cover both sides of the sale date. That way, an investor can't buy the identical stock within 30 days just before the sale and then realize a short-term loss for tax purposes.

Discovering the Softer Side of the IRS: Tax Deductions for Investors

In the course of managing your portfolio of stocks and other investments, you'll probably incur expenses that are tax-deductible. The tax laws allow you to write off certain investment-related expenses as itemized expenses on Schedule A — an attachment to IRS Form 1040. Keep records of your deductions and retain a checklist to remind you which deductions you normally take. IRS Publication 550 ("Investment Income and Expenses") gives you more details.

The following sections explain common tax deductions for investors: investment interest, miscellaneous expenses, and donations to charity. I also list a few items you *can't* deduct.

Investment interest

If you pay any interest to a stockbroker, such as margin interest or any interest to acquire a taxable financial investment, that's considered investment interest and is usually fully deductible as an itemized expense.

Keep in mind that not all interest is deductible. Consumer interest or interest paid for any consumer or personal purpose isn't deductible. For more general information, see the section covering interest in IRS Publication 17.

Miscellaneous expenses

Most investment-related deductions are reported as miscellaneous expenses. Here are some common deductions:

- Accounting or bookkeeping fees for keeping records of investment income
- Any expense related to tax service or education
- Computer expense — you can take a depreciation deduction for your computer if you use it 50 percent of the time or more for managing your investments

✔ Investment management or investment advisor's fees (fees paid for advice on tax-exempt investments aren't deductible)

✔ Legal fees involving stockholder issues

✔ Safe-deposit box rental fee or home safe to hold your securities, unless used to hold personal effects or tax-exempt securities

✔ Service charges for collecting interest and dividends

✔ Subscription fees for investment advisory services

✔ Travel costs to check investments or to confer with advisors regarding income-related investments

You can deduct only that portion of your miscellaneous expenses that exceeds 2 percent of your adjusted gross income. For more information on deducting miscellaneous expenses, check out IRS Publication 529.

Donations of stock to charity

What happens if you donate stock to your favorite (IRS-approved) charity? Because it's a noncash charitable contribution, you can deduct the market value of the stock.

Say that last year you bought stock for $2,000 and it's worth $4,000 this year. If you donate it this year, you can write off the market value at the time of the contribution. In this case, you have a $4,000 deduction. Use IRS Form 8283, which is an attachment to Schedule A, to report noncash contributions exceeding $500.

To get more guidance from the IRS on this matter, get Publication 526, "Charitable Contributions."

Knowing what you can't deduct

Just to be complete, here are some items you may think you can deduct, but, alas, you can't:

✔ Financial planning or investment seminars

✔ Any costs connected with attending stockholder meetings

✔ Home office expenses for managing your investments

Taking Advantage of Tax-Advantaged Retirement Investing

If you're going to invest for the long term (such as your retirement), you may as well maximize your use of tax-sheltered retirement plans. Many different types of plans are available; I touch on only the most popular ones in the following sections. Although retirement plans may not seem relevant for investors who buy and sell stocks directly (as opposed to a mutual fund), some plans, called self-directed retirement accounts, allow you to invest directly.

IRAs

Individual Retirement Accounts (IRAs) are accounts you can open with a financial institution, such as a bank or a mutual fund company. An IRA is available to almost anyone who has earned income, and it allows you to set aside and invest money to help fund your retirement. Opening an IRA is easy, and virtually any bank or mutual fund can guide you through the process. Two basic types of IRAs are traditional and Roth.

Traditional IRA

The traditional Individual Retirement Account (also called the deductible IRA) was first popularized in the early 1980s. In a traditional IRA, you can make a tax-deductible contribution of up to $5,000 in 2011 (some restrictions apply). Individuals age 50 and older can make additional "catch-up" investments of $1,000. For 2012 and beyond, the limits will be indexed to inflation.

The money can then grow in the IRA account unfettered by current taxes, because the money isn't taxed until you take it out. Because IRAs are designed for retirement purposes, you can start taking money out of your IRA in the year you turn 59½. (Hmm. That must really disappoint those who want their money in the year they turn 58¾.) The withdrawals at that point are taxed as ordinary income. Fortunately, you'll probably be in a lower tax bracket then, so the tax shouldn't be as burdensome.

Keep in mind that you're required to start taking distributions from your account when you reach age 70½ (that's gotta be a bummer for those who prefer the age of 71⅞). After that point, you may no longer contribute to a traditional IRA. Again, check with your tax advisor to see how this criteria affects you personally.

If you take out money from an IRA too early, the amount is included in your taxable income, and you may be zapped with a 10 percent penalty. You can avoid the penalty if you have a good reason. (The IRS provides a list of reasons in Publication 590, "Individual Retirement Arrangements.")

To put money into an IRA, you must earn income equal to or greater than the amount you're contributing. *Earned income* is money made either as an employee or a self-employed person. Although traditional IRAs can be great for investors, the toughest part about them is qualifying — they have income limitations and other qualifiers that make them less deductible based on how high your income is. See IRS Publication 590 for more details.

Wait a minute! If IRAs usually involve mutual funds or bank investments, how does the stock investor take advantage of them? Here's how: Stock investors can open a self-directed IRA with a brokerage firm. This means that you can buy and sell stocks in the account with no taxes on dividends or capital gains. The account is tax-deferred, so you don't have to worry about taxes until you start making withdrawals. Also, many dividend reinvestment plans (DRPs) can be set up as IRAs as well. See Chapter 19 for more about DRPs.

Roth IRA

The Roth IRA is a great retirement plan that I wish had existed a long time ago. Here are some ways to distinguish the Roth IRA from the traditional IRA:

- ✔ The Roth IRA provides no tax deduction for contributions.

- ✔ Money in the Roth IRA grows tax-free and can be withdrawn tax-free when you turn 59½.

- ✔ The Roth IRA is subject to early distribution penalties (although there are exceptions). Distributions have to be qualified to be penalty- and tax-free; in other words, make sure that any distribution is within the guidelines set by the IRS (see Pub. 590).

The maximum contribution per year for Roth IRAs is the same as for traditional IRAs. You can open a self-directed account with a broker as well. See IRS Publication 590 for details on qualifying.

401 (k) plans

Company-sponsored 401(k) plans (named after the section in the tax code that allows them) are widely used and very popular. In a 401(k) plan, companies set aside money from their employees' paychecks that employees can use to invest for retirement. Generally, in 2012 you can invest as much as $17,000 of your pretax earned income and have it grow tax-deferred. Those over age 50 can contribute more as a "catch-up" contribution. For 2013 and beyond, check with the IRS and/or your tax advisor.

Usually, the money is put in mutual funds administered through a mutual fund company or an insurance firm. Although most 401(k) plans aren't self-directed, I mention them in this book for good reason.

Because your money is in a mutual fund that may invest in stocks, take an active role in finding out the mutual funds in which you're allowed to invest. Most plans offer several types of stock mutual funds. Use your growing knowledge about stocks to make more informed choices about your 401(k) plan options. For more information on 401(k) and other retirement plans, check out IRS Publication 560.

If you're an employee, you can also find out more about retirement plans from the Department of Labor at www.dol.gov/ebsa/publications/wyskapr.html.

Keep in mind that a mutual fund is only as good as what it invests in. Ask the plan administrator some questions about the funds and the types of stocks the plan invests in. Are the stocks defensive or cyclical? (For more information on defensive and cyclical stocks, see Chapter 13.) Are they large cap or small cap? (See Chapter 1 for more about these types of stocks.) If you don't make an informed choice about the investments in your plan, someone else will (such as the plan administrator), and that someone probably doesn't have the same ideas about your money that you do.

Part V
The Part of Tens

In this part . . .

This wouldn't be a *For Dummies* book if I didn't include a Part of Tens. Here you find quick reference lists of many basic stock investing ideas and strategies. I point out what nonstock strategies go well with stocks and what great opportunities exist for today's investor. I also include considerations for when your portfolio is down — and also when it's up. Check the information in this part when you don't have time to read the denser parts of the book or when you just need a quick refresher on what to do before, after, and even during your stock investing pursuits.

Chapter 22

Ten Considerations When Your Stock Portfolio Is Down

Your stock portfolio is down, or perhaps one stock has taken a tumble. Considering the ways of the world in recent years, is that so shocking? At the very least, it is unsettling, and all stockholders have experienced setbacks in some, if not all, of their holdings. The best in the business saw some heavy losses, and even legendary investors such as Warren Buffet took it on the chin in 2008. But fast forward to today . . . what should you do in the event of lower stock prices? This chapter provides ten actions for you to consider.

Do Nothing

Doing nothing doesn't sound good to you, I bet. "Do nothing?! Here I am trying not to freak out, and there you are Mr. Stay-calm-author!" Well, before you dismiss the idea outright, think it over.

Selling should be a matter tied to other factors (you need the money, tax considerations, and so forth), not tied to the intricate idea that the stock itself is wrong. Look . . . if you've chosen a solid company that's fundamentally strong (you read Parts II and III, right?), then there's no need to be impulsive and sell emotionally. If history is any indication, good stocks come back. You don't want to sell a stock when *everyone* is selling; you want to consider doing the opposite of what the crowd is doing.

Too often I've seen people go through the "woulda, coulda, shoulda" when they buy a stock and it goes down. Then they sell it. Guess what? When it later returned to new highs they went through the "woulda, coulda, shoulda" syndrome again. Look, patience and discipline are important for investors in good times . . . but they're even more important in bad times.

Evaluate the Big Picture

If the company whose stock you own is a solid company and looking good, you may need to look beyond that and ask about the big picture. Is there anything ominous on the economic and political landscape that could be like a meteor aimed at your stock portfolio? That's certainly possible. What does the big picture look like?

Sometimes, the big picture tells us that stocks — any stocks! — may not be a good place. That moment is, of course, rare, but it can happen. Can current economic conditions lead to the idea that stocks in general are bad to hold on to? That remains to be seen, but certainly investors can be in conditions that are bearish for stocks in general. I regularly review some websites that do a great job of informing or alerting me to the big picture, including www. financialsense.com, www.kingworldnews.com, www.marketwatch. com, and www.grandfathereconomicreport.com.

If it looks that way, it behooves you to tilt your stock portfolio toward dividend-paying stocks (such as utilities), which will at least give you cash flow until the coast is clear. For more information about dividends, check out Chapters 3 and 9.

Assess Your Needs

No matter how badly or how well a stock is doing, the issue may really be your personal situation. Many folks panicked and sold stocks during 2008–2009 because they needed the money! People lost their jobs or saw their debt or cash flow getting out of hand. You never want to sell a stock out of weakness, but if you need the money, what do you do? You end up selling because your immediate financial needs certainly trump any considerations tied to the stock's value or prospects.

Make sure that you have an emergency fund in addition to a good stock portfolio, as I explain in Chapter 2. You want to sell a stock because it's no longer a desirable holding, not because you need the cash.

Check the Stock Periodically

If a company is good and its prospects look good, then I wouldn't sweat the short-term gyrations in its price. A stock price moves up and down as buyers and sellers get in and out of it. There will be days when it looks like everyone is racing for the exits. But the bottom line is that good stocks will ultimately zigzag upwards.

Periodically review the stock. If no news has come out about the stock, check once every three or six months. How is it progressing? How are its sales and profits? Are they getting better, or not? How about its balance sheet? Is it better or worse now than it was a year ago? If the stock's fundamentals are deteriorating and its industry is issuing some gloomy reports, reconsider owning it. (Flip to Part III, which includes chapters to help you research and pick stocks.)

Buy More Stock

"Buy more stock? Are you crazy, Mr. Author-sez-buy-more-stock?" Yeah . . . I'm serious. Look, stock investing is a long-term pursuit. A stock price is only a snapshot of how much the market says it values the stock at a given moment. It's not the be-all and end-all that says what the underlying stock is actually worth.

If the company's fundamentals indicate real value that is higher than the current quoted stock price, why not buy more? Think about it this way: If you love bread and you bought bread yesterday for $3 a loaf, and today you find that bread is on sale for $2.50, do you panic about the value of bread? No, of course not. The value of that bread is indeed $3, but the current price is $2.50. Where I come from, that's called a "sale!" Get some more!

A stock's price is not always a determinant of the stock's (and hence the company's) current value. If the value of the underlying company is greater than the stock's price, consider that a "sale" or "buying opportunity" to pick up more value for less out-of-pocket cost. (Chapter 11 has details on determining a stock's value.)

Consider a Stop-Loss Order

A *stop-loss order* instructs your broker to sell a particular stock in your portfolio only when the stock reaches a particular price. The idea of putting a stop-loss order on a stock that's already down sounds like closing the barn door after the horse is gone. Well, just maybe, there's another horse inside the barn that could also race out and be gone. In other words, is there potential for a greater downside with this particular stock?

It's bad enough if a stock plummets from $50 to $40, but there are many examples of stocks that have gone to zero. Better to save some of your money than to lose all of it.

Chapter 17 goes into greater detail about stop-loss orders. Don't forget to make it a "good-til-canceled" order so the protection covers the stock for an extended period of time.

Think about a Trailing Stop

If you're considering a stop-loss order (see the preceding section), take a look again at the trailing stop. It still has the downside protection of the stop-loss order, but this particular order is more dynamic than the stop-loss order because it has the potential to ride the stock in the event of a rebound in its price. When the rebound unfolds, the trailing stop keeps increasing the "floor" to the stock's price, and you increase the chance of either seeing your stock zigzag upward or selling (when the stop order is triggered) at a higher level. Flip to Chapter 17 for more details.

Survey Small Caps

In the event that some of your stocks are down, I mention the idea of buying more stock of that particular company earlier in this chapter. Why not? If everything about the stock is positive and the only negative is that the stock's price is down, then buying more stock is a good idea. Here's a twist on that point for those investors who are a little bit more venturous: Buy small cap stocks.

If the stock is down and (presumably) the industry or sector is down, then more buying opportunities are at hand. If you're a little more aggressive in your approach (say, you're a 30-something with a long-time horizon), why not buy some small cap stocks in that same industry or sector? (A *small cap stock* is the stock of a company valued between $250 million and $1 billion; see Chapter 1 for the scoop.)

In the event of a sharp pullback in stock prices, typically the prices of small cap stocks are more volatile, and they tend to fall by a greater percentage. Of course, when a bullish up-move in that sector occurs, small cap stocks have the tendency to go up sharply as well.

If you're seeking value and are more aggressive than the average investor, pick up small cap stocks that are undervalued (due to being oversold in a correction or market pullback) and have the realistic potential of giving you much greater gains when the rebound does occur.

Explore Exchange-Traded Funds

In the preceding section, I give you the idea of picking up small cap stocks in the event of a market pullback (a buying opportunity), to take advantage of the coming upturn in stock prices. That's fine if you're more growth-oriented or aggressive, but what if you're more conservative in your approach? What if you're in your pre-retirement years and won't (or can't) tolerate the risk? Then consider a safer way of playing that plunge with the expectation of the eventual rebound.

Say that the energy sector gets battered in a stock market that has fallen sharply; of course, there may then be buying opportunities in energy stocks. But conservative investors certainly have choices that are suitable. At that point, why not "buy the whole industry" (so to speak) by simply buying an energy exchange-traded fund (ETF)? An ETF gives you the ability to buy in a single security a portfolio that includes the top 40–50 stocks in a particular sector. More guidance on buying ETFs is in Chapter 5.

Sell the Losers

Even the best investors have had to get rid of losers in their portfolios. There's no shame in selling a stock at a loss (just remember to keep the winners!). All portfolios need adjusting from time to time, and your biggest concern is that the overall portfolio is trending upward.

When that "loser" is showing no signs of promise for the future, you may as well take advantage in other ways. When you sell that losing stock, the money can be reinvested in a better stock and have the opportunity to be a winner. In addition, that losing stock may benefit you taxwise because net losses give you tax benefits (at the very least). Find out more about capital losses in Chapter 21.

Chapter 23

Ten Considerations When Your Stock Portfolio Is Up

In This Chapter

▶ Using long-term investing strategies

▶ Considering orders, triggers, and options

*A*ll of your research and incisive decision-making has paid off! Your stock is up, and you're feeling good about that. But hold on! The world's events and shaky conditions keep you on your toes. What should you do? This chapter lists ten considerations to make when your stock portfolio is doing well (and you want to help it stay that way!).

Reassess Your Portfolio Periodically

If you see that your stock portfolio is zigzagging upward, it's a good time to reassess and make sure that it's on the right track. Are there any stocks that look wobbly? Have you seen any disconcerting reports on a particular stock or industry that's in your portfolio?

When you get a chance, redo the process that got you to buy that stock or exchange-traded fund (ETF; see Chapter 5). Does it still have the plusses that you saw when you initially acquired that stock? Are the fundamentals still good? Are sales and profits still looking good? Is the industry still on a long-term uptrend? (Flip to Parts II and III for a refresher on researching and picking winners.)

If all the positives are still there, there's probably little to do (for now anyway). Just jot a reminder on your calendar to reassess quarterly (or when a major event occurs, such as a major financial crisis, an act of war, or another far-reaching or impactful event).

Figure Out Whether Your Needs Have Changed

Sometimes the issue isn't your portfolio. Maybe what needs to be reassessed is you! Consider what's happening in your life, your work, or your family. Imagine what a genius you'd look like to your spouse if you cashed in a winning stock just before it pulled back — at the right time to take advantage of that sale at the big-box home improvement store to fix up your bathroom!

If that winning stock in your portfolio is a growth stock, would you still hold it if you came across a milestone event in your life? If, for example, you're nearing retirement age, why not remix your portfolio to become a little more defensive? Perhaps that "hot growth stock" that has performed so well over the years is good enough to cash out. Then you can use the proceeds to buy a good income stock from the same sector or industry.

The bottom line is stocks and stock strategies can vary widely, and a change may be necessary based on personal changes you may be experiencing. Check out Chapter 2 for pointers on assessing your current financial situation and goals.

Use the Almighty Trailing Stop Order

Getting jittery about the market? What's happening with your stock? Keep in mind that success with your stocks isn't just based on what you invest in — it's also based on how you invest. What better way to protect your gains than with the trailing stop?

A *trailing stop* is a stop-loss order that an investor actively manages by moving it up along with the stock's market price. The stop "trails" the stock price upward. As the stop goes upward, it protects more and more of the stock's value from declining. In the event that the stock does fall, the trailing stop stays put at the last point, and it triggers a sale when the stock hits that price.

The trailing stop is one of my favorite strategies, especially if the market grows uncertain (or maybe the investor becomes uncertain!). You can easily add it, and you can remove or extend it as you see fit. For more details on trailing stops, go to Chapter 17.

Add Stability with Exchange-Traded Funds

If the hot stocks in your portfolio look like they've been overbought (I discuss this condition in Chapter 10), consider some ways to protect your gains and add some stability to your portfolio.

If, for example, you have a great energy stock that has performed well in recent months or years, why not switch to an energy stock ETF? That way you can continue to be bullish on the same sector while switching gears to a more conservative strategy (food for thought!). I talk about ETFs in detail in Chapter 5.

A good time to make this type of switch is when the stock has a long-term capital gain (in other words, when the stock has given you a nice profit, which, in turns, becomes a taxable gain). That way, you lock in a lower tax cost while simultaneously going from a growth stock to a more stable position. Flip to Chapter 21 for more about taxes.

Apply Long-Term Logic

Maybe, just maybe, buying more of your hot stocks is a good idea. If you are indeed a long-term investor and you don't need the money until years from now, why not increase your holdings of a winner?

Maybe you have 200 shares of that winning stock; why not have 300 shares? It doesn't necessarily mean a riskier holding because other strategies can kick in very easily (such as trailing stops or covered call writing, both of which I discuss in this chapter). If the long-term picture still looks bright for that stock and the industry/sector that it's in, consider increasing your holdings. Keep in mind that no stock holding should be greater than 5 percent of a total financial portfolio for the average investor.

Place a Limit Order

Assuming you like a stock and plan on holding it for the long term, consider putting on a limit order at a lower price and making it good-til-canceled (GTC). If the stock does take a breather and corrects as surely as most stocks do, the limit order gives you a way to accumulate more stock on the cheap when a price break presents itself.

Limit orders give you the ability to get your specific price (up or down), but they can sometimes vary from broker to broker on how they get triggered. Some brokers buy (or sell) the stock at an exact price while others treat the limit order as a trigger that turns into a market order and makes that purchase (or sale) at a different price from what you expected. Make sure you check with your broker about the specifics of limit orders. More on limit orders is in Chapter 17.

Set Up Triggers

Don't be gun-shy about *broker triggers* (like that pun?). These are just orders and/or e-mail alerts that brokers use to help their customers navigate the market environment. Is some news hitting your stock or its particular industry? Triggers act like an early warning system when certain events and conditions occur so that you can act on them (by buying or selling your stock). Many brokerage firms have websites that allow you to customize your orders. In addition, websites such as www.marketwatch.com and www.bloomberg.com can e-mail you news alerts on stocks and market news. You can find out more about broker orders (such as trade triggers) in Chapter 18.

Consider the Protective Put

A *put option* is a bet you make that a particular investment (such as a stock or commodity) will go down in price during a specific period of time. It has been used as a speculative vehicle by those who are "bearish" on a particular investment. In the context of this chapter, the put option has an entirely different use: as a tool to protect you from loss.

The type of put option that I'm referring to is called a *protective put*. You typically buy it on a stock (or ETF or other investment) you already own. Of course, if you own that particular stock, you certainly aren't hoping that it goes down, but that protective put acts like a form of insurance in case the stock does decline.

If your stock goes down (temporarily), your protective put goes up. You can then continue holding on to the stock and sell the put option at a profit. The profit you make on the put can offset (wholly or partially) the temporary decline in the stock.

Protective puts are a relatively common strategy, and you can easily find out about them using a simple search online. A good place to get tutorials on the protective put is the Chicago Board Options Exchange (CBOE) website (www.cboe.com/strategies/pdf/protectiveputsstrategy.pdf). If this specific sub-address is no longer valid, do a search for "protective put" from the CBOE's main page at www.cboe.com.

Check Out the Covered Call Option

Writing covered call options is a good way to generate income from an existing stock in your portfolio. Simply stated, a *covered call option* is a vehicle that gives you a chance to make money from stocks in your brokerage account. It's an ultra-safe way to generate more income — as much as 10 percent, 15 percent, or more — from your stock position.

If you have stocks that have experienced a strong rise, it may be an opportune time to do a covered call, which will help you generate some good income.

Covered call options are beyond the scope of this book, but I strongly recommend that you look into them because they can be a safe wealth-building feature, even in portfolios that are temporarily down. You can find excellent tutorials and beginners' information on covered call options at the Chicago Board Options Exchange (www.cboe.com/strategies/pdf/covered calls.pdf). Another educational source for you is the Options Industry Council (www.888options.com). It's easy to do a search for "covered call" on the home page.

For more on options in general, see *Trading Options For Dummies* by George A. Fontanills (published by Wiley).

Think about a Zero-Cost Collar

A *zero-cost collar* is an option combination that you do on your stock: simultaneously buying a put option and selling a covered call. The goal of this strategy is to protect or "collar" the price of your stock so that it has little wiggle room. The covered call limits the upside of the stock, but the put option increases in value should the stock decline.

Where does the "zero-cost" come in? Well, if you do it right, the income from the covered call that you receive can be enough money to buy the put so you can easily avoid any out-of-pocket costs. It's like free "price insurance" for your stock. Cool!

To find out more about this strategy, go to the CBOE and Options Industry council for their tutorials. In addition, you can get full details on this strategy in *Trading Options For Dummies* (see the preceding section for more on these resources).

Chapter 24

Ten Challenges and Opportunities for Stock Investors

Stock investing doesn't happen in a vacuum; it operates in a world swirling with issues and events that affect your stocks and stock investing decisions. Issues and events?! Oh man . . . what a time to be alive! Since 2008, indeed it has been a "brave, new world" and stock-picking is no longer a rational or (somewhat) easy pursuit. Fortunately, it can still be profitable if you see clearly what the stock market faces today.

Events and conditions in today's economic and social landscape will either help or hurt your stock picks. Queue into today's unfolding challenges and opportunities for wiser stock investing; I present ten of them in this chapter.

Debt, Debt, and More Debt

Virtually all categories of debt (personal, corporate, government, and so forth) are either at record highs or pretty darn close; for example, I recently saw a headline that college debt has reached a mind-boggling $1 trillion. To view the scary show (coming to a wallet near you!) go to www.usdebt clock.org. Chilling!

We are living in the age of overindebtedness (just talk to someone from Greece or California!). For stock investors, the point is loud and clear. If a company is too overindebted or has customers that are overindebted, the risk to the economic health of that company becomes obvious. If you invest in a stock that's exposed to debt problems, directly or indirectly, you'll be at risk.

Take a close look at the company's financials with the help of Chapters 11 and 12, and ask yourself how exposed the company is to excessive debt. Too much debt means too much risk for its stock. Look elsewhere for potential investments, because there are plenty of stocks with low (or controllable) levels of debt.

Inflation

Inflation is related to the preceding section on debt, especially government debt. When governments spend beyond their means, they, of course, go into debt (like the rest of us). However, when push comes to shove, they can print (in other words, create) money to pay this debt (unlike the rest of us). Most governments that produce their own currency, such as the United States and Japan, tend to overproduce (what an understatement!) money. When you have too much money chasing too few goods and services, you have inflation.

Given this reality, it's important to keep some things in your portfolio that benefit from inflation, such as gold- and silver-related stocks and exchange-traded funds (ETFs) as well as other stocks that stand to benefit, such as energy and grain companies. Flip to Chapter 5 for more about ETFs; I touch on precious metals and energy in Chapter 14.

Unfunded Liabilities

The public hears enough about the country's debt, but it doesn't understand that the stated debt is only part of the liability issues the country faces. One of the least well-known but most troubling aspects of today's massive debt picture is unfunded liabilities. The future liabilities of paying government pensions (such as Social Security) and Medicare/Medicaid actually dwarf the national debt. The national debt (as I write this) recently passed $16 trillion (and is still galloping along), but the federal government's total unfunded liabilities are north of $100 trillion, and climbing. Add to that nosebleed-level number the unfunded liabilities of state and local governments (around $2.5 trillion as of mid-2012).

The point is that those pensioners and payees who think that money is coming their way had better rethink that. When these folks need money that they were counting on for their bills and don't get it . . . what then? You'll hear lots of clicking at brokerage sites ("confirm sell order here").

Your best bet is to assume that the money from these shaky sources won't be there and act accordingly. It sounds extreme, but if you become as self-reliant as possible (for example, by bulking up your portfolio with quality, dividend-paying stocks; see Chapters 3 and 9), you'll be less susceptible to the coming difficulties. And hey, if nothing really bad happens, you'll be that much better off!

The Growth of Government

When you invest in stocks, you invest in companies. These companies, along with their customers and investors, are producers in the private economy. The private economy, in turn, supports government — its programs, public sector employees, dependents, and so on. From a functional point of view, the government is a burden that must be carried by the private sector. This specific point about being a burden is neither a negative nor positive point; it's just a reality.

The private sector has been able to shoulder the government and its related programs for decades, and it has generally worked well. However, the growth has crossed a troublesome line. The federal government's debt has recently exceeded 100 percent of the country's gross domestic product (GDP) and has grown dramatically in recent years (I touch on this debt earlier in this chapter). Additionally, the federal annual budget (in terms of outlays or spending) is now greater than 28 percent of the country's GDP, the highest level in half a century.

History (and places like Greece in 2011) tells us that this type of development is unsustainable and that it can have profound and troubling effects on the private sector (translation: the stock market goes down). What's an investor to do?

Investing in quality stocks is part of an overall, long-term, wealth-building strategy, but along the way, and especially during perilous times, prudent safeguards should be utilized. Be sure to visit Chapter 4 (on risk and volatility) and Chapter 17 (covering stop-loss orders).

International Challenges

The world's stability seems to be getting more fragile; issues with financial crises, government mismanagement, and regional conflicts in Europe, China, the Middle East, and other corners of the globe will ultimately affect your stock portfolio. Given that, stock investors are more apt to push the panic button when the headlines scream doom. Therefore, check to see to what extent that company whose stock you're considering is dependent on those troubled lands.

Investing in a company that does business internationally isn't a bad thing; it can be good because it shows that the company makes money in a diversified range of countries. But it's a good idea to contact the company's shareholder department or visit its website to see what exposure (if any) it may have to the world's trouble spots. Of course, if the company does business with a country or region that's generally stable politically and economically, that's a plus.

Recession/Depression

As I write this, various sources have pointed out that the U.S. is in a very slow recovery in the wake of the worst recession in decades. In addition, still more sources are warning that it's in danger of relapsing into a second recession (the so-called "double-dip recession").

I certainly have my own views on the matter, but no matter how you slice it, the economy is having its toughest times in modern history. The economy has so many headwinds that it could easily stumble further in a treacherous decline. What's an investor to do?

Throughout the book I have referenced "human need" investing, and that should be the cornerstone of your investing, especially in tough times. No matter how good or bad times are, people will continue to buy what they need from the companies that fill their needs. See Chapters 13 and 14 for more information.

Technology

One great thing about the United States is that it still has a vibrant technology sector, for various reasons. Technology just makes some of our social and business activities that much more productive or enjoyable. No matter how bad the economy is, people will use their technology to ease the pain. If the economy is bad, technology blunts the difficulties. How many businesses have migrated to the Internet because the old ways became too expensive or unwieldy? A good example is the newspaper industry.

To me, technology is best broken up into two categories: technology that fills "wants" and technology that fills "needs." Even though "wants" seem to have done very well in recent years (just ask Apple devotees), I prefer that investors stick to technology that people and businesses need, such as technology for data storage, accounting, and telecommunications. It's a safer way to go. Your common sense here, coupled with research, will help you. Websites such as www.forbes.com, www.pcworld.com, and www.wired.com keep an eye on technology.

Commodities

In 2011, the world population crossed the 7 billion mark. That's a lot of people to feed, clothe, shelter, and so forth. The point is that demographics play a powerful role in the world of investing. These people represent "demand," and investors think about "supply." Another way of looking at it is in terms of "consumption" and "production." Production means that someone — such as public companies — can prosper by satisfying that growing demand.

All of these people need more of what we can summarize in one word: commodities (or natural resources). Commodities include corn, soybeans, cotton, cocoa, rice, copper, zinc, and so much more.

Stocks (and related ETFs) of profitable companies that provide and prepare commodities for general consumption will do well, and investors should participate. 'Nuff said. Flip to Chapter 14 for the scoop.

Energy

Energy has morphed into both a challenge and an opportunity. Energy as we have known it for decades — oil — is indeed running toward empty. Specifically, our economy has been running on sweet crude (don't taste it) since before I came along. But supplies of sweet crude have been more and more difficult to come by, and the U.S. is having difficulty finding enough to meet its almost insatiable appetite. The days are numbered for this type of energy investment. The talk about peak oil is more than scuttlebutt — it's a real issue. (*Peak oil* is a reference to the condition in which the world no longer has cheap and easily accessible sweet crude, which has been a mainstay of modern economies for decades.)

Fortunately, new opportunities are opening up. New technologies are helping the country find new energy supplies (such as natural gas and shale oil), and this is a very encouraging area for investors to research for new stock opportunities.

Energy will always be a vital part of a modern economy, no matter what form it may take. Energy is a necessity for businesses and consumers, and it belongs to some extent in almost any portfolio. See Chapter 14 for more information.

Dangers from Left Field

No one knows what tomorrow brings, but investors and society as a whole remain wary. Potential exists not only for bad conditions, but also for good to the extent that investment opportunities can arise from some negative conditions and crises.

Think in terms of cause and effect. When the devastating terrorist attacks took place on September 11, 2001, many "effects" were sent into motion. After the people mourned and prayed, they acted. Forward-thinking investors shifted money out of stocks and industries that were to be affected negatively (such as airlines) and into appropriate alternatives (such as defense). When it comes to investing (and everything else!), maintain your ability to analyze and discern with logic and reason.

Crises, by their very nature, are unpredictable. I don't recommend that you get a crystal ball to figure out what profound event or catastrophe will strike tomorrow, but I do advise you to be prepared to act when something earth-shaking does happen (and I think these events *will* happen).

Chapter 25

Ten Great Strategies That Go Well with Stocks

I think that stock investing is indeed an essential part of an overall wealth-building program, but I think that reminders about the other pieces of the puzzle are important so that you have a complete financial picture (nice wrap-up, right?). In today's financial markets, hedging is an important accompaniment to your stock-investing pursuits. Hedging can take a variety of forms, but the point is to have vehicles that help you diversify and protect you against the potential downside of pure stock investing. The ten strategies in this chapter are good accompaniments to your stock investing pursuits.

Gold

If you think that I'm including gold because I wrote *Precious Metals Investing For Dummies,* published by Wiley (a shameless plug, I know), you're wrong! Actually I wrote the book because I think that we're in a huge bull market for precious metals. Gold went from under $300 per ounce in 2001 to more than $1,700 in 2012 for a gain of more than 466 percent (sweet!). Gold (and I mean the physical bullion) is important for all investors in today's times. Gold has been a store of value for centuries, and it outlives paper assets. Virtually all paper assets (stocks, bonds, currencies, and so on) have counter-party risk — something that physical gold does not.

What do I mean by counter-party risk? The value of a paper investment is directly tied to the promise or performance of the counter-party; a *counter-party* is the entity that makes the promise or is tied to the performance. A stock is only as good as the performance of the underlying company. A bond's value depends on the counter-party (issuer) to make good on its promise to pay back principal and interest. The value of currency (such as dollars or euros) depends on the issuing government's ability to manage the currency to keep it from losing value (for example, the currency's value falls when inflation rises).

Physical gold bullion (coins or bars) is one of the very few investments that doesn't have counter-party risk the way that stocks, exchange-traded funds (ETFs), and other paper investments do. Acquire some to truly diversify away from the risks of paper investments.

See the next section for purchase recommendations; gold and silver are available via the same resources.

Silver

Silver is a long-time favorite of mine, and it quietly became one of the top performers of the past dozen years. From 2001 to 2012, silver went from under $5 per ounce to more than $33 for a gain of more than 560 percent. Some investments that derive their value from silver (such as silver mining stocks) did even better.

The reasons for investing in silver that I most often cite for stock investors are that silver has no counter-party risk (like gold; see the preceding section) and the supply and demand fundamentals are fantastic. Silver has the dual identity of being a monetary metal (as is gold) and an industrial metal (like copper). The fact that silver is constantly being used up and consumed by worldwide industry bodes well for silver's long-term investment potential.

In other words, silver has value in both good and bad times. Considering that it has a 2,000+-year track record as a store of value and a means for exchange helps too!

As with gold, buy the physical bullion to play it safe. At this writing, silver is much more affordable than gold for investors. Eagle bullion coins issued by the U.S. Mint are one of the easiest ways to acquire physical silver bullion; for details, check out www.usmint.gov/mint_programs/american_eagles/index.cfm?action=american_eagle_bullion.

1 Bonds

I'm worried about inflation that I think is coming, and I want to see people minimize its impact. I mention gold and silver earlier in this chapter as part of your arsenal of inflation hedges, but you can add other "weapons" too. One of my favorites is straight from the U.S. Treasury: the I bond (the "I" is a reference to inflation).

You may remember the old savings bonds from days gone by. But fortunately the latest versions are worth considering. The interest rate on the I Bond is tied to the government's official consumer price index (CPI) rate. If the CPI rate goes up, so does the rate for the I Bond. It's guaranteed by the federal government, and you can buy it for as low as $50 directly from the U.S. Treasury (see its website at www.treasurydirect.gov).

Consider buying at least one a month (at $50 per purchase, it's not a heavy deal) and accumulate them. After one year, you can redeem them with no penalty if you need the money. Go to the Treasury's website for more details.

Nonstock ETFs

Stocks are good, and they're an important part of any long-term portfolio, but your brokerage account gives you the ability to buy other securities to diversify away from general stock market risks. Good diversification means that you (hopefully) add quality positions to hedge the risks that may be present in the rest of your portfolio.

The stock market usually doesn't move in lock step with other markets (such as some currencies and precious metals), and it's a good idea to consider adding some of these other markets by using exchange-traded funds (ETFs). Some nonstock ETFs can be in areas such as energy, precious metals, and currencies. Check out Chapter 5 for the scoop.

Inverse ETFs

Exchange-traded funds (ETFs) are a great companion to your stock investing pursuits, partly because different objectives can be established very easily right in your stock brokerage account. ETFs can be a good part of a diversified portfolio. But let me add another wrinkle to the mix: inverse ETFs.

An inverse ETF is just what it sounds like: It acts inversely to what it corresponds to. For example, if you get an inverse ETF on the S&P 500, that particular inverse ETF will go up if the S&P 500 index goes down (and vice versa).

In other words, if the S&P 500 goes down, the inverse ETF will go up accordingly. Of course, if the S&P 500 goes up, that inverse ETF will go down. You get the picture.

There are inverse ETFs on many stock vehicles ranging from major market indexes (such as the S&P 500 and the "Dow") all the way to specific sectors (such as financial stocks or technology). The same sources that I provide on ETFs in Chapter 5 and in Appendix A provide information and guidance on inverse ETFs, and I certainly hope you discuss this type of security with an investing professional or someone you trust. The bottom line is that an inverse ETF can be a good way to hedge against severe recessions or extended bear markets.

Protective Puts

A put option gives you the ability to gain when the underlying security (in this case, a stock) goes down in value. When the stock goes down, the put option increases in value, and you can sell or cash out the put option for a profit. Cashing out the put option gives you a profit that offsets most (if not all) of the downward move of your stock. You end up still owning the stock, but at least you have the gain from cashing out the put, too. This strategy offers you a way to hedge against the stock's fall. It's referred to as a *protective put,* and it's a nice way to augment your stock investing in these days of risk and volatility.

If your stock is still a good value, consider using the proceeds from cashing out your put option to buy more of that stock. If the stock is down, you'll be able to pick up some shares at a good price. Then if the stock gets back on track to zigzag upward, you'll have built up a nice position for more gains. Oh, man! Tell your brother-in-law about that nice move!

You can find out more about protective puts at the Chicago Board Options Exchange website (www.cboe.com/strategies/pdf/protective putsstrategy.pdf).

Covered Calls

Writing a covered call is a great — and generally safe — way for the average (or above-average) investor to create added cash flow from a stock or ETF in an existing portfolio. Giving this strategy the attention needed to adequately explain it to you would take too much space and go beyond the scope of this book. But take my word for it; it's a great strategy that adds safety and income to a stock portfolio.

Great free tutorials are available on exactly what a covered call is and how to deploy it. Sources such as the educational section of the Chicago Board Options Exchange (www.cboe.com) or the Options Industry Council's website (www.888options.com) give any novice the full details on the topic of covered call writing. You can easily go to their sites and do a quick search for "covered call writing" to get some great guidance for beginners.

You can also check out *Trading Options For Dummies* by George A. Fontanills (Wiley).

Zero-Cost Collars

I can't get into too much detail here because it would require too much writing to make you say "Oh! That's a great idea!" but trust me . . . this technique would impress your financial advisor (or your brother-in-law). A zero-cost collar is a combination of two elements: buying a put option and writing a call option (I discuss both strategies earlier in this chapter). You do this simultaneously on a stock that you own.

The essential point of a zero-cost collar is that it puts a "collar" on your stock's price and insulates it from a decline (either entirely or partly). It's a great way to protect your stock from a sudden or temporary drop in price. In the event that the stock goes down, the net effect is that both the put you bought and the call you wrote end up being profitable. This "double profit" usually offsets the downward move of the stock.

Part of the genius of the zero-cost collar is that it can be easily structured so that it doesn't cost you anything. The money you receive for doing the covered call portion of this combination can pay for the put that you buy (hence the name "zero-cost" collar). Seriously, you'll make your broker or your brother-in-law envy your savviness. Websites such as www.cboe.com and www.888options.com have the information you need to master this one.

Tangibles

Hold on to your hat. I'm about to tell you to get stuff that will make you think that your author will soon wear a tin-foil hat. But I'm serious. Consider beefing up your pantry, along with other tangibles that are related to the world of human necessities. Look . . . the reason you own stocks is to help you deal with human necessities in the future (fund your retirement, buy food, pay utilities, and so forth). But the economy is so fragile right now that difficulties in acquiring necessities (food, water, medicines, and so on) could happen at any time. Let's face it — when folks panic, they do all sorts of things (besides panic-selling their stocks à la 2008).

When times are good, I tell folks to have emergency funds someplace safe, such as a bank savings account. But when times look as bad as they have in recent years (trending toward potentially more difficult times), it's better to be prepared. I personally keep extra essentials on hand (nonperishable food, water, candles, and other items that are necessities during difficult times). Even the government encourages this practice with websites such as www. ready.gov.

Cash

I leave the boring one for last! Seriously, cash in the form of savings or an amount parked in a secure money market fund is part of your arsenal for overall financial well-being. As a direct investment, it's good in a deflationary environment and very bad in an inflationary environment, but that's not why I mention it here. I mention it because investors need cash on the sidelines for a variety of reasons: chief among those reasons are short-term emergencies and as capital for buying opportunities. Chapter 2 has more on the topic of having cash on hand (such as in an emergency fund).

Part VI
Appendixes

"I read about investing in a company called Unihandle Ohio, but I'm uneasy about a stock that's listed on the NASDAQ as UhOh."

In this part . . .

Check out the appendixes in this part for resources
that aid you in making informed investment decisions. Whether the topic is stock investing terminology,
economics, or avoiding capital gains taxes, I include a
treasure trove of resources to assist you in your research,
including some of my favorite blogs. Whether you go to a
bookstore, the library, or the Internet, Appendix A gives
you some great places to turn to for help. In Appendix B, I
explain financial ratios. These important numbers help
you better determine whether to invest in a particular
company's stock.

Appendix A

Resources for Stock Investors

● ●

Getting and staying informed are ongoing priorities for stock investors. The lists in this appendix represent some of the best information resources available.

Financial Planning Sources

To find a financial planner to help you with your general financial needs, contact the following organizations:

Certified Financial Planner Board of Standards
1425 K St. NW, Suite 500
Washington, DC 20005
Phone 800-487-1497
Website www.cfp.net
Get a free copy of the CFP Board's pamphlet *10 Questions to Ask When Choosing a Financial Planner*. Be sure to ask for a financial planner who specializes in investing.

Financial Planning Association (FPA)
7535 E. Hampden Avenue, Suite 600
Denver, CO 80231
Phone 800-322-4237
Website www.fpanet.org
This is the largest organization of financial planning professionals.

National Association of Personal Financial Advisors
3250 N. Arlington Heights Rd., Suite 109
Arlington Heights, IL 60004
Phone 847-483-5400
Website www.napfa.org
This is the leading organization for fee-based financial planners (in other words, they don't get paid through commissions based on selling insurance/investment products).

The Language of Investing

Standard & Poor's Dictionary of Financial Terms
By Virginia B. Morris and Kenneth M. Morris
Published by Lightbulb Press, Inc.
A nicely laid out A-to-Z publication for investors mystified by financial terms.
It explains the important investing terms you come across every day.

Investing for Beginners
Website `http://beginnersinvest.about.com`
This site offers good basic information for novice investors.

Investopedia
Website `www.investopedia.com`
An excellent site with plenty of information on investing for beginning and intermediate investors.

Investor Words
Website `www.investorwords.com`
One of the most comprehensive sites on the Internet for beginning and intermediate investors for learning words and phrases unique to the financial world.

Textual Investment Resources

Stock investing success isn't an event; it's a process. The periodicals and magazines listed here (along with their websites) have offered many years of guidance and information for investors, and they're still top-notch. The books provide much wisdom that's either timeless or timely (covering problems and concerns every investor should be aware of now).

Periodicals and magazines

Barron's
Website `http://online.barrons.com/home-page`

Forbes magazine
Website `www.forbes.com`

Investor's Business Daily
Website `www.investors.com`

Kiplinger's Personal Finance magazine
Website `www.kiplinger.com`

***Money* magazine**
Website www.money.cnn.com

SmartMoney
Website www.smartmoney.com

Value Line Investment Survey
Website www.valueline.com

The Wall Street Journal
Website www.wsj.com

Books

Common Stocks and Uncommon Profits and Other Writings
By Philip A. Fisher
Published by John Wiley & Sons, Inc.
Although the book is from 2003, the information and guidance are still valuable for today's investors.

Elliott Wave Principle: Key to Market Behavior
By A. J. Frost and Robert R. Prechter
Published by New Classics Library
Robert Prechter is one of the leading technicians and has had some very accurate forecasts about the stock market and the general economy.

Forbes Guide to the Markets: Becoming a Savvy Investor
By Marc M. Groz
Published by John Wiley & Sons, Inc.
This book is a solid investing guide from the folks at Forbes.

Fundamental Analysis For Dummies
By Matt Krantz
Published by John Wiley & Sons, Inc.
I had the good fortune to review this book, and it's very worthwhile for serious investors. The author "drills down" into the financials of a company, which any serious investor would need to know.

How to Pick Stocks Like Warren Buffett: Profiting from the Bargain Hunting Strategies of the World's Greatest Value Investor
By Timothy Vick
Published by McGraw-Hill Professional Publishing
When you're investing, it's good to see what accomplished investors like Warren Buffett do, and this book explains his approach well.

The Intelligent Investor: The Classic Text on Value Investing
By Benjamin Graham
Published by HarperCollins
This is a classic investing book that was great when it was published and is very relevant in today's tumultuous stock market.

Secrets of the Great Investors (audio series)
Published by Knowledge Products
Phone 800-876-4332
Website `www.knowledgeproducts.net/html/inv_files/invest.cfm`
I have this audio series, and it offers classic lessons on investing from great investors.

Security Analysis: The Classic 1951 Edition
by Benjamin Graham and David L. Dodd
Published by the McGraw-Hill Companies
This book is a classic, and most investors in this uncertain age should acquaint themselves with the basics.

Standard & Poor's Stock Reports (available in the library reference section)
Website `www.netadvantage.standardandpoors.com`
Ask your reference librarian about this excellent reference source, which gives one-page summaries on the major companies and has detailed financial reports on all major companies listed on the New York Stock Exchange and Nasdaq.

The Wall Street Journal Guide to Understanding Money & Investing
By Kenneth M. Morris and Virginia B. Morris
Published by Lightbulb Press, Inc.
This is a neat little book that offers a good overview of investing.

Special books of interest to stock investors

The Collapse of the Dollar and How to Profit from It: Make a Fortune by Investing in Gold and Other Hard Assets
By James Turk and John Rubino
Published by Doubleday
Turk and Rubino give a good overview of our currency problems coupled with strategies to deal with them.

Crash Proof 2.0: How to Profit from the Economic Collapse
By Peter D. Schiff with John Downes
Published by John Wiley & Sons, Inc.
A great "crash course" on the problems facing our modern economy and how to strategize with your portfolio.

The ETF Book: All You Need to Know About Exchange-Traded Funds
By Richard A. Ferri
Published by John Wiley & Sons, Inc.
Considering the marketplace, ETFs are better choices than stocks for some investors, and this book does a good job of explaining them.

Hot Commodities: How Anyone Can Invest Profitably in the World's Best Market
By Jim Rogers
Published by Random House
The cornerstone of "human need" investing includes commodities, and Rogers provides great insights in this book.

Precious Metals Investing For Dummies
By Paul Mladjenovic
Published by John Wiley & Sons, Inc.
My shameless plug for another great book. Seriously, the book covers an area that will become an important part of the financial landscape in the coming months and years (can you say "inflation"?). Yes, common stocks and exchange-traded funds (ETFs) involved in precious metals are covered.

Investing Websites

How can any serious investor ignore the Internet? You can't, and you shouldn't. The following are among the best information sources available.

General investing websites

Bloomberg
www.bloomberg.com

CNN Money
www.money.cnn.com

Financial Sense
www.financialsense.com

Forbes
www.forbes.com

Invest Wisely: Advice From Your Securities Industry Regulators
www.sec.gov/investor/pubs/inws.htm

MarketWatch
www.marketwatch.com

MSN Money
www.money.msn.com

SmartMoney
www.smartmoney.com

Stock investing websites

AllStocks.com
www.allstocks.com

CNBC
www.cnbc.com

Contrarian Investing.com
www.contrarianinvesting.com

DailyStocks
www.dailystocks.com

Morningstar (known for mutual funds but has great research available on stocks as well)
www.morningstar.com

Quote.com
www.quote.com

Raging Bull
www.ragingbull.com

Standard and Poor's
www.standardandpoors.com

The Street
www.thestreet.com

Yahoo! Finance
www.finance.yahoo.com

Stock investing blogs

These blogs offer a wealth of opinions and insights from experts on investing. Peruse them to round out your research (you may even find some articles from me as well).

Minyanville
www.minyanville.com

StockMarketToday
www.stockmarkettoday.com

StreetAuthority
www.streetauthority.com

Seeking Alpha
www.seekingalpha.com

Zero Hedge
www.zerohedge.com

Technorati
www.technorati.com
Note: I include this site because it's a popular search engine for blogs. There are many excellent financial and stock market blogs that I can't fit in this space, so do a search on Technorati.

Other blogs that are useful for stock investors

Freedom & Prosperity Blog
www.mladjenovic.blogspot.com
(My economic and financial market commentaries)

HoweStreet
www.howestreet.com

King World News
www.kingworldnews.com

Mish's Global Economic Trend Analysis
http://globaleconomicanalysis.blogspot.com

SafeHaven
www.safehaven.com

Investor Associations and Organizations

American Association of Individual Investors (AAII)
625 N. Michigan Ave.
Chicago, IL 60611-3110
Phone 800-428-2244
Website www.aaii.com

National Association of Investors Corp. (NAIC)
711 W. 13 Mile Rd.
Madison Heights, MI 48071
Phone 877-275-6242
Website www.betterinvesting.org

Stock Exchanges

Chicago Board Options Exchange (CBOE)
Website www.cboe.com
Note: The CBOE is an options exchange, but I include it here because options have been mentioned throughout this book, and the CBOE options learning center has lots of information about how options can enhance your stock investing.

Nasdaq
Website www.nasdaq.com
The main site for Nasdaq. You'll find lots of information and guidance for stock investors here.

New York Stock Exchange/Euronext
Website www.nyse.com
The NYSE's site has a wealth of information for stock investors.

OTC Bulletin Board
Website www.otcbb.com
If you decide to research small cap stocks, this is the site to go to for data and research on small publicly-traded companies.

Finding Brokers

The following sections offer sources to help you evaluate brokers and an extensive list of brokers (with telephone numbers and websites) so that you can do your own shopping.

Choosing brokers

SmartMoney magazine
Website www.smartmoney.com
SmartMoney does a comprehensive annual review and comparison of stockbrokers.

Stock Brokers
Website www.stockbrokers.com
This site tracks and reviews brokers.

Brokers

Charles Schwab & Co.
Phone 800-435-4000
Website www.schwab.com

E*TRADE
Phone 800-387-2331
Website www.etrade.com

Fidelity Brokerage Services
Phone 800-343-3548
Website www.fidelity.com

Muriel Siebert & Co.
Phone 800-872-0444
Website www.siebertnet.com

Options Xpress
Phone 888-280-8020
Website www.optionsxpress.com

Scottrade
Phone 800-619-7283
Website www.scottrade.com

TD Ameritrade
Phone 800-669-3900
Website www.tdameritrade.com

thinkorswim
Phone 866-839-1100
Website www.thinkorswim.com

TradeKing
Phone 877-495-5464
Website www.tradeking.com

Vanguard Brokerage Services
Phone 877-662-7447
Website: https://personal.vanguard.com/home

Wall Street Access
Phone 800-709-5929
Website www.wsaccess.com

Wells Fargo Securities
Phone 866-224-5708
Website www.wellsfargoadvisors.com

Fee-Based Investment Sources

The following are fee-based subscription services. Many of them also offer excellent (and free) e-mail newsletters tracking the stock market and related news.

The Bull & Bear
Website www.thebullandbear.com

The Daily Reckoning (Agora Publishing)
Website www.dailyreckoning.com

Elliott Wave International
Phone 770-536-0309
Website www.elliottwave.com

Hulbert Financial Digest
Website www.marketwatch.com/premium-newsletters/hulbert-financial-digest
(Part of MarketWatch.com)

InvestorPlace
Website www.investorplace.com

Louis Rukeyser's Wall Street
Website www.shepherdswallstreet.com

Mark Skousen
Website www.mskousen.com

The Motley Fool
Website www.fool.com

Richard C. Young's Intelligence Report
Website www.intelligencereport.investorplace.com

Richard Russell's Dow Theory Letters
Website www.dowtheoryletters.com

The Value Line Investment Survey
Phone 800-654-0508
Website www.valueline.com

Weiss Research's Money and Markets
Website www.moneyandmarkets.com

Dividend Reinvestment Plans

BUYandHOLD (a division of Freedom Investments)
Website www.buyandhold.com

DRIP Central
Website www.dripcentral.com

DRIP Investor
Website www.dripinvestor.com

First Share
Website www.firstshare.com

ShareBuilder (ING Direct)
Website www.sharebuilder.com

Sources for Analysis

The following sources give you the chance to look a little deeper at some critical aspects regarding stock analysis. Whether it's earnings estimates and insider selling or a more insightful look at a particular industry, these sources are among my favorites.

Earnings and earnings estimates

Earnings Whispers
Website www.earningswhispers.com

Thomson Reuters
Website www.thomsonreuters.com

Yahoo's Stock Research Center
Website http://biz.yahoo.com/r/

Zacks Investment Research
Website www.zacks.com

Sector and industry analysis

Hoover's
Website www.hoovers.com

MarketWatch
Website www.marketwatch.com

Standard & Poor's
Website www.standardandpoors.com

Stock indexes

Bloomberg's list of stock indexes worldwide
www.bloomberg.com/markets/indexes

Dow Jones Indexes
www.djindexes.com

Investopedia's tutorial on indexes
www.investopedia.com/university/indexes/#axzz2BZGFhYpT

Note: If these direct links don't work, do a search for indexes from the site's home page. Also, keep in mind that many of the resources in this appendix offer extensive information on indexes (such as MarketWatch and Yahoo! Finance).

Factors that affect market value

Understanding basic economics is so vital to making your investment decisions that I had to include this section. These great sources have helped me understand the big picture and what ultimately affects the stock market (see Chapters 13, 14, and 15 for more details).

Economics and politics

American Institute for Economic Research (AIER)
Website www.aier.org
Note: AIER also has great little booklets for consumers on budgeting, Social Security, avoiding financial problems, and other topics.

Center for Freedom and Prosperity
Website www.freedomandprosperity.org

Federal Reserve Board
Website www.federalreserve.gov

Financial Sense
Website www.financialsense.com

Foundation for Economic Education
Website www.fee.org

Grandfather Economic Report
Website www.grandfathereconomicreport.com

Ludwig von Mises Institute
518 W. Magnolia Ave.
Auburn, AL 36832
Phone 334-321-2100
Website www.mises.org

Moody's Analytics
Website www.economy.com

Securities and Exchange Commission (SEC)
Phone 800-732-0330
Websites www.sec.gov and www.investor.gov
The SEC has tremendous resources for investors. In addition to providing information on investing, the SEC also monitors the financial markets for fraud and other abusive activities. For stock investors, it also has EDGAR (Electronic Data Gathering, Analysis, and Retrieval system), which is a comprehensive, searchable database of public documents that are filed by public companies.

Federal laws

Go to any of these sites to find out about new and proposed laws. The on-site search engines will help you find laws either by their assigned number or a keyword search.

Library of Congress (Thomas legislative search engine)
Website http://thomas.loc.gov/home/thomas.php

U.S. House of Representatives
Website www.house.gov

U.S. Senate
Website www.senate.gov

Technical analysis

Big Charts (Provided by www.marketwatch.com)
Website www.bigcharts.com

Elliott Wave International
Website www.elliottwave.com

LiveCharts
Website www.livecharts.com

StockCharts.com
Website www.stockcharts.com

Insider trading

Free EDGAR
Website www.freeedgar.com

ProCon
Website www.procon.org

Securities and Exchange Commission (SEC)
Website www.sec.gov

StreetInsider
Website www.streetinsider.com

10-K Wizard
Website www.10kwizard.com
Note: This site takes you to Morningstar's Document Research site, which can help you find the filed documents.

Tax Benefits and Obligations

Americans for Tax Reform
Website www.atr.org

Fairmark
Website www.fairmark.com

Fidelity Investments
Website www.401k.com

J.K. Lasser's series of books on taxes
By J.K. Lasser
Published by John Wiley & Sons, Inc.
Website www.jklasser.com

National Taxpayers Union
Website www.ntu.org

TaxMama
Website www.taxmama.com

Fraud

Federal Citizen Information Center
Website www.pueblo.gsa.gov
Investing publications for consumers from the Federal Citizen Information Center catalog are available for free downloading at this website.

Financial Industry Regulatory Authority (FINRA)
1735 K St. NW
Washington, DC 20006
Phone 800-289-9999 or 301-590-6500
Website www.finra.org
This website gives you information and assistance on reporting fraud or
other abuse by brokers.

National Consumers League's Fraud Center
Website www.fraud.org

North American Securities Administrators Association
Phone 888-846-2722
Website www.nasaa.org

Securities and Exchange Commission (SEC)
Website www.sec.gov
The government agency that regulates the securities industry.

Securities Industry and Financial Markets Association (SIFMA)
1101 New York Ave. NW, 8th Floor
Washington, DC 20005
Phone 202-962-7300
Website www.sifma.org

Securities Investor Protection Corporation (SIPC)
Website www.sipc.org
SIPC has the role of restoring funds to investors with assets in the hands of
bankrupt and otherwise financially troubled brokerage firms (make sure that
your brokerage firm is a member of SIPC).

Appendix B

Financial Ratios

• •

Considering how many financial catastrophes have occurred in recent years (and continue to occur in the current headlines), doing your homework regarding the financial health of your stock choices is more important than ever. This appendix should be your go-to section when you find stocks that you're considering for your portfolio. It lists the most common ratios that investors should be aware of and use. A solid company doesn't have to pass all these ratio tests with flying colors, but at a minimum, it should comfortably pass the ones regarding profitability and solvency:

✔ **Profitability:** Is the company making money? Is it making more or less than it did in the prior period? Are sales growing? Are profits growing?

You can answer these questions by looking at the following ratios:

- Return on equity
- Return on assets
- Common size ratio (income statement)

✔ **Solvency:** Is the company keeping debts and other liabilities under control? Are the company's assets growing? Is the company's net equity (or net worth or stockholders' equity) growing?

You can answer these questions by looking at the following ratios:

- Quick ratio
- Debt to net equity
- Working capital

While you examine ratios, keep these points in mind:

✔ Not every company and/or industry is the same. A ratio that seems dubious in one industry may be just fine in another. Investigate and check out the norms in that particular industry. (See Chapter 13 for details on analyzing sectors and industries.)

✔ A single ratio isn't enough on which to base your investment decision. Look at several ratios covering the major aspects of the company's finances.

✔ Look at two or more years of the company's numbers to judge whether the most recent ratio is better, worse, or unchanged from the previous years' ratios. Ratios can give you early warning signs regarding the company's prospects. (See Chapter 11 for details on two important documents that list a company's numbers — the balance sheet and the income statement.)

Liquidity Ratios

Liquidity is the ability to quickly turn assets into cash. Liquid assets are simply assets that are easy to convert to cash. Real estate, for example, is certainly an asset, but it's not liquid because converting it to cash can take weeks, months, or even years. Current assets such as checking accounts, savings accounts, marketable securities, accounts receivable, and inventory are much easier to sell or convert to cash in a short period of time.

Paying bills or immediate debt takes liquidity. Liquidity ratios help you understand a company's ability to pay its current liabilities. The most common liquidity ratios are the current ratio and the quick ratio; the numbers to calculate them are located on the balance sheet.

Current ratio

The current ratio is the most commonly used liquidity ratio. It answers the question, "Does the company have enough financial cushion to meet its current bills?" It's calculated as follows:

Current ratio = Total current assets ÷ Total current liabilities

If Schmocky Corp. (SHM) has $60,000 in current assets and $20,000 in current liabilities, the current ratio is 3, meaning the company has $3 of current assets for each dollar of current liabilities. As a general rule, a current ratio of 2 or more is desirable.

A current ratio of less than 1 is a red flag that the company may have a cash crunch that could cause financial problems. Although many companies strive to get the current ratio to equal 1, I like to see a higher ratio (in the range of 1–3) to keep a cash cushion should the economy slow down.

Quick ratio

The quick ratio is frequently referred to as the "acid test" ratio. It's a little more stringent than the current ratio in that you calculate it without inventory. I'll use the current ratio example discussed in the preceding section. What if half of the assets are inventory ($30,000 in this case)? Now what? First, here's the formula for the quick ratio:

Quick ratio = (Current assets less inventory) ÷ Current liabilities

In the example, the quick ratio for SHM is 1.5 ($60,000 minus $30,000 equals $30,000, which is then divided by $20,000). In other words, the company has $1.50 of "quick" liquid assets for each dollar of current liabilities. This amount is okay. *Quick liquid assets* include any money in the bank, marketable securities, and accounts receivable. If quick liquid assets at the very least equal or exceed total current liabilities, that amount is considered adequate.

The acid test that this ratio reflects is embodied in the question, "Can the company pay its bills when times are tough?" In other words, if the company can't sell its goods (inventory), can it still meet its short-term liabilities? Of course, you must watch the accounts receivable as well. If the economy is entering rough times, you want to make sure that the company's customers are paying invoices on a timely basis.

Operating Ratios

Operating ratios essentially measure a company's efficiency. "How is the company managing its resources?" is a question commonly answered with operating ratios. If, for example, a company sells products, does it have too much inventory? If it does, that could impair the company's operations. The following sections present common operating ratios.

Return on equity (ROE)

Equity is the amount left from total assets after you account for total liabilities. (This can also be considered a profitability ratio.) The *net equity* (also known as shareholders' equity, stockholders' equity, or net worth) is the bottom line on the company's balance sheet, both geographically and figuratively. It's calculated as

Return on equity (ROE) = Net income ÷ Net equity

The net income (from the company's income statement) is simply the total income less total expenses. Net income that isn't spent or used up increases the company's net equity. Looking at net income is a great way to see whether the company's management is doing a good job growing the business. You can check this out by looking at the net equity from both the most recent balance sheet and the one from a year earlier. Ask yourself whether the current net equity is higher or lower than the year before. If it's higher, by what percentage is it higher?

For example, if SHM's net equity is $40,000 and its net income is $10,000, its ROE is a robust 25 percent (net income of $10,000 divided by net equity of $40,000). The higher the ROE, the better. An ROE that exceeds 10 percent (for simplicity's sake) is good (especially in a slow and struggling economy). Use the ROE in conjunction with the ROA ratio in the following section to get a fuller picture of a company's activity.

Return on assets (ROA)

The return on assets (ROA) may seem similar to the ROE in the preceding section, but it actually gives a perspective that completes the picture when coupled with the ROE. The formula for figuring out the ROA is

Return on assets = Net income ÷ Total assets

The ROA reflects the relationship between a company's profit and the assets used to generate that profit. If SHM makes a profit of $10,000 and has total assets of $100,000, the ROA is 10 percent. This percentage should be as high as possible, but it will generally be less than the ROE.

Say that a company has an ROE of 25 percent but an ROA of only 5 percent. Is that good? It sounds okay, but a problem exists. An ROA that's much lower than the ROE indicates that the higher ROE may have been generated by something other than total assets — debt! The use of debt can be a leverage to maximize the ROE, but if the ROA doesn't show a similar percentage of efficiency, then the company may have incurred too much debt. In that case, investors should be aware that this situation can cause problems (see the section "Solvency Ratios," later in this appendix). Better ROA than DOA!

Sales-to-receivables ratio (SR)

The sales-to-receivables ratio (SR) gives investors an indication of a company's ability to manage what customers owe it. This ratio uses data from both the income statement (sales) and the balance sheet (accounts receivable, or AR). The formula is expressed as

Sales-to-receivables ratio = Sales ÷ Receivables

Say that you have the following data for SHM:

Sales in 2011 are $75,000. On 12/31/11, receivables stood at $25,000.

Sales in 2012 are $80,000. On 12/31/12, receivables stood at $50,000.

Based on this data, you can figure out that sales went up 6.6 percent (sales in 2012 are $5,000 higher than 2011 and $5,000 is 6.6% of $75,000), but receivables went up 100 percent (the $25,000 in 2011 doubled to $50,000, which is a move up of 100%)!

In 2011, the SR was 3 ($75,000 divided by $25,000). However, the SR in 2012 sank to 1.6 ($80,000 divided by $50,000), or was nearly cut in half. Yes, sales did increase, but the company's ability to collect money due from customers fell dramatically. This information is important to notice for one main reason: What good is selling more when you can't get the money? From a cash flow point of view, the company's financial situation deteriorated.

Solvency Ratios

Solvency just means that a company isn't overwhelmed by its liabilities. Insolvency means "Oops! Too late." You get the point. Solvency ratios have never been more important than they are now because the American economy is currently carrying so much debt. Solvency ratios look at the relationship between what a company owns and what it owes. The following sections discuss two of the primary solvency ratios.

Debt-to-net-equity ratio

The debt-to-net-equity ratio answers the question, "How dependent is the company on debt?" In other words, it tells you how much the company owes and how much it owns. You calculate it as follows:

Debt-to-net-equity ratio = Total liabilities ÷ Net equity

If SHM has $100,000 in debt and $50,000 in net equity, the debt to net equity ratio is 2. The company has $2 of debt to every dollar of net equity. In this case, what the company owes is twice the amount of what it owns.

Whenever a company's debt-to-net-equity ratio exceeds 1 (as in the example), that isn't good. In fact, the higher the number, the more negative the situation. If the number is too high and the company isn't generating enough income to cover the debt, the business runs the risk of bankruptcy.

Working capital

Technically, working capital isn't a ratio, but it does belong to the list of things that serious investors look at. *Working capital* measures a company's current assets in relation to its current liabilities. It's a simple equation:

Working capital = Total current assets – Total current liabilities

The point is obvious: Does the company have enough to cover the current bills? Actually, you can formulate a useful ratio. If current assets are $25,000 and current liabilities are $25,000, that's a 1-to-1 ratio, which is cutting it close. Current assets should be at least 50 percent higher than current liabilities (say, $1.50 to $1.00) to have enough cushion to pay bills and have some money for other purposes. Preferably, the ratio should be 2 to 1 or higher.

Common Size Ratios

Common size ratios offer simple comparisons. You have common size ratios for both the balance sheet (where you compare total assets) and the income statement (where you compare total sales):

✓ **To get a common size ratio from a balance sheet,** the total assets figure is assigned the percentage of 100 percent. Every other item on the balance sheet is represented as a percentage of total assets.

Total assets equal 100 percent. All other items equal a percentage of the total assets.

For example, if SHM has total assets of $10,000 and debt of $3,000, then debt equals 30 percent (debt divided by total assets, or $3,000 ÷ $10,000, which equals 30 percent).

✓ **To get a common size ratio from an income statement** (or profit and loss statement), you compare total sales.

Total sales equal 100 percent. All other items equal a percentage of the total sales.

For example, if SHM has $50,000 in total sales and a net profit of $8,000, then you know that the profit equals 16 percent of total sales ($8,000 ÷ $50,000, which equals 16 percent).

Keep in mind the following points with common size ratios:

- ✔ **Net profit:** What percentage of sales is it? What was it last year? How about the year before? What percentage of increases (or decreases) is the company experiencing?

- ✔ **Expenses:** Are total expenses in line with the previous year? Are any expenses going out of line?

- ✔ **Net equity:** Is this item higher or lower than the year before?

- ✔ **Debt:** Is this item higher or lower than the year before?

Common size ratios are used to compare the company's financial data not only with prior balance sheets and income statements but also with other companies in the same industry. You want to make sure that the company is not only doing better historically but also as a competitor in the industry.

Valuation Ratios

Understanding the value of a stock is very important for stock investors. The quickest and most efficient way to judge the value of a company is to look at valuation ratios. The type of value that you deal with throughout this book is the *market value* (essentially the price of the company's stock). You hope to buy it at one price and sell it later at a higher price — that's the name of the game. But what's the best way to determine whether what you're paying for now is a bargain or is fair market value? How do you know whether your stock investment is undervalued or overvalued? The valuation ratios in the following sections can help you answer these questions. In fact, they're the same ratios that value investors have used with great success for many years.

Price-to-earnings ratio (P/E)

The price-to-earnings ratio (P/E) can double as a profitability ratio because it's a common barometer of value that many investors and analysts look at. I cover this topic in Chapter 11, but because it's such a critical ratio, I also include it here. The formula is

P/E ratio = Price (per share) ÷ Earnings (per share)

For example, if SHM's stock price per share is $10 and the earnings per share are $1, the P/E ratio is 10 (10 divided by 1).

The P/E ratio answers the question, "Am I paying too much for the company's earnings?" Value investors find this number to be very important. Here are some points to remember:

- Generally, the lower the P/E ratio, the better (from a financial strength point of view). Frequently, a low P/E ratio indicates that the stock is undervalued, especially if the company's sales are growing and the industry is also growing. But you may occasionally encounter a situation where the stock price is falling faster than the company's earnings, which would also generate a low P/E. And if the company has too much debt and the industry is struggling, then a low P/E may indicate that the company is in trouble. Use the P/E as part of your analysis along with other factors (such as debt, for instance) to get a more complete picture.

- A company with a P/E ratio significantly higher than its industry average is a red flag that its stock price is too high (or that it's growing faster than its competitors). If the industry's P/E ratio is typically in the range of 10–12 and you're evaluating a stock whose P/E ratio is around 20, then you may want to consider avoiding it. A company's P/E ratio not only needs to be taken in context with its industry peers but also based on its year-over-year performance.

- Don't invest in a company with no P/E ratio (it has a stock price, but the company experienced losses). Such a stock may be good for a speculator's portfolio but not for your retirement account.

- Any stock with a P/E ratio higher than 40 should be considered a speculation and not an investment. Frequently, a high P/E ratio indicates that the stock is overvalued.

When you buy a company, you're really buying its power to make money. In essence, you're buying its earnings. Paying for a stock that's priced at 10 to 20 times earnings is a conservative strategy that has served investors well for nearly a century. Make sure that the company is priced fairly, and use the P/E ratio in conjunction with other measures of value (such as the ratios in this appendix).

Price-to-sales ratio (PSR)

The price-to-sales ratio (PSR) helps to answer the question, "Am I paying too much for the company's stock based on the company's sales?" This is a useful valuation ratio that I recommend using as a companion tool with the company's P/E ratio (see the preceding section). You calculate it as follows:

PSR = Stock price (per share) ÷ Total sales (per share)

This ratio can be quoted on a per-share basis or on an aggregate basis. For example, if a company's market value (or market capitalization) is $1 billion and annual sales are also $1 billion, the PSR is 1. If the market value in this example is $2 billion and annual sales are $1 billion, then the PSR is 2. Or, if the share price is $76 and the total sales per share are $38, the PSR is 2 — you arrive at the same ratio whether you calculate on a per-share or aggregate basis. For investors trying to make sure that they're not paying too much for the stock, the general rule is that the lower the PSR, the better. Stocks with a PSR of 2 or lower are considered undervalued.

Be very hesitant about buying a stock with a PSR greater than 5. If you buy a stock with a PSR of 5, you're paying $5 for each dollar of sales — not exactly a bargain.

Price-to-book ratio (PBR)

No, this doesn't have anything to do with beer, although I am enjoying a cold Pabst Blue Ribbon as I write this! The price-to-book ratio (PBR) compares a company's market value to its accounting (or book) value. The book value refers to the company's net equity (assets minus liabilities). The company's market value is usually dictated by external factors such as supply and demand in the stock market. The book value is indicative of the company's internal operations. Value investors see the PBR as another way of valuing the company to determine whether they're paying too much for the stock. The formula is

Price-to-book ratio (PBR) = Market value ÷ Book value

An alternate method is to calculate the ratio on a per-share basis, which yields the same ratio. If the company's stock price is $20 and the book value (per share) is $15, then the PBR is 1.33. In other words, the company's market value is 33 percent higher than its book value. Investors seeking an undervalued stock like to see the market value as close as possible to (or even better, below) the book value.

Keep in mind that the PBR may vary depending on the industry and other factors. Also, judging a company solely on book value may be misleading because many companies have assets that aren't adequately reflected in the book value. Software companies are a good example. Intellectual properties, such as copyrights and trademarks, are very valuable yet aren't fully covered in book value. Just bear in mind that, generally, the lower the market value is in relation to the book value, the better for you (especially if the company has strong earnings and the outlook for the industry is positive).

Index

Apple & Mac

Pad 2 For Dummies,
rd Edition
78-1-118-17679-5

Phone 4S For Dummies,
th Edition
78-1-118-03671-6

Pod touch For Dummies,
rd Edition
78-1-118-12960-9

Mac OS X Lion
or Dummies
78-1-118-02205-4

Blogging & Social Media

CityVille For Dummies
78-1-118-08337-6

Facebook For Dummies,
th Edition
78-1-118-09562-1

Mom Blogging
or Dummies
78-1-118-03843-7

Twitter For Dummies,
nd Edition
78-0-470-76879-2

WordPress For Dummies,
th Edition
78-1-118-07342-1

Business

Cash Flow For Dummies
78-1-118-01850-7

Investing For Dummies,
th Edition
78-0-470-90545-6

Job Searching with Social
Media For Dummies
978-0-470-93072-4

QuickBooks 2012
For Dummies
978-1-118-09120-3

Resumes For Dummies,
6th Edition
978-0-470-87361-8

Starting an Etsy Business
For Dummies
978-0-470-93067-0

Cooking & Entertaining

Cooking Basics
For Dummies, 4th Edition
978-0-470-91388-8

Wine For Dummies,
4th Edition
978-0-470-04579-4

Diet & Nutrition

Kettlebells For Dummies
978-0-470-59929-7

Nutrition For Dummies,
5th Edition
978-0-470-93231-5

Restaurant Calorie Counter
For Dummies,
2nd Edition
978-0-470-64405-8

Digital Photography

Digital SLR Cameras &
Photography For Dummies,
4th Edition
978-1-118-14489-3

Digital SLR Settings
& Shortcuts
For Dummies
978-0-470-91763-3

Photoshop Elements 10
For Dummies
978-1-118-10742-3

Gardening

Gardening Basics
For Dummies
978-0-470-03749-2

Vegetable Gardening
For Dummies,
2nd Edition
978-0-470-49870-5

Green/Sustainable

Raising Chickens
For Dummies
978-0-470-46544-8

Green Cleaning
For Dummies
978-0-470-39106-8

Health

Diabetes For Dummies,
3rd Edition
978-0-470-27086-8

Food Allergies
For Dummies
978-0-470-09584-3

Living Gluten-Free
For Dummies,
2nd Edition
978-0-470-58589-4

Hobbies

Beekeeping
For Dummies,
2nd Edition
978-0-470-43065-1

Chess For Dummies,
3rd Edition
978-1-118-01695-4

Drawing For Dummies,
2nd Edition
978-0-470-61842-4

eBay For Dummies,
7th Edition
978-1-118-09806-6

Knitting For Dummies,
2nd Edition
978-0-470-28747-7

Language &
Foreign Language

English Grammar
For Dummies,
2nd Edition
978-0-470-54664-2

French For Dummies,
2nd Edition
978-1-118-00464-7

German For Dummies,
2nd Edition
978-0-470-90101-4

Spanish Essentials
For Dummies
978-0-470-63751-7

Spanish For Dummies,
2nd Edition
978-0-470-87855-2